CUMBERLAND AND WESTMORLAND ANTIQUARIAN AND
ARCHAEOLOGICAL SOCIETY

SOCIETY OF ANTIQUARIES OF NEWCASTLE UPON TYNE

HADRIAN'S WALL 1989-1999

A Summary of Recent Excavations and Research

prepared for

The Twelfth Pilgrimage of Hadrian's Wall, 14-21 August 1999

Edited by

Paul Bidwell

1999

Published at Carlisle by the Cumberland and Westmorland
Antiquarian and Archaeological Society and the
Society of Antiquaries of Newcastle upon Tyne

First published in Great Britain 1999

© Paul Bidwell and the various contributors 1999

ISBN 1 873124 29 5

Printed by Titus Wilson & Son, Kendal

CONTENTS

ORGANIZING COMMITTEE FOR THE TWELFTH PILGRIMAGE OF
HADRIAN'S WALL

D.J. BREEZE, B.A., Ph.D., F.S.A., F.S.A.Scot., F.R.S.E. (Chairman)

FOREWORD

It is 150 years since John Collingwood Bruce, for many years the doyen of mural studies, led the first Pilgrimage along Hadrian's Wall. His was a larger version of the family holiday on the Wall the previous year. Then he had been prevented from undertaking a continental holiday because of the unrest which is characterised as the Year of Revolutions. The core of the first Pilgrimage was only about 20 strong and it was to be another 37 years before the next, but by the end of the century, this new tour had become an established event in the calendar of the two northern archaeological societies.

The purpose of the Pilgrimage is to give an opportunity to be reminded of the familiar and to learn about new work over the last decade. It is also, in keeping with the first Pilgrimage, a convivial occasion. This is underlined by the mix of the Pilgrims, from all parts of Britain and abroad. Hadrian's Wall is the best preserved, most explored and most famous of all the frontier installations erected by the Romans. It stands today as magnificent if mute testimony to the power of one of the world's great civilisations. It is entirely appropriate, therefore, that in 1987 Hadrian's Wall was designated a World Heritage Site.

Thousands of visitors come to Hadrian's Wall every year. Some visit a few main sites, others walk the Wall. The importance of providing appropriate facilities for all visitors has been recognised by the Government which in 1994 announced that it would establish a National Trail along the Wall. This action is closely associated with the Management Plan for Hadrian's Wall prepared by English Heritage in association with all interested local parties. These two, the Trail and the Management Plan, should ensure the physical well being of Hadrian's Wall for decades to come.

There is no doubt that the single most important discovery on Hadrian's Wall over the last 50 years has been the Vindolanda writing tablets. These have enriched our understanding of the northern frontier in two ways. Firstly, they directly illuminate life on the frontier in the years immediately before the building of Hadrian's Wall. Secondly, although the archive contains new and unique documents, the basic similarities with other military records from the Eastern provinces validates the use of that material to help understand life on the northern frontiers of the empire.

Work elsewhere, at South Shields and Birdoswald in particular, have challenged our preconceived views. In both cases the discoveries have been made during excavations undertaken as part of programmes to improve interpretation. We thus have the added bonus of not only learning more about Hadrian's Wall, but being able to see the discoveries as well.

Here is the fascination of archaeology. Just as it seems as if little more will be found, an unsuspected discovery offers not only new information but also a new challenge. Long may it continue thus!

DAVID J. BREEZE
Chairman, Hadrian's Wall 1999 Pilgrimage Committee
April 1999

PREFACE AND ACKNOWLEDGEMENTS

This book has the same purpose as previous Pilgrimage publications: to summarise the previous decade's work and to provide illustrations of the sites to be visited. Its greater length is explained by the steady growth in our knowledge of Hadrian's Wall; as in the past, this has been achieved mainly by excavation, but for the first time in these decennial publications it has been possible to include important and extensive results from analytical field survey and geophysical prospection.

These matters are covered in the final chapter. Three other chapters deal with topics of particular importance: the Vindolanda writing-tablets, the environment of Hadrian's Wall and the Hadrian's Wall World Heritage Site Management Plan. There is also the usual overview of recent work and, to mark the 150th anniversary of the First Pilgrimage in 1849, a brief consideration of its originator, John Colligwood Bruce. The print-run of the last Pilgrimage publication by Charles Daniels exceeded by some hundreds the copies issued to Pilgrims, but the surplus sold quite rapidly. In the hope that there is likewise a wider public for this publication, the Pilgrimage Committee has approved some minor alterations to the previous format, notably the omission of instructions to Pilgrims and the itinerary. The main additions are a comprehensive bibliography and a systematic referencing system in the main body of the work.

I am grateful to the Pilgrimage Committee for advice and suggestions on the scope of this publication and to the various authors for their speedy responses to my requests for contributions. The following readily supplied information on specific points: Mark Bowden, Georgina Plowright, David Sherlock, Graeme Stobbs and Alan Whitworth. Nick Hodgson read the whole text and I thank him particularly for his comments on Chapter 2. I am grateful to Dave Whitworth for preparing the text and illustrations for publication and to Roger Oram for devising several additional illustrations. The following are also acknowledged for supplying illustrations: Paul Austen (58-9), Alan Biggins (27, 51-2), Robin Birley (38-40), David Breeze (1), Ian Caruana (62), Jim Crow (35-7, 42, 63-5), Jacqui Huntley (6-8), Mike McCarthy (55-7), David Taylor (26), Mary Todd (67), Tony Wilmott (46-50), the RCHME (23, 32) and Tyne and Wear Museums (2-5, 10-19, 22, 29, 33).

PAUL BIDWELL   7 June 1999

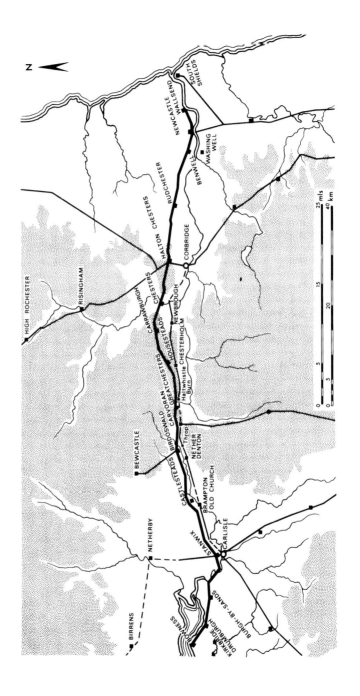

Figure 1. Hadrian's Wall and the Stanegate forts.

1. THE PILGRIMAGES OF HADRIAN'S WALL

P. Bidwell

John Collingwood Bruce and the First Pilgrimage of Hadrian's Wall

In 1848 John Collingwood Bruce had hoped to visit Rome, but much of Europe was in revolutionary turmoil. Instead he explored the Roman Wall from end to end in the company of the artists Charles and Henry Richardson and his son Gainsford. In the autumn he delivered five lectures on the Wall to the Literary and Philosophical Society of Newcastle upon Tyne and then, encouraged by their enthusiastic reception, he announced a pilgrimage along the line of the Wall to take place in the following year. Twenty-three gentlemen, three accompanied by their wives, met at Wallsend at one in the afternoon on Monday 25 June 1849, and later dined in the Castle, Newcastle upon Tyne (Fig.2). 'All went merry as a marriage-bell, while we discussed and re-discussed the eighteen toasts set down for our consideration', as Bruce recalled. The Pilgrims reached Bowness on Saturday 30 June and on their return journey by train visited Langley Castle, Corbridge and Dilston Tower and Hall.

Bruce quickly established himself as the leading authority on the Wall, publishing three editions of *The Roman Wall* (in 1851, 1853 and 1867), *The Wallet-Book of the Roman Wall* (1863, revised and re-named *Handbook to the Roman Wall* in 1884, with a further edition in 1885), *Lapidarium Septentrionale* (1875), and many pamphlets and articles.

Pilgrimage by the Roman Wall.

OPENING DINNER

IN THE

Great Hall of the Castle of Newcastle-upon-Tyne,

ON MONDAY, 25 JUNE, 1849,

☞ DINNER ON THE TABLE AT HALF-PAST FOUR O'CLOCK.

Figure 2. Invitation to the opening dinner of the First Pilgrimage. Bruce Collection, South Shields Museum (Tyne & Wear Museums).

On the occasion of the Sesquicentennial Pilgrimage, a brief sketch of the founder of the Pilgrimages is called for. John Collingwood Bruce (1805-1892) was born in Newcastle upon Tyne. His father was a schoolmaster who from small beginnings had established a very successful school in Percy Street. Bruce studied at Glasgow University from 1821 to 1829 and qualified as a Presbyterian minister. For a while he was a travelling preacher in northern England and London, but in 1831 gave up his ministry and went into partnership with his father. He remained a deeply religious man and continued active in the Presbyterian Church of England, being elected Moderator of the Synod in 1881. His father died in 1834 and under Bruce's management the Percy Street Academy, otherwise known as Bruce's Academy, continued to flourish.

By the time of the first Pilgrimage in 1849 Bruce was already active in antiquarian studies. He had been elected to the Society of Antiquaries of Newcastle upon Tyne in 1846 and was immediately involved in the restoration of the Keep and Black Gate. He served as Secretary from 1856 to 1870 and remained prominent, and often dominant, in the affairs of the Society until his death. His antiquarian interests were wide, encompassing not only the Roman Wall but the history of Newcastle upon Tyne, Northumbrian music and the small-pipes, the Bayeux Tapestry and prehistoric rock art. His championing of philanthropic causes, particularly schemes of religious, educational and moral improvement, brought him wider fame. At his funeral the carriage procession was half a mile in length and most of the public bodies in northern England passed resolutions lamenting his loss.

The title of Expounder-General given to Bruce by the Pilgrims sums up his main contribution to Wall studies. He published the first clear and well-illustrated descriptions of the Wall and his lectures were popular with general and learned audiences. He was welcome as a guest at Alnwick Castle and Chesters, where he cultivated and guided the antiquarian tastes of the fourth Duke of Northumberland and John Clayton, to the enduring benefit of Wall studies. After his death his reputation lost some of its lustre. A wide-ranging rather than profound scholar, his work seemed superficial and, when it descended to detail, sometimes unreliable.

Bruce was very much a man of his age, combining tremendous energy with high moral purpose. There is no doubt that his reputation suffered in the reaction against all things Victorian that lasted until quite recently. But even one of his severest judges conceded that Bruce had 'one overriding merit, a missionary fervour and supreme skill at arousing and maintaining general interest in the subject' (Birley 1961, 61-4). That in itself, in the present age when the future of the Wall depends above all on the part it is seen to play in the economic, social and cultural life of its region, is enough to ensure respect and admiration for the life of John Collingwood Bruce. It is fitting that on the first day of the Twelfth Pilgrimage the Pilgrims will climb from the Quayside at Newcastle to lay a wreath at Bruce's monument in the Cathedral of St Nicholas.

Later Pilgrimages

Bruce had suggested further Pilgrimages in 1855 and 1857, but it was not until 1886 that the Second Pilgrimage took place (Fig. 3). Organised by the

Figure 3. Menu of the opening dinner of the Second Pilgrimage, 26 June 1886. J.C. Bruce Collection, South Shields Museum (Tyne & Wear Museums).

Society of Antiquaries of Newcastle upon Tyne and the Cumberland and Westmorland Antiquarian and Archaeological Society, the Pilgrimage lasted eight days and was accompanied throughout by Bruce, the Chief Pilgrim, then aged 80. There were further Pilgrimages in 1896 and 1906; the Fifth Pilgrimage was deferred until 1920 because of the First World War; the Sixth Pilgrimage was in 1930, but again because of war the Seventh Pilgrimage did not take place until 1949, since when it has been possible to arrange a Pilgrimage every decade.

The length and content of the Pilgrimages have varied, but they have all served the same purposes. First, all have been acts of veneration for the best-known Roman monument in Britain. In modern times they have been opportunities to study and discuss discoveries made in the previous decade and have been a spur to further research. They have also been tours of inspection, examining the condition of the remains. Finally, they have all been convivial, allowing a large group of people sharing a common interest to spend a pleasant and instructive week together.

The history of the first eight Pilgrimages was written by Eric Birley (1961, 25-47). In 1949 the Seventh Pilgrimage, starting at South Shields and ending at Maryport, lasted six days. The 1959 and 1969 Pilgrimages were shorter, but in 1979 the Tenth Pilgrimage restored South Shields and Maryport to the itinerary. The Twelfth Pilgrimage will see the addition of at least one outpost fort to the route and the revival of the boat trip up the River Tyne which figured in the 1949 Pilgrimage.

The Pilgrimage Handbooks
Bruce and his successors had issued brief prospectuses of forthcoming Pilgrimages containing nothing more than details of the programme (Fig. 4), but in 1930 R. G. Collingwood compiled *The Book of the Pilgrimage*, a substantial booklet of 54 pages supplied as a guide for the Pilgrims. Eric Birley prepared a larger guide of 83 pages for the Centenary Pilgrimage in 1949. He had intended a guide of comparable length for the 1959 Pilgrimage, but a printing strike prevented its production. Instead he produced *Research on Hadrian's Wall* (Birley 1961), a stocktaking of four centuries' work on the Wall. It is one of the three texts which the student of the Wall must always

4

CUMBERLAND & WESTMORLAND

Antiquarian & Archaeological Society.

AND THE

SOCIETY OF ANTIQUARIES

OF NEWCASTLE-UPON-TYNE,

DETAILED & AMENDED PROGRAMME

OF THE CUMBERLAND PORTION OF THE

Seven Days Pilgrimage

ALONG THE ROMAN WALL,

TO COMMENCE

ON SATURDAY, JUNE 26th,

AND END ON

SATURDAY, JULY 3rd, 1886.

Committee for Local Arrangements in Cumberland:

J. A. CORY, CARLISLE.
ISAAC CARTMELL, CARLISLE.
R. S. FERGUSON, F.S.A., CARLISLF.
Rev. T. LEES, F.S.A. WREAY.

General Committee:

J. C. BRUCE, LL.D., F.S.A., NEWCASTLE.
C. J. BATES, M.A., HEDDON.
R. S. FERGUSON, F.S.A., CARLISLE.
R. O. HESLOP, CORBRIDGE.
C. C. HODGES, HEXHAM.
THOMAS HODGKIN, D.C.L., &c., NEWCASTLE.
C. J. SPENCE, NORTH SHIELDS.
ROBERT BLAIR, F.S.A., SOUTH SHIELDS, (Hon. Secretary).

Figure 4. Front page of the prospectus for the Second Pilgrimage. J.C Bruce Collection, South Shields Museum. (Tyne & Wear Museums).

have at hand (the others, of course, being *The Handbook to the Roman Wall* and Breeze and Dobson's *Hadrian's Wall*). The guides that accompanied the 1969 and 1979 Pilgrimages were briefer (Birley 1969; Dobson 1979), but Daniels (1989) produced a more substantial publication for the 1989 Pilgrimage (95 pages) which has been the inspiration for the present work.

These guides are often referred to as the Pilgrimage Handbooks, although none has had that title. Confusion with the *Handbook to the Roman Wall* can arise and the title of the present work makes plain that it is essentially a summary of the last decade's research.

In Memoriam

' *Felix qui potuit rerum cognoscere causas*', Virgil, *Aeneid*, IV, 490.

Sadly there are several additions to be made to the Roll of Honour of past Pilgrims prominent in the study of Hadrian's Wall. **Eric Birley** (1906-1995) was for many decades the foremost authority on the Wall. He will be remembered also for his wider contributions to Roman archaeology, particularly in the field of prosopography and as founder of the International Limes Congresses, and, beyond archaeology, for his distinguished war service in military intelligence. **Charles Daniels** (1932-1996) was the editor of the thirteenth edition of the *Handbook to the Roman Wall* (1978) and prepared the guide for the last Pilgrimage. His most important excavations were at Wallsend and Housesteads; in a life full of travel on the frontiers of the Roman Empire, Hadrian's Wall was an abiding passion. **Michael Jarrett** (1934-1994) excavated at Ebchester, Halton Chesters and Maryport; he is best known for his revision of Nash-William's *The Roman Frontier in Wales* (1969). **Richard Wright** (1908-1992) in 1939 took over R. G. Collingwood's work on the *Roman Inscriptions of Britain*, published in 1965. **Charles Anderson** (1909-1998) must also be mentioned, not for research but for his many years as Charge Hand for the Ministry of Works and its successors, supervising the masons who uncovered and preserved the Wall.

We must also remember other past Pilgrims not directly concerned with research on Hadrian's Wall, prominent amongst them Miss **Anne Robertson** (1910-1997), excavator of many Roman sites in Scotland and author of the authoritative guide to the Antonine Wall, and **John Philipson** (1910-1995), editor of *Archaeologia Aeliana* for over thirty years.

2. A SUMMARY OF RECENT RESEARCH ON HADRIAN'S WALL

P. Bidwell

Introduction
This chapter concentrates on recent discoveries and research which have advanced the study of Hadrian's Wall, with a particular emphasis on its function and structural history. Succeeding chapters deal with the environment of the Wall and the Vindolanda writing-tablets, but much else of importance has been excluded for reasons of space, for example research on pottery, small finds, coins and sculpture.

Excavation
During the last decade there have been excavations on a large scale at five forts (South Shields, Wallsend, Newcastle, Vindolanda and Birdoswald) and in the civilian areas at Carlisle, and work on a smaller scale at other forts, some of which has been very informative, as at Stanwix, Burgh-by-Sands and High Rochester. The bridges at Chesters and Corbridge have been investigated and on the Cumbrian coast tower 2B and milefortlet 21 have been completely excavated. Little work has taken place on the line of the Wall: the only large-scale excavation has been at Wallsend where an 80m length of the Wall is being exposed for permanent display, and sections have been cut across the Wall and Vallum at Black Carts. Small-scale work has taken place at two milecastles, but no turrets have been excavated.

In the wider context of British archaeology at the end of the century, it is remarkable and heartening that so much excavation continues to take place on the Wall, especially as much of it is undertaken essentially for research purposes rather than as rescue work in advance of development. Admittedly the research is rarely pure. Sites are excavated in order to display and interpret them to visitors, as at South Shields and Vindolanda, or to allow them to be managed properly, as at Black Carts. Their selection will be dictated by non-archaeological needs, for example economic and social regeneration or conservation, but once a site is chosen work can proceed according to a research strategy based largely on archaeological considerations. The main disadvantage of this applied research is that it can entirely pass by some of the most important questions about the Wall. There are for example fundamental uncertainties about the use of milecastle gateways and whether civilian traffic was confined to major routes passing through the Wall, as at Portgate, matters which are at the root of any understanding of how the Wall was intended to function and are discussed at the end of this chapter. Such problems cannot be solved by digging forts. Answers are only likely to come from problem-driven excavations undertaken in a spirit of pure research, for which there are at present no resources. We can only hope that the research strategy for the Hadrian's Wall World Heritage Site will recognise the need for this work (p. 70).

Work by RCHME
The RCHME Hadrian's Wall Project, a revision of the Ordnance Survey records, was undertaken between January 1988 and September 1990, with some additional work continuing into 1993. It covered the length of the Wall as far east as turret 7B. The separate RCHME Cumberland Coast Project, carried out between January 1993 and February 1994, surveyed the remains of the coastal defences, including the site of the fort at Maryport (Lax and Blood 1997). Finally, the RCHME Hadrian's Wall Archive Project has compiled a national index to archaeological and antiquarian records of the Wall.

User Guides for the Projects are available from RCHME and some of the results have been published (noted here under individual site entries). Part of the Commentary in the User Guide for the Hadrian's Wall Project is published in Chapter 6 under Wall Miles 26, 40/41, 43, 43/44 and 72.

The RCHME publication of *Roman Camps in England* (Welfare and Swan 1995) has been the culmination of survey work over many years. Of the 95 isolated camps or groups of camps in the Inventory, 37 are in Northumberland and 19 in Cumbria. This study will long remain one of the essential texts for the study of Hadrian's Wall and its environs.

Excavation reports and other studies
Volumes describing excavations at South Shields, Vindolanda, Birdoswald and Carlisle have appeared since 1989; accounts of numerous smaller excavations have been published in county and national journals. There still remains a back-log of post-excavation work on several major excavations,

but in almost every instance the preparation of final reports for publication is in progress. The next few years should see a fine harvest of reports which is certain to improve our understanding of the Wall.

General surveys of finds are not noted under the individual site entries in Chapter 6. Over a period of six years from 1990 to 1995, there have been published nine fascicules, including an index, which make up the second volume (*Instrumentum Domesticum*) of *The Roman Inscriptions of Britain* (*RIB* II). Of particular importance to Wall studies are the fascicules dealing with diplomas and lead sealings (1) and with military tile stamps (4). The first volume of *RIB* has been reprinted with addenda and corrigenda by Tomlin. Snape (1993) has produced a *corpus* of brooches from the Stanegate sites; Allason-Jones (1991) has used small finds to examine Roman and native interaction in Northumberland and, with Dungworth (1997), has assembled the evidence for metal-working on Hadrian's Wall. Swan's work on the legionary pottery of York (1992) should be noted because some of these products appear at the eastern end of Hadrian's Wall. Finally, Jarrett (1994) has produced a comprehensive survey of the history and postings of non-legionary units in Britain.

Guide books and maps
The continuing popularity of the Wall is reflected by the number of guide books now offered for sale to visitors. There is now a German-language *Reiseführer* published in Switzerland which deals with the central sector of the Wall (Masé 1995). Other guides adopt varying approaches: Richards' *The Wall Walk* (1993) is heavily influenced by Wainwright's Lakeland and Pennine guides and Hopkins' *Walking The Wall* (1993) combines a sometimes inaccurate account of the Wall with more engaging descriptions of the natural history of its modern environs. Green's *Discovering Hadrian's Wall* (1992) is straightforward and conscientious. De la Bédoyère's *Hadrian's Wall: History and Guide* (1998) is a sound archaeological guide, well illustrated and taking account of recent research. Breeze's *Souvenir Guide to the Roman Wall* (1993) is the best short introduction.

Nothing that has been published in the last ten years can be regarded as a substitute for the *Handbook to the Roman Wall* or Breeze and Dobson's

Hadrian's Wall. Fortunately, arrangements have been made for the preparation of the fourteenth edtion of the *Handbook* and a new edition of *Hadrian's Wall* will appear shortly.

The new edition of the *Ordnance Survey Map of Hadrian's Wall* which appeared at the time of the last Pilgrimage was widely criticised. Much more useful is the 1997 *Ordnance Survey Outdoor Leisure Map 43* which includes the Wall from Sewingshields as far west as turret 51b. The earlier *Ordnance Survey Map of Hadrian's Wall* (1964 and 1972 editions) is still the best available, although only to be bought second-hand.

The late prehistoric period

The general picture of later prehistoric settlement in our area has become clearer in the last decade, mainly through studies of the environmental evidence which are fully discussed by Huntley in Chapter 4. Here it is worth emphasising how the building of the Wall and its associated works has preserved a huge transect of the prehistoric and early Roman landscape of northern England, protecting it from degradation by later cultivation, plant growth and erosion.

Recent discoveries illustrate the enormous potential of these pre-Wall deposits. Beneath the Roman levels at South Shields the well preserved remains of a round house dating to the third century BC have been found and it now seems possible that a hill fort lies beneath the annexe of the fort at High Rochester. The South Shields round house had been burnt down, producing a large deposit of charred grain and debris from the structure of the house. Similar remains in an open landscape would not have survived more than two millennia of natural and agricultural processes. At Wallsend and Denton it has been possible to show that the Roman builders had appropriated fields prepared with narrow rig and furrow for the next crop, the preliminary levelling layers having filled the freshly-cut furrows. This simple stratigraphical relationship (which has also been recorded at Rudchester) dispels the belief that ard marks found beneath the Wall might be connected with Roman clearance of the site rather than with native agriculture.

Note also: Bewley 1994, a survey of prehistoric and Romano-British settlement on the Solway plain, sceptical about the Roman impact on native settlement patterns.

The Flavian and Trajanic periods

The earliest Roman military occupation

Timbers from the rampart and other primary structures in the first fort at Carlisle have been dated by dendrochronology to the second half of 72 or early in 73 (Caruana 1992, 104-5). This establishes beyond much doubt that the fort was established in the governorship of Q. Petillius Cerialis (71-4), overturning a widely but not universally held view that it was only under Agricola that forts were established beyond Chester and York. At the very least forts as early as Carlisle might be expected on the route from York, across Stainmore and up the Eden valley. However, a single line of forts a hundred miles in length, crossing the Pennines by a route even now sometimes closed to traffic in winter, seems an inadequate method of controlling a huge tract of Brigantian territory. A more extensive system of forts is likely, and Caruana (1997) has put forward arguments not only for the possible Cerialan date of some forts on the line of Dere Street and in north-west England but also for the placing of forts in southern Scotland. Pottery collected by field-walking at Blennerhasset in Cumbria (Evans and Scull 1990) could well be consistently of early Flavian date, but none of the other forts discussed by Caruana has yet produced enough early material to do more than hint at the possibility of an origin in the early 70s.

The only sites in the Tyne-Solway corridor which can be unequivocally associated with Agricola are Corbridge (Red House) and Carlisle, where the original fort continued in occupation. Writing tablets from the fort at Carlisle suggest that it was occupied by the *ala Gallorum Sebosiana* during Agricola's governorship (*Tab. Luguval.* 44 and possibly 46).

The Stanegate

The Stanegate (the medieval name for parts of the Roman road connecting Corbridge with Carlisle) became the northern limit of Roman military occupation in Britain by *c.* 105, and then, following the building of Hadrian's Wall, it served as the main east-west road, even after forts were placed on the line of the Wall. It originated as a cross-country route between the two main roads running into Roman Scotland, even if the building of a proper road came later, as now seems likely (see below). The earliest fort known along its line is at Vindolanda, where a construction date in the mid-80s, first proposed in the 1930s, is now supported by new evidence (Birley 1994, 18-35). The scarcity of samian ware form 29s, common on Agricolan sites, confirms that occupation began well into the 80s (but note R. Birley's suggestion of an earlier fort north of the Stanegate, p.131). The Period I fort, however, was demolished in *c*. 90, the date of a large group of unused samian ware found in the west ditch of the fort. Nether Denton is probably another fort of this period; it cannot be closely dated, but its position, roughly equidistant between Carlisle and Vindolanda, suggests that it too originated in the mid-80s.

The building of these two forts took place at about the same time as Roman forts north of the Forth-Clyde isthmus were abandoned. Many of the forts south of the isthmus, it seems, remained in occupation. An alternative view has been outlined by Jones (1991): by the early 90s a series of large forts had been established in a line running from Corbridge westwards, possibly to the Solway. These included Corbridge, Vindolanda, Nether Denton and Carlisle, possibly also Newbrough, Carvoran and Burgh-by-Sands I. Such a powerful concentration of forces would imply that many forts in southern Scotland had also been given up as well as those further north; the few forts in southern Scotland where occupation running into the 90s is proved would have served as outposts.

This interpretation has to be assessed in the light of Table 1 which presents the periods of occupation at Corbridge, Vindolanda and Carlisle, running up to the building of Hadrian's Wall. At Carlisle and Vindolanda the dates of several construction periods are established by dendrochronology, allowing a degree of precision which excavators forced to rely on pottery and coins for dating their sites will certainly envy. The closest correspondences in the histories of these three forts occur in *c*. 105 when they were all rebuilt. Since the 1950s much has been made of the rebuilding of the fort at Corbridge, dated to 103 or later by a coin of Trajan found in its east rampart; as Breeze and Dobson noted (1987, 25), this provided the only good evidence for the date at which the remaining forts in southern Scotland were given up (although the absence of samian from Les Martres-de-Veyre at these forts suggests that they were not occupied for very long after the beginning of Trajan's reign: Hartley 1972, 15). Now that rebuilding at Carlisle (Caruana 1992, 104) and Vindolanda (Birley 1994, 111) can be dated by dendrochronology to *c*. 105, the conventional date for the withdrawal to the Stanegate is vindicated, providing it is assumed that that the simultaneous rebuilding of these forts resulted from the movement of units to new postings, following the abandonment of southern

Scotland. Indeed, at Vindolanda *cohors VIIII Batavorum* seems to have been replaced by *cohors I Tungrorum*. In contrast the early 90s, the date by which Jones has argued withdrawal from Scotland was largely complete, saw complete rebuilding only at Vindolanda; at Carlisle, although the south gate was rebuilt, the buildings in the interior remained unaltered; no building activity is known at Corbridge.

The need to strengthen control of the new frontier zone provides the most plausible reason for the building of forts at Brampton and Carvoran. Nothing further has been learnt about the small forts at Throp, Haltwhistle Burn and Newbrough.

So much for the forts. A perceptive contribution by Poulter (1998) sets out the reasons why the construction of the Stanegate road might not have occurred until the Trajanic period. Its course, rather than following the easiest lines cross-country, runs from fort to fort, requiring traverses of some difficult country. The implication is that the forts, including the small forts at Haltwhistle Burn and Throp (generally agreed to be of Trajanic date), were already there

CORBRIDGE (Bishop and Dore 1988, 140-1)			VINDOLANDA (Birley 1994)			CARLISLE (Caruana 1992, 104; Tomlin 1998, 32)		
Period	Date AD	Unit(s)	Period	Date AD	Unit(s)	Period	Date AD	Unit(s)
						3A/1	**72/3**	
Red Ho.	**78?**					3A/2	78/82	A SEB
I	**c. 86**	A PETR	**I**	**c. 85**		3B/1	83-4	
			II	**c. 90/92**	C I T/ C IX B	3B/2	93/4	
			III	**97**	C IX B			
II	**c. 105**		**IV**	**105**	C I T	**5A**	**105**	
			V	*c.* 112	C I T			
III	*c.*122							

Table 1: Dated structural periods at Corbridge, Vindolanda and Carlisle. Building, rebuilding or major internal re-planning of forts shown in **bold.** Abbreviations of unit titles: *A PETR*: *ala Petriana*; *A SEB*: *ala Gallorum Sebosiana*; *C I T*: *cohors I Tungrorum*; *C IX B*: *cohors VIIII Batavorum*. At some periods these forts may have accommodated more than one unit: the *equites Vardulli* are known to have been at Vindolanda in Period IV or V, and legionaries are known at Carlisle and Vindolanda.

when the Stanegate was built, and dictated its line. Bishop (1995) has similarly concluded from the discovery of a fort controlling the river crossing of the River Ure at Roecliffe that Dere Street was not built until at least the mid-80s, when the Roecliffe fort, occupied from *c*. 71, was replaced by another fort at Aldborough, 2km to the east and on the line of Dere Street.

Was the Stanegate a frontier?
W. H. Forster suggested as early as 1913 that the Stanegate forts were associated with a frontier line established after the withdrawal from Scotland, and this has been accepted until quite recently. Except in the Solway area (see below), there is no question of the frontier being represented by a continuous barrier. Instead, what is meant is a frontier as defined by Dobson (1986, 2-3), specifically in considering the Stanegate: 'a disposition of forces along the frontier line in a greater concentration than elsewhere, with sometimes the addition of observation posts (towers) and fortlets accommodating small groups of men'. Having examined its supposed components, Dobson concluded that there was no firm evidence for the existence of such a system on the Stanegate. The forts on its line merely marked the limit of Roman ocupation and the zone was held in no greater strength than, for example, Dere Street or the road across Stainmore to Carlisle.

Yet some continue to regard the Stanegate as a frontier system. Woolliscroft (1989b), for example, has attempted to show that the forts and the occasional towers such as Mains Rigg were intervisible, so that signals could be passed along the system. There is also the question of the 'Western Stanegate', an apparent extension which ran as far as Kirkbride and which seems to have been accompanied, at least in places, by a ditch and palisade. The most recent summary was published in the previous Pilgrimage Handbook (Jones in Daniels 1989, 92-5; see also Jones 1989 and 1994-5). A frontier running from Kirkbride to Burgh-by-Sands, formed at least in places by a continuous barrier, would make little sense unless movement from the north was also rigorously controlled further to the west.

The Tyne valley east of Corbridge
An extension of the Stanegate to the east of Corbridge has been sought but there is no sign of one, either to the north or south of the Tyne. Any scheme that is proposed will be highly speculative, having to depend on the slender evidence of a pre-Hadrianic fort at Washing Wells and the uncertain foundation

Period	Events	Eastern Extension to Wallsend	Newcastle to Willowford	Willowford to Bowness	Cumbrian Coast	Outpost forts	Hinterland forts
	Governor, A. Platorius Nepos.		Broad Wall, turrets, milecastles, bridges started.	Turf Wall and mile-castles, stone turrets.	Forts, mile-fortlets and towers.	Bewcastle (also Birrens and Netherby?).	Vindolanda (?) and Corbridge rebuilt.
IA, Hadrianic, c. 122-138.	A. Platorius Nepos.		Forts added to Wall. Vallum begun.				Hardknott built (or earlier in Hadrian's reign?).
		Extension to Wallsend.	Narrow Wall.				
			Forts added at Carraw-burgh and Great Chesters.				
			Carvoran rebuilt in stone.	Birdoswald and Wall nearby rebuilt in stone.			Hardknott replaced by Raven-glass.
	Antonine Wall begun early in Pius' reign and Hadrian's Wall abandoned, although some forts may have still been manned on a reduced scale. Vallum slighted.					High Rochester and Risingham built.	Corbridge rebuilt.
Antoninus Pius (138-161).	Hadrian's Wall re-occupied from c. 158.	Wall repaired and some rebuilding in forts (eg Wallsend).	Remainder of Turf Wall and forts rebuilt in stone.	Most towers and milefortlets not re-occupied.		S. Shields rebuilt on new site. New forts at Lanchester, Chester-le-St.	
		Vallum abandoned, Military Way built, road bridge at Chesters					
M Aurelius (161-180). Commodus (180-192).	Warfare in northern Britain.	Many turrets out of use (doors blocked). Milecastle gates narrowed.				Birrens and Newstead abandoned.	
Septimius Severus (193-211).	Warfare succeeded by invasion of Scotland.	Repairs to Wall, many turrets demolished.				Fortress built at Carpow; Cramond re-occupied. Both abandoned by 211.	S. Shields rebuilt as supply base; legionaries at Corbridge (and Carlisle?).
Caracalla (212-217).	Withdraw-al from Scotland.	Beginning of a period of apparent stability. No overall programmes of repairs or modifications to the Wall known.					

Table 2: This represents the standard view of the structural sequence of Hadrian's Wall, for the most part differing only in a few details from Breeze and Dobson (1987). The major change is acceptance of a single occupation of the Antonine Wall (Hodgson 1995).

date of a fort at South Shields (not on the site of the mid-Antonine stone fort), which could be Flavian or Trajanic (Bidwell and Speak 1994, 14).

The following sections comment in detail on the structure and history of the Wall which are both of great complexity. For the convenience of the reader, the general sequence down to the Severan period is summarised on Table 2.

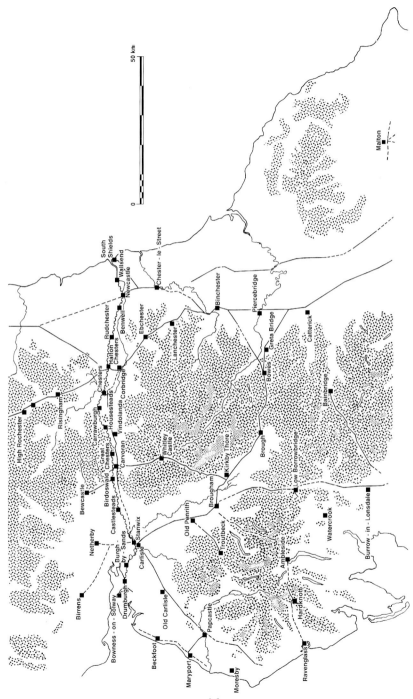

Figure 5. Forts in northern England, Hadrianic and later.

16

The origins of Hadrian's Wall
In 1997 a fragment of a tombstone was found at Vindolanda which recorded the death '*in bell*[*o*]' of a centurion associated with a unit of Tungrians. A. Birley (1998) has argued that the text probably refers to *cohors I Tungrorum*, possibly at Vindolanda in as many as three of the five pre-Hadrianic periods; the centurion seems to have been a legionary in command of the unit. According to Birley the war in which he fell was that which preceded and brought about the building of Hadrian's Wall, a war otherwise attested only by two oblique literary references and the issue in 119 of a coin bearing the image of Britannia, probably to mark a victory over the Britons.

A British war early in Hadrian's reign might have been the immediate reason why the Wall was built, but the emperor's general policy was to define the permanent limits of the empire. On his first great tour of the provinces, after visting the German frontier, he crossed to Britain in 122. This episode has been examined in the only full, modern biography of Hadrian recently published by A. Birley (1997b). The extent to which Hadrian involved himself personally in the design of the Wall will probably always remain uncertain. Birley portrays a difficult man, touchily proud of his many real accomplishments, who sought the company of those learned in his areas of interest, sometimes only to heap sarcasm on them. An experienced soldier obsessed with architecture and a restless traveller with a taste, it seems, for wild and mountainous country (the product of his passion for hunting), he would surely have relished the prospect of planning new and uniquely elaborate frontier works in northern Britain.

The building of Hadrian's Wall
The chronology of the building programme
A hitherto unknown governor of Britain in Hadrian's reign, L. Trebius Germanus, is named on a diploma of unknown provenance, and now in a private collection at Munich; it was issued on 20 August 127 (Nollé 1997, 299-75 including an addendum by M. Roxan). This establishes the last possible date for the departure of his predecessor, A. Platorius Nepos; indeed, he probably left Britain in late 126, if not earlier, by which time forts were being built on the line of the Wall, as is demonstrated by inscriptions from Benwell and Halton Chesters which bear his name. Another result of identifying Germanus as Nepos's successor has been to strengthen the case for restoring

the latter's name on a poorly-recorded Hadrianic building inscription from the outpost fort at Bewcastle (*RIB* 995; *Britannia* 29 (1998), 443, where R. Tomlin shows that Germanus' names cannot posssibly fit the recorded letters). It is thus likely that Bewcastle and perhaps the other two western outpost forts at Birrens and Netherby, which have also produced Hadrianic building inscriptions, were built during the early stages of work on the Wall.

Note also: Bennett 1998, proposing a new sequence of construction at the eastern end of the Wall, unfortunately not supported by recent discoveries (p. 97).

The architecture of the Wall
It is now generally (but not universally) accepted that there was a walkway along the top of the Wall. The presence of foot-bridges on the line of the Wall where it crosses the Rivers North Tyne and Irthing (Bidwell and Holbrook 1989, 134-5), together with other long-known features suggesting a Wall-walk, seems to have resolved the issue. Much has been made of the absence of capping stones which would prove the existence of crenellations (Hill and Dobson 1992, 32); there are other methods of finishing the tops of merlons, for example a mortar capping, which has been employed successfully on the reconstructions at Vindolanda and Wallsend. It is now known that at least in places the Wall had a decorative finish. Remains of whitewash have been noted on a chamfered slab from Peel Gap (Crow 1991, 46, fig. 8.2), and wall-plaster fallen from the rear of the Wall has been found at Denton (Bidwell and Watson 1996, 23-8, figs 18-20).

These sorts of decorative treatment are entirely normal in Roman building construction (Bidwell 1996a). Entirely abnormal are the construction techniques of the Broad and Narrow Walls. The use of clay rather than mortar was first observed by Richmond (1950, 43) at turret 26b in 1948 and now instances of the use of clay far outnumber occurrences of the mortared core. Dissection of the core at Denton, west of Benwell, and at Chesters has shown that clay provided the main body of the core, with the rubble serving as a filler (Bidwell and Watson 1996, 19). In the central sector of Hadrian's Wall mortar is absent from the core of the Narrow Wall (Crow 1991, 55). Mortar was usually employed in the Broad and Narrow Walls only to point the facing stones, and then very sparingly. That it was feasible, given enough time and labour, to build the Wall with an orthodox mortared core is demonstrated of course by the the Extra-Narrow or 'Severan' Wall. The techniques of construction used in the original Wall have few parallels in Roman stone defensive architecture and were presumably adopted because the building programme was too compressed to allow time for conventional techniques.

Evidence for the design of turrets has been thoroughly reviewed by P. Hill (1997) and several alternative reconstructions proposed.
Note also: Crow 1991, on building phases of the Curtain Wall in the central sector, with comments on sources of building materials; Hill 1991, on interruptions in the work programme and the possibility that a legion might be switched to a different sector to complete work begun by another legion; Hill and Dobson 1992, reviewing evidence for the form and function of the Wall, turrets and milecastles; Johnson 1997, a comprehensive guide to the geology of the Wall area, particularly useful for sources of building stone; Kendal 1996, an interesting examination of transport logistics and quantity surveys for the building of the Wall; Mann 1990a, on *legio VI Victrix* rebuilding the Turf Wall in stone between milecastles 49 and 54 late in Hadrian's reign.

The fort decision
The decision to add forts to the Wall after most of the turrets and milecastles had been built (or at least had been partly built, cf. Hill 1991, 35-6), some then having to be demolished to make way for the forts, can now be seen in a new light. It has long been thought that at the same time forts on the Stanegate were abandoned and their units moved up to the new forts on the Wall. What actually happened was more complicated.

In the eastern part of the Wall and its immediate vicinity there were no pre-Hadrianic forts north of the Tyne to be abandoned, and the units for the forts at Wallsend, Benwell and Rudchester would presumably have been drawn from postings further south. The large Stanegate forts south of the central sector at Corbridge (Bishop and Dore 1988, 135, 140) and Vindolanda (Bidwell 1985, 6-10; Birley 1994, 14-5) now seem to have continued in occupation throughout the Hadrianic period. From Carvoran westwards only four forts, Birdoswald, Stanwix, Drumburgh and Bowness-on-Solway, were added to the Wall when the fort decision was taken. The pre-Hadrianic forts at Carvoran, Carlisle and Burgh- by- Sands (Burgh I or III), all in close proximity to the Wall, remained in occupation. Castlesteads might also have been of pre-

Hadrianic origin: its position, isolated from the Wall, certainly resembles those of the other early forts in the western part of the Wall.

Although this account rests partly on interim statements rather than full publication of the evidence, it is certainly no longer possible to claim with confidence that 'all [the] Stanegate posts were given up and their garrisons transferred to the Wall' (Daniels 1978, 28). In the western sector three of the Stanegate period forts (or four if Castlesteads is early) survived, so that part of the pre-Hadrianic system of forts, and perhaps even a nascent Trajanic frontier, were incorporated in the Wall system. In the central sector it would also have been a matter of augmentation rather than substitution when forts were added to the Wall, if Corbridge and Vindolanda remained in occupation. East of Corbridge the position remains obscure. The apparent absence of forts from where men could have been sent to control the Wall in its initial phase is one of the reasons why J. Crow (1995, 18-22) has argued that from the very first it had been intended to place forts on the Wall, the building of turrets and milecastles on sites forts were to occupy being simply a mistake. False starts are common enough in Roman building projects, but it will be difficult to prove Crow's hypothesis of delayed intention by means of archaeology. In any event the change to Narrow gauge in the construction of the Wall, which took place at the same time as the forts were added or shortly afterwards, was certainly a major modification to the original design.

It seems safer to accept the reality of the fort decision, even if it can now be seen much more as an augmentation of the number of units in the Wall zone rather than the transfer of units from the Stanegate to new forts on the line of the Wall.

A connection between the fort decision and warfare in northern Britain in the mid-120s, discounted since the 1970s, has been revived by J. Casey in a study of the coinage of Alexandria (1987). The city produced an annual coinage dated by regnal years; issues of the *Nike* type seem to be confined to years when major conflicts were in progress, and Casey (*ibid.*, 71) has connected the large issue of this type in Years 9 and 10 of Hadrian's reign (124/5-125/6) with conflict in Britain, specifically resistance to the building of the Wall. According to Casey, this led to strengthening of the Wall by the addition of forts on its line and the consequent increase in the number of units in the Wall zone.

Note also: Bennett 1998 (see also Bennett 1990), arguing for a lengthy hiatus in the construction of the Wall when the fort decision was taken. The Vallum is seen as a temporary measure, closing off the line of the Wall while work on the forts was in progress, and redundant once the curtain was completed later in Hadrian's reign.

The forts

It now seems likely that all the forts associated with the Turf Wall were originally built in turf and timber. This can now be demonstrated, or is strongly indicated, at Birdoswald (Wilmott 1997, 53) and Stanwix (Dacre 1985). It has long been known that the original forts at Castlesteads, Drumburgh and Bowness-on-Solway were of turf and timber.

Since 1989 there has been much more excavation at forts than on the Wall itself. Although many of the excavations have not penetrated below the later Roman levels, some new information about the Hadrianic fort plans has been recovered.

At Wallsend the two barracks recently re-excavated in the *retentura* were found to have originally been built in timber and the stone hospital was also preceded by a timber building of uncertain function (p.84). Hitherto, Hadrianic timber buildings have only been encountered in the western forts where the defences were also originally of turf and timber, as at Bowness-on-Solway, although at Chesters J. Gillam saw postholes under the barracks when they were being consolidated. This raises the question of to what extent we can rely on the stone buildings as a guide to the original plans of the forts. For example, at Halton Chesters the plan recovered by geophysical survey (Fig. 26) shows barracks in the *retentura* aligned east-west, while the buildings in the *praetentura* run north-south. Perhaps the latter were preceded by timber buildings on an east-west alignment and the insertion of a bath building in the western part of the *praetentura* meant that this part of the fort had to be entirely re-planned.

The Vallum

There have been excavations on the Vallum at Burgh-by-Sands, Denton and Black Carts. Metalling was found on the north berm at Burgh-by-Sands (Austen 1994, 41, fig. 2) and at Black Carts, but was absent at Denton, where the berm was revealed for a length of 9.5m (Bidwell and Watson 1996, 38).

The cobbles and sand at Burgh-by-Sands were thought to represent the Military Way, but the very thin metalling at Black Carts finds a parallel at Appletree in Wall-mile 50 (Daniels 1978, 217). Five instances of metalling on the south berm are also known, although it is clear that on both berms the metalling is more often absent than present (Heywood 1965, 89-90). Its infrequent occurrences hardly suggest that there was regular traffic along the Vallum berms.

Note also: Bowden and Blood 1991, 30, explaining that at Rudchester the course of the Vallum established by an RCHME survey implies that it was actually under construction to the west when the site of the fort was chosen, and that its course was simply shifted south of the fort by means of a single dog-leg.

Lateral communications

The question of lateral communication behind the Wall before the construction of the Military Way was reviewed in 1989 (Bidwell and Holbrook 1989, 150-3). Between Corbridge and Willowford, a little to the east of Birdoswald, the arrangements are clear: there were branch roads from the Stanegate to the forts, and when the Vallum was constructed openings and causeways opposite the forts were the only means of approaching the Wall from the south, except at specially-provided gates through the Wall at Portgate on Dere Street, north of Corbridge (there may have been other such gates on major north-south routes). To the west of Willowford, where the Wall lies north of the River Irthing, a new road would have been needed immediately south of the Wall, for the Stanegate lies wholly south of the Irthing. A new road was probably also supplied to the east of Portgate, running between the Wall and the River Tyne.

A new feature in the anatomy of the frontier is a metalled track running close behind the Wall at Denton, which was traced for a distance of 170m (Bidwell and Watson 1996, 20-2, 31, 33-5, figs 12, 17A and 22). It had been resurfaced twice; the uppermost surface produced a *denarius* of Septimius Severus issued in AD 202-10, perhaps pressed into the metalling by traffic. The survival of the track after the construction of the Military Way, which apparently ran some 30.0-40.0m south of the Wall at Denton, might suggest that it was used mainly for maintenance and patrols. It would thus be comparable to the

Limesweg on the Upper German and Raetian frontiers. In 1976 an unmetalled hollow way was seen behind the Turf Wall at Tarraby Lane, east of the fort at Stanwix (Smith 1978, 23-4, fig. 7), but further excavations nearby suggest that it is not of Roman date (information from M. McCarthy) and thus the Denton track stands as an isolated discovery.

Bellhouse (1989, 7-9) has questioned the identification of the coastal road on the Cardurnock peninsula, but work at tower 2B uncovered two layers of metalling, the lower preceding the construction of the stone tower and presumably contemporary with one or both of the successive timber towers (Jones 1993, 37, fig. 2). This was advanced as evidence for the existence of an early patrol road.

The Antonine period

The evidence for a second Antonine occupation of Scotland beginning in *c*.158 has been carefully examined by Hodgson (1995) and found wanting. He has suggested that withdrawal from the Antonine Wall began in *c*.155-8; this was perhaps a gradual process, so that some forts, for example Mumrills and Castlecary, effectively served as outpost forts while the bulk of the army fell back on Hadrian's Wall. The virtues of this new view lie in its economy of hypothesis, rejecting the Brigantian revolt of *c*.155 and therefore any reason to withdraw temporarily to northern England, and in its plausible interpretation of the structural sequences at forts in Scotland.

When Hadrian's Wall was reoccupied, the Cumbrian coastal system of towers and milefortlets was largely abandoned. This can now be stated more confidently because milefortlet 21 (Swarthy Hill) has produced only Hadrianic pottery (Turnbull 1991, 3), and reassessment of the published pottery from milefortlet 1 (Biglands) by the writer suggests that there is only one sherd which is certainly of post-Hadrianic date (a samian Dr. 45: Potter 1977, 173, no. 10). West of the Irthing work was resumed on rebuilding the Turf Wall in stone; the only indication of the date of this rebuilding is the pottery from Turf Wall levels at milecastle 79 and turret 54A which includes nothing necessarily later than the mid-Antonine period. Some, most recently Hassall (1984), have associated the rebuilding with Severus.

Following further excavations at Chesters in 1990-1, the Severan date proposed for the road bridge by Bidwell and Holbrook (1989, 28, 138-40) must now be rejected: a dump of pottery associated with early occupation of the newly-discovered tower at the west end of the bridge is of early to mid-Antonine date (p.120). At Corbridge the bridge which carries Dere Street across the River Tyne can be tied in even more closely with Chesters because of exact correspondences in techniques of construction noted during survey and excavation in 1995 by the writer and M. Snape. In recent decades it has been assumed that the Military Way was added when Hadrian's Wall was re-occupied in the mid-Antonine period and that it was inspired by a similar road serving the Antonine Wall. The re-dating of the road bridge at Chesters supports a mid-Antonine date for the Military Way, and the contemporaneous bridge-building at Corbridge suggests that this was part of general improvements made to lines of communications in northern Britain following the abandonment of the Antonine Wall. However, survey of the Military Way by RCHME in Wall miles 40 and 41 (p.137-9) has shown that in some stretches steepness of gradients and narrowness of the roadway would have prevented its use by wheeled traffic. This emphasises the continuing importance of the Stanegate as the main east-west route behind the Wall.

As might be expected after a period of abandonment, there was rebuilding in forts, as, for example, at Wallsend where timber buildings were replaced in stone. The fort at South Shields was rebuilt on a new site. New forts at Lanchester (Casey *et al.* 1992, 70-1) and Chester-le-Street (Bishop 1993, 81) were probably also built following the withdrawal from the Antonine Wall, strengthening control of the eastern hinterland of Hadrian's Wall. Most important of all, a new fort was added to the Wall at Newcastle (p. 99).

An important diploma listing part of the British garrison has been found in Bulgaria. It was issued to a Dacian cavalryman of *cohors II Gallorum veterana* and is dated 23 March 178 (*Britannia*, **26** (1995), 390). The cavalryman had served in Britain, for the commander named on the diploma, Domitius Hieron, also dedicated an altar of *cohors II Gallorum* at Old Penrith (*RIB* 917). The wider importance of the diploma lies in its naming Ulpius Marcellus as governor. Hitherto, Marcellus' governorship was thought to have begun in *c.* 180.

Note also: Daniels 1991, arguing on historical grounds that a military crisis on the Danube in 168-9 led to the final abandonment of the Antonine Wall.

The Severan period

Extensive repairs to the Wall, most evident in the central sector, are represented by the Extra-Narrow Wall, six feet in width and built with a core of rubble and hard lime-rich mortar. At Peel Gap the Extra-Narrow Wall was later than a limited repair which was associated with a deposit containing later second-century pottery (Crow 1991, 55). Dating evidence is lacking elsewhere, and the Severan date attributed to the Extra-Narrow Wall otherwise depends on the late sources which credit Severus with building a Wall in Britain, taken to be exaggerated references to repairs to Hadrian's Wall carried out by that emperor. The Wall-fort at Burgh-by-Sands (Burgh II, p.179) now seems to be a third-century addition which also involved the re-alignment of the Wall.

The circular buildings inside Stone Fort 1 at Vindolanda, two further examples of which have been discovered in excavations carried out by the Vindolanda Trust in 1997 (p.135), are likely to have been connected with Severan work on Hadrian's Wall and in its vicinity. These buildings, unique in Roman military architecture, are a well-known type in Romano-British civilian contexts, particularly at villas (Bidwell 1985, 28-31). They seem best interpreted as accommodation for forced labour from southern Britain, which may be connected with building stones from the Wall mentioning some of the southern *civitates*, and perhaps also the Brigantes (*RIB* 1672-3, 1843-4, 1962, 2022).

Birdoswald, it has been suggested (Wilmott 1997, 404), was not fully manned until the Severan period because it was not until then that the fort was supplied with granaries. The argument depends essentially on the literal truth of an inscription of *c.* 205-8 (*RIB* 1909) recording a '*horreum fec(erunt) coh(ortes) I Ael(ia) Dac(orum) et I T(h)racum c(ivium) R(omanorum)*'; the stratigraphical evidence does not seem to require such a late date for the building of the granaries. Thomas and Witschel (1992) have shown that sometimes Roman building inscriptions prove to have grossly exaggerated the scale of the work or have misrepresented its nature, when the structures to which they refer are analysed. One reason for this seems to be that a building inscription might be much more than a bald statement of the work done: it could be an opportunity to deliver a much broader statement about the virtues, for example a zeal for renewal, of the emperor or body credited with the work. Accurate descriptions might thus be subordinated to propaganda (cf. *ibid.*, 152-6 for military building inscriptions). A parallel in historical writing is the claim by late Roman writers that Severus built a wall in Britain, which, as noted above, is surely an exaggerated reference to repairs carried out in his reign on Hadrian's Wall.

Hadrian's Wall after Severus

No overall programmes of renovation are known after the Severan period, but a certain amount has recently been learnt about the state of the Wall in the later third and fourth centuries. At Sewingshields a cist burial, likely to be of late-Roman date, was cut through soil that had accumulated at the base of the Wall and was later sealed by Wall collapse (Crow and Jackson 1997, 64). A more precise *terminus post quem* for the dereliction of the Wall came from Sycamore Gap where a coin hoard of the 350s was found buried in soil at the base of the Wall and covered by Wall collapse (Crow in Daniels 1989, 51). Repairs to the Wall in the later Roman period have been recorded at Wallsend and Denton. A re-facing of the south side of the Wall at Wallsend contained material reused from a shrine or temple and was thus probably of the later third or fourth centuries (p. 96). The repair was effected by adding a new face which projected beyond the line of the original Wall face. A repair of similar character was indicated by the limits of the robbing trench on the south face of the Wall at Denton (Bidwell and Watson 1996, 28-30); the re-facing of the Wall presumably followed the collapse which sealed a coin of Severus. Along the rear of the Wall west of Housesteads insets and outsets are visible in several places; they probably represent repairs similar to those at Wallsend and Denton rather than gang-lengths of differing widths, as they are currently explained.

The Severan rebuilding was the last of a series of comprehensive renovations of the Wall, usually thought to have been undertaken with imperial authority and conceivably in emulation of the grand Hadrianic project. The Wallsend and Denton repairs are makeshift and limited in extent: they represent routine maintenance rather than a programme of renovation and bear witness to the continuing use of the Wall in the later Roman period.

The forts in the later Roman period

Excavations at Halton Chesters in 1960-1 (shortly to be published) and at Rudchester in 1972 gave rise to an expectation of episodes of reduced occupation or abandonment of Wall forts. The remainder of the third century following the Severan campaigns has been regarded as the least troubled period in the history of the Wall; units or parts of units could thus be withdrawn for service elsewhere. None of the forts excavated since the early 1970s, with the possible exception of Birdoswald, has produced any evidence to support this theory. At Housesteads, Wallsend, Vindolanda and South Shields, there is plenty of post-Severan and pre-fourth century activity, and no suggestion in the coin series of gaps in occupation.

Thinking about the state of forts in the later third and early fourth centuries has always been strongly influenced by the Tetrarchic inscription from Birdoswald, which describes the restoration of the *praetorium* which '*erat humo copert(um) et in lab(em) conl(apsum)*' along with the *principia* and baths (*RIB* 1912). It now has to be considered in the light of Thomas and Witschel's (1992) paper which casts a sceptical eye on epigraphic claims that buildings were extensively restored or rebuilt. Wilmott (1997, 201), while rejecting the literal truth of the inscription, was inclined to accept that the *praetorium* might have needed major repair after a period of abandonment. Evidence for this possible abandonment was the rarity of coins of Carausius and Allectus, also scarce at most Wall forts, and silting at the west gate resulting from neglect of the drainage systems. The *praetorium* was in a low-lying part of the fort and might have been damaged by flooding.

Essential for understanding the function of the Wall in the late third and fourth centuries is the question of unit sizes and status (for a recent review of the evidence, see Coello 1996). The so-called 'chalet' barracks at Housesteads and elsewhere can now be associated with a type of later Roman barrack which originates in the 220s or 230s (Bidwell 1991). Its main characteristic is a reduction in the number of *contubernia* from ten (the usual number in earlier auxiliary barracks) to five or six. Side passages, as at Vindolanda and at South Shields in several periods, and *contubernia* built as separate units, as at Vindolanda, are often features of this type, but also occur in earlier barracks. 'Chalet' barracks were connected by Daniels (1980) with the presence of family groups, each *contubernium* being occupied by a single family. It would follow that the garrisons of the forts had shrunk to about 10% of their numbers in the earlier Empire: Hadrian's Wall would thus have been held by little more than a token force. In the later Roman barracks at South Shields and Wallsend there were no signs of the presence of families in the *contubernia*, apart from a mid fourth-century infant burial at South Shields. Allason-Jones (1989, 60-1) has detected no increase in the number of objects with female associations in fourth-century levels at the Wall-forts; if anything, such objects seem to be less common in the late period.

In the 1960s Birley and Wilkes had taken the straightforward view that the reduction in the number of *contubernia* in the late barracks at Housesteads meant that there had been a corresponding reduction in the size of the century. Bidwell (1991, 14) followed this in his analysis of the plans of later Roman barracks which he took to signify a halving of the numbers in a century. 'Chalet' barracks are still seen as a type distinct from the later Roman barracks at South Shields and Vindolanda by Crow (1995, 88, 92), but he rejects any necessary connection between 'chalets' and the presence of families. Whatever differences there might be about the typology of the barracks, there is agreement that the army on the Wall in the later Roman period, although reduced in numbers, amounted to much more than a token force.

In their discussion of the coins from High Rochester, Casey and Savage (1980) argued for the abandonment of the outpost forts in 312, or possibly 314, a case which has been strengthened by the publication of the coins and pottery from Bewcastle (Austen 1991b; Gillam *et al.* 1993).

The only fort in the Wall zone to have been laid out to a new plan in the later Roman period was South Shields. At some date between *c*. 286 and 320 ten barracks of the later Roman type and a courtyard house were built in the south-eastern half of the fort. They were disposed on plots delimited by two intersecting streets; at the head of the street leading from the *porta praetoria* a new *principia* was built. The closest parallel to this plan occurs in the Camp of Diocletian at Palmyra, but other forts and fortresses in the East had similar plans (Bidwell and Speak 1994, 40-2, fig. 2.12). Furthermore, examination of the plans at Corbridge, Vindolanda and Risingham suggests that new fort plans had begun to develop as early as the Severan period (Bidwell 1996b).

South Shields establishes that the northern frontier was by no means isolated from developments in military architecture elsewhere in the later Roman Empire (see also the late Roman courtyard house at South Shields, the plan of which has clear links with the late-imperial Mediterranean *domus*: Hodgson 1996). Therefore it might be expected that some of the forts on the northern frontier might contain churches, common enough in forts on other late Roman frontiers. The only secure identification of a church in a British fort has been at Richborough, but in the last decade churches have also been claimed at South Shields (Bidwell and Speak 1994, 44-5, 103-4, figs 3.39, 3.48), Housesteads (Crow 1995, 95-8), Vindolanda and, most tentatively, at Birdoswald. In none of these instances can the identification be regarded as secure (although, predictably, the writer favours South Shields). Also, the meagre harvest of objects with supposedly Christian associations from the Wall area has been winnowed by Mawer (1995), discarding some chaff.

Note also: studies of fort names, garrisons and related topics, based mainly on late Roman sources. Hodgson (1991) assesses the evolution of the later Roman garrison in Britain in the light of the *Notitia Dignitatum*. Mann (1989b) considers the evidence for fort names and late Roman units from Birdoswald to Ravenglass, suggesting that Maryport was *Praesidium*, the location of the prestigious *equites Dalmatae* (cf. the presence of late military fittings of probable Danubian or Dalmatian type at Maryport: Webster 1986, 63-5, fig. 7, nos. 41-2); Mann (1992a) has also examined the question of *loca*. Finally, Smith (1997) attempts a bold re-ordering of fort names on the Cumbrian coast and elsewhere, which to a certain extent has been overtaken by the publication of the Ravenglass diploma (p.187).

The *vici*

Vici are dealt with late in this summary because it is their ending which has recently commanded the most attention. Daniels (1980, 190) was the first to realise that occupation in several *vici* on Hadrian's Wall was much reduced in the fourth century. A summary of the coins from Vindolanda published by Casey (1985) demonstrated that the *vicus* had been abandoned by *c*. 270, and Bidwell (1991, 14) listed other *vici* as far south as Manchester where there are few signs of fourth-century occupation (Wallsend can now be added to the list, p.94). Daniels (1980, 190) thought that the *vicani* might have moved into abandoned areas of forts in the later third century (cf. p. 26) and that 'chalet' barracks were introduced during the Diocletianic rebuilding of forts so that the *vicani* could remain in the forts; the assumption was that a large element in the *vicus* population consisted of soldiers' families. Bidwell (1991, 12) proposed as decisive factors reductions in the size of garrisons (also adduced by Casey and Hoffmann (1998, 13) in their report on Greta Bridge) and changes in methods of supply and payment to soldiers. This explanation depends on the assumption that *vici* existed mainly to supply the forts (cf. Snape 1991). From the second half of the third century, most forts were perhaps supplied from a smaller number of larger centres, for example the towns at Corbridge and Carlisle, although there is a clear exception at Malton where occupation continued through the fourth century (Wenham and Heywood 1997).

Research on the *vici* in the last decade has produced some significant negative results, principally at High Rochester where survey and limited excavation has found no traces of an extra-mural settlement (p.195).

Post-Roman

For Breeze and Dobson (1976, 232 = 1987, 234), the end of Roman Britain was effectively the end of Hadrian's Wall as a defended frontier. 'The soldiers of the Wall returned to the soil from which they had sprung', and occupation of the forts dwindled away. This view was formed in the mid-1970s, before two forts produced sequences of early post-Roman activity. The south-west gate at South Shields was isolated by a ditch no earlier than the last decade of the fourth century and then restored to use by building a causeway over the ditch and by the insertion of a timber portal in the north-west carriageway of the ruinous gate (Bidwell and Speak 1994). At Birdoswald, where at some stage a timber portal had also been inserted into the north carriageway of the west gate (Wilmott 1997, 216, fig. 153), two phases of timber buildings were found overlying the northern granary and adjacent areas *(ibid.*, 209-17, figs 146-52). Coins of the House of Valentinian from the demolition of the granary show that the first phase of timber buildings dates from no earlier than the last quarter of the fourth century. The best-defined building, of the second phase, was interpreted as a timber hall similar to examples of fifth- and sixth-century date in western and northern Britain.

On any reasonable reckoning the sequences at South Shields and Birdoswald continued into the fifth century. A narrative which fits post-Roman occupation of the Wall-forts has been brilliantly constructed by Casey from a wide-ranging survey of the historical, archaeological and environmental evidence (1993; 1994). The incursion of woodland onto areas cleared for agriculture seems to have begun about a century after the end of Roman rule. That century saw the establishment of British kingdoms; communities still surviving in the Roman forts, and perhaps the conscious inheritors of Roman military traditions, might have been important elements in the social and military systems of those kingdoms (see also Wilmott 1997, 224-31). Dark (1992) goes much further, proposing that after a period of abandonment Hadrian's Wall was re-fortified as a defence between two British kingdoms in the late fifth and sixth century. A view of the environmental evidence contrary to that of Casey and Wilmott was taken: widespread reversion to woodland occurred in the Hadrian's Wall area in the fifth century, 'probably even the early fifth century' (Dark and Dark 1996, 65-9).

This is a period when, in order to say anything at all, a great deal has to be made of very little. The archaeologist of Hadrian's Wall, accustomed to dealing with a mass of information which rarely yields clear-cut answers, will be inclined to caution. Due weight should be given to negative evidence. Three sites, Corbridge, Benwell and Wallsend (p.93), were used for Anglo-Saxon burials in the sixth century, by which time they had presumably been deserted, and Carlisle has produced nothing to support the continuity of occupation often assumed likely from the references to the *civitas* in the anonymous late seventh-century Life of St Cuthbert. Even where occupation clearly continued into the fifth century, the evidence can be ambiguous: at South Shields the sequence at the south-west gate has to be balanced against the individuals buried in the abandoned courtyard house following violent deaths in the early fifth century. Many of the chronologies proposed for the post-Roman period rely on dead reckoning, an assumption that each phase of activity would be separated by several decades. There may be little warrant for this in a period when society was being rapidly and traumatically transformed: after all, in the period of Roman conquest and pacification structural phases could follow rapidly, as at Vindolanda, where the original fort was rebuilt four times in less than four decades. The neat, dismissive sentence quoted at the start of this section might still be very much to the point.

The function of Hadrian's Wall.
The publication in 1976 of Breeze and Dobson's *Hadrian's Wall* crystallised two opposing points of view about the function of the Wall. Their view was that the Wall served as a 'non-defensive barrier ... to control movement in and out of the province, and allow the peaceful economic exploitation of the northern part of the province' (Breeze and Dobson 1976, 143). The contrary view, as expressed by the late Charles Daniels (1979, 360), was that the Wall was 'undoubtedly military [and] had a defensive capability from the start'. Since the 1970s more extreme views have been expressed. Donaldson (1988, 1989) has argued that the Wall was built to impede and deter enemy incursions:

as originally planned its garrisons undertook only limited forward patrolling and were perhaps even aided in defence by artillery mounted in turrets. For Mann (1990b) the Wall was '... militarily ... merely a piece of rhetoric', a product of particular circumstances, not least the direct intervention of Hadrian; once built it had little defensive value, the security of the frontier depending on outpost forts and, for local problems, the milecastles. Thus after the reign of Hadrian the Wall became a historical curiosity which survived as an example of idealised military engineering. The parts that served a real purpose, the forts and milecastles, remained in use. The rest was gradually abandoned, first the Vallum, then the turrets and finally the curtain itself.

Fundamental to any consideration of how the Wall functioned is the perception of threat: was there any prospect of attacks which might threaten Roman control of the frontier? Can such a prospect explain the disposition of Roman forces and the design and structural history of the Wall? The starting point has to be the now largely discounted claims that not only were there threats to the Wall but three separate attacks which actually resulted in widespread destruction of the Wall and its forts. Even as late as twenty years ago, at the time of the Tenth Pilgrimage, it was still accepted that there were two periods of destruction on the Wall, in the 180s or 197, and in 367 (Dobson 1979, 31). But many had already rejected destruction in 296, doubts continued to grow, and less than a decade later the only destruction levels accepted by Breeze and Dobson (1987, 130) were those of the 180s at Corbridge, Halton Chesters and Rudchester. The last Pilgrimage Handbook (Daniels 1989, 11) made no mention of destruction, noting only Dio's statement that a crossing of the northern frontier occurred in *c*. 180. A wider scepticism has also developed about the threats in general posed by peoples beyond the frontiers: Whittaker (1994, 210-14), for example, concluded that the barbarian invasions which began in the later third century only exceptionally involved very large numbers.

Belief in the destruction of the Wall having ebbed so far, it is startling to find that at least parts of the fort at South Shields were burnt down at some date between *c*. 273 and *c*. 318, wilfully and it seems with hostile intent. More generally, some have emphasised the serious nature of conflicts between the Roman army and the peoples of northern Britain, as in the case of the war which preceded the building of the Wall (see A. Birley, pp. 15-17), and Casey (p. 20) has revived the idea that renewed warfare led to the fort decision in the mid-120s. The withdrawal from the Antonine Wall, according to Hodgson

(1995, 41-3), might have been caused as much by military difficulties in Scotland as by the need to transfer units to deal with trouble in Germany. Growing scepticism about the scale of barbarian incursions across frontiers elsewhere has surely been checked by the discovery in 1992 of the Augsburg altar recording the successful interception of an army of Semnones and Iuthungi returning from Italy in 260 with 'many thousands' of Italian captives (Bakker 1993).

Two papers by Breeze illustrate how Roman forces were disposed to control the population beyond the Wall, not just when the Wall was was built but following the movement of units in the following decades. He noted that the largest concentration of forces was in the central sector of the Wall, beyond which extend areas where few native settlements are known (1985). In the more densely settled lowlands beyond the east and west ends of the Wall, it seems that there was a social system which in normal circumstances the Roman army could control, allowing a thinner spread of units along the Wall in these sectors. Breeze (1992) subsequently compared the location of cavalry units (*alae*) on Hadrian's Wall with that on other Roman frontiers; for tactical reasons the *alae* on the Wall had been placed in forts on or near cross-country routes, allowing for their speedy deployment. In the Eighth Horsley Memorial Lecture Baatz (1997) described how auxiliary forts were disposed to control the Upper German and Raetian *limites*. Of particular interest is his discussion of double forts which allowed one of the units to be moved away to deal with emergencies without disrupting routine control of the frontier. This is a possible explanation for the proximity of the forts at Corbridge and Halton Chesters, Vindolanda and Housesteads, and Carlisle and Stanwix. Comparative studies of frontiers are rarely undertaken at a detailed level, and an unpublished PhD thesis by Hodgson (1993) illustrates the potential of this very taxing field of study. Concentrating on the linear frontiers, he argues that the gradual strengthening of frontier works from the Flavian period onwards resulted from persisting opposition to Roman control at the European limits of empire.

If the Roman army was faced with military problems serious enough to challenge its control of the northern frontier, the Wall should be seen as more than 'merely a piece of rhetoric'. Recent advances in understanding how the Wall was meant to function include strengthening of the likelihood that it had a walkway along its top, presumably with a parapet (p. 18), and Woolliscroft's (1989) demonstration that in the original design variations in the standard spacing of milecastles and turrets can be accounted for by the need for them to be intervisible with forts on the Stanegate or with towers which could relay signals to those forts. The structural history of the Wall will establish whether it still served a purpose in the later Roman period. After the renovations that continued down to the early third century, little is known of its building history, although late repairs have now been seen at the east end of the Wall and at two points in the central sector the Wall can be shown to have been kept or to have remained in good repair at a late date (pp. 25-6).

More general factors also have to be taken into account. If the Cumbrian coatal system of milefortlets and towers was not re-occupied after the withdrawal from the Antonine Wall, as seems increasingly likely (p.23), it is hard to accept that its purpose had been primarily to regulate and tax trade across the Solway (see, for example, Shotter 1996, 80). If such a trade had existed, the need to control it would have been ever-present. On the other hand, if the coastal system had been devised to meet a specific threat, diplomacy or warfare could have removed that threat, rendering the system redundant. Also of importance is the likelihood that unit strengths in the later third and fourth centuries were maintained at higher levels than some have previously thought, implying that the Wall was of continuing importance (p.27).

A positive result of the debate about the function of the Wall which began in the late 1970s has been to focus interest on its structural archaeology. The results can be seen in various studies cited in this chapter, particularly those by Crow, Dobson and Hill. There is much more that archaeology can contribute to our understanding of the Wall and, in conclusion, a problem will be presented which will only be solved by further excavation and survey. When the Vallum was constructed, access to the Wall from the south was restricted to causeways opposite forts, except at the Wall gates such as Portgate. A track immediately behind the Wall has been seen at Denton, but otherwise no lateral routes are known until, following the abandonment of the Vallum, the Military Way was built in the mid-Antonine period (for metalling on the Vallum berms, see p. 21). There were secondary causeways across the Vallum opposite the milecastles and gaps, apparently primary, in the north mound, but no gaps in the south mound. Along the Wall itself, causeways across the Wall ditch in front of the milecastle gateways are known only at Turf Wall milecastle 50 and perhaps at Turf Wall milecastle 54.

The abandonment of the Vallum and construction of the Military Way in the mid-Antonine period would seem to have allowed general access right up to the rear of the Wall, but there were still no causeways across the Wall ditch in front of the milecastles. Recent survey by RCHME has also shown that in places, for example Wall mile 41, the Military Way was little more than a footpath 2m wide, sometimes with gradients as steep as 1:3, impossible for wheeled traffic. The possibility of anything more than pedestrian traffic passing through the milecastles, even if there had been some means of crossing the Wall ditch, was finally removed when their gates were narrowed, probably in the 180s.

The absence of any clear lines of access across the Wall challenges the commonly-held view that Hadrian's Wall was intended to control but not prevent movement, thus allowing cross-frontier trade and transhumance to continue interrupted. Breeze and Dobson, who follow the conventional interpretation in *Hadrian's Wall*, inserted a cautionary paragraph in the third edition (1987, 41) on the problems caused by the absence of causeways in front of milecastles. Elsewhere, Dobson (1986, 12) confessed uncertainty 'on civilian use of milecastles as a way through [the Wall]'. Much hangs on this, for if civilians could not use the milecastle gates, Hadrian's Wall would be virtually a closed frontier, with civilian access confined only to the very few Wall gates.

This is an archaeological problem, arising directly from the observable state of the Wall and its associated works, and can only be resolved by further archaeological work. For example, causeways across the Wall ditch might have been removed and have left no trace, but excavation or geophysical survey might locate road metalling on the berm or north of the Wall ditch if there had originally been access northwards.

Note also: general surveys of recent work: Breeze 1989, 1991; Daniels 1989b. For comparative discussions of frontiers, see Hodgson 1995b, Maxfield 1990 and Whittaker 1994.

3. THE VINDOLANDA WRITING-TABLETS

A. R. Birley

State of Publication

Twenty-five years after the first tablets were discovered, it is probably still too early to assess their impact - in any case, only a few of those found in the last series of excavations in the deep sections (1991-4) have been published; and the stylus-tablets still have to be deciphered.[1] The ink-tablets from the 1985-9 excavations are now (virtually)[2] all published, by Alan K. Bowman and J. David Thomas, with contributions by J. N. Thomas (1994, abbreviated *Tab. Vindol.* II). The editors also republished in this volume the tablets found in the 1970s, which they edited in 1983 (Bowman and Thomas 1983). Naturally enough, some revision to the edition of 1983 was possible in the light of new finds and further modifications will obviously be needed. Alan Bowman has also published a very readable 'popular' work based on the tablets, *Life and Letters on the Roman Frontier: Vindolanda and its People* (1994).

Since then a good many more have been found. So far, seven of the most interesting texts from the excavations of 1991-4 have been published. For

---

1. Cf. below, next n., on some of the stylus-tablets. Of the new ones, one may note that Inv. 1228 has an at least partially legible ink rim-inscription, registering that a soldier called Billo owed money.
2. A fair number of the tablets from the 1985-9 excavations were not worth photographing: 366, 392, 395, 413, 417-419, 435, 440-1, 446, 450, 452-3, 478, 482-3, 497, 505, 513, 517-519, 521, 523, 524-6, 528-531, 533, 536, 545, 553-4, 559, 566, 569, 572, 580-2, 601, 611-612,619-620, 626, 628-9, 633-5, 641-3, 645, 652-4, 656, 658-9, 664, 669-673, 676-8, 681, 690-1, 693, 697-9, 708-710, 715, 717, 719-720, 729, 732-6, 749-750, 757-8, 760-1, 768, 772-9, 785, 791, 793, 795, 799-801, 808, 847, 852, 864, 870, 878-880, 883, 885, 890, 920, 930-2, 934, 976-7, 984-8; or blank: nos. 11, 38A, 40, 70, 133-4, 154-6, 178, 184, 212, 232, 241, 258, 284, 298, 310, 333, 342, 484, 565, 609, 683, 727, 765, 784; or so abraded that nothing legible remains: 115, 174, 179, 191, 390, 481, 640, 756, 771, 798, 982. 961 was not a tablet. There remain over eighty stylus tablets, a few of which have already been mentioned in preliminary publications but of which the editing is still outstanding (Inv. 532, 561+562, 575, 689, 722, 725, 743, 787, 789, 797, 805, 822, 836, 851, 863, 923, 958, 974 are certainly important).
Of the unpublished ink-tablets from 1985-9 one might note Inv. 218 (perhaps reading *optio..Feli—,* hence possibly from a *renuntium*); 251 (?*tu...em*); 438 (?*val*[ ]); 762 (? [ ] *et..eni*); 846 (? *et primo et fere.r...*); 952 (some six lines partially legible, e.g. ?.*co tibi...sed...ut*); 953 (? *rogo ad puxes ut eum crusticium per..*).

four from those found in 1991-2 (most of which were fragmentary, Inventory nos. 91/998 to 92/1206), see Birley and Birley 1994:

Inv. 91/1022 is a letter from Major to Cocceiius (sic) Maritimus (period IV), dealing with business matters involving the *Caesariani*, i.e. imperial slaves and freedmen from the *familia Caesaris*, and written while the writer was 'making the bed warm'. On the address, *Vindoland(a)e*, cf. below.

91/1091A (period II) is a list of names from part of an account.

92/1108 (period II) is a partially legible letter about supply of *bracis*, a cereal used for making beer, including mention of 'wagons of the Britons', and *vecturae*, 'transport fees', and *velatura*, 'transport business' (a word only attested once in Latin literature), technical terms from the Roman transport business.

92/1187 (period II) is page 2 of a letter (with most of the address on the back) from Aspanius Comicianus to Mensor, referring to the *conscientiam praefecti* and greeting *omnes cives et amicos*.

Of those found in 1993 (Inventory numbers from 1207-1566), three important examples (all period III) have been published by Bowman and Thomas (1996):

93/1398 is two sheets (the reverse too abraded to read) of an account with interesting commodities, including *infiblatoria* (cloaks with attached brooches, a word hitherto known only in Greek transliteration from a Trajanic inscription at Pessinus in the province of Asia), *corticia* (thought to mean clothing made from tree bark), and a *scordiscus*; with prices both per item and totals; and an unexampled set of symbols for *denarius* fractions.

93/1474A is the *expensa* of Flavius Cerialis, not named, but clearly identifiable from the entertainment of known friends and correspondents of his, including Brocchus, Niger and September and the fact that it derives from period III, indeed from a bonfire of a pile of rubbish representing a clear-out at the end of this period. In a total of 112 lines, spread over five sheets, four written on both sides, it gives two consular dates, AD 103 (*Traiano v*) and 104 (*Sex. Attio Subur[ano]*), and mentions the arrival of the governor, *adventu consu[laris]*, a legate, consumption of considerable quantities of poultry (*pulli* and *anseres*), at least one religious festival (the Matronalia, 1st March), a brewer (*cervesar[io]*), a veteran, and much else besides. This tablet requires the date of the departure of coh. VIIII Batavorum equitata, and thus the end of period III, to be put slightly later, probably summer 105.

93/1544 is a letter of the decurion Masclus to Cerialis, whom he addresses as *regi suo*, 'his king', and whom he asks to be *mihi propitius*, before adding a PS, 'the comrades have no beer, I ask that you order some to be sent', *cervesam commilitones non habunt, quam rogó iubeas mitti*. This is useful not least in confirming that the Ninth Batavians drank plenty of beer, and that they were a *cohors equitata*. Masclus' usage *habunt* instead of the normal *habent* at last convinced the editors that *qui debunt* in the *renuntia* was a variant for *qui debent* (rather than intended as an abbreviation for *q(ui) videbunt*, as they interpreted it in *Tab. Vindol.* II). They take 'king' to be standard flattery; still, some have a residual wish to see Cerialis as 'king of the Batavians', descended from the royal stock like Julius Civilis, the leader of the Batavian Revolt (Tacitus, *Hist.* 4.13).

Bowman and Thomas in this article also offer a few useful improvements to the text of the Major letter (Inv. 91/1022, cf. above), in particular reading *si itá* instead of *spicá* in line 7, which makes much better sense.[3] The editors also express their hope 'to publish within the next three years' a further volume of tablets - hence there is a chance that *Tab. Vindol.* III may be available by the time of the Pilgrimage or shortly afterwards.

Comments on the Tablets [4]

a) <u>Latin</u>

The editors of *Tab.Vindol.* II have a very full discussion of what the tablets

---

3. But their wish to take the recipient's name as *Coccelió* — instead of the 'hypercorrect' *Coceiio - Coccelió* — with 'I *longa*' - must be rejected. The *I* in the name of one '*Coccelia*' *Severa* , the only parallel they can find for the *nomen* 'Coccelius', an inscription from Norba (Càceres) in Spain, is a misprint for I *longa*, as noted in the edition they cite, J. Vives, *ILER* 4781. It is in fact another example of the hypercorrect double I in Cocceiius (and, incidentally, *materterae* on the Norba stone is not a second *cognomen* for Trebia Vegeta, the woman commememorated by Cocceiia Severa. It means 'maternal aunt').

4. It should be stressed that in what follows comments on and quotations from unpublished tablets are provisional, based on readings by A.R. and R.E. Birley. Some views expressed here were already put forward in Birley *et al.* (1993, 18ff, produced without the benefit of consulting *Tab. Vindol.* II, where, it hardly needs to be added, the readings are in many cases superior).

have revealed on the Roman army and many other matters, not least palaeographical. This has been supplemented by J.N. Adams' article on the language of the Vindolanda writing tablets (1995). He discusses a great variety of questions such grammar, syntax, spelling, vocabulary, punctuation, accents (the *apex*). It is important to register his conclusion that general literacy of army personnel, not least in spelling and grammar, was exemplary. One exception, *debunt* and *habunt* instead of *debent* and *habent*, was produced by 'a social class (probably that of the *optiones*) who regularly used [a] substandard form, *yet were literate* '. On the whole the standard of spelling is pronounced to be very good. (One may here once again stress the startling discovery that Virgil's *Aeneid* was being read at Vindolanda, evidently as a school author for the son of Flavius Cerialis, *Tab. Vindol.* II, 118.) Jim Adams does note also examples of Celtic loan-words and one of Celticized pronunciation, and the Octavius letter (*Tab. Vindol.* II, 343) is referred to repeatedly as being an exception to the general high standard. He also discusses a whole range of linguistic items of interest for army life in the period just before the Wall was built, too numerous to summarise here, e.g. the use of *frater*, *collega* and *soror* by correspondents of the same social class.[5]

b) The army

Three particular tablets are important in showing, respectively, a much reduced garrison (*Tab. Vindol.* II,154: 296 men of coh. I Tungrorum present, 456 absent, of whom 337 were *Coris*, presumably Corbridge), and a mixed garrison (180, *militibus legionaribus* and 181, the *equites Vardulli*: in both cases clearly there at the same time as the 'main' garrison, by then the Tungrians again). The *renuntia* (127-152, 165?) of the Ninth Batavians seem to be a new type of document,[6] and the formulaic leave requests to Cerialis and other officers (166-177) are also instructive. Could the regular mention of *curatores* as well as *optiones* in the former may indicate that the *curator* was the cavalry equivalent of the *optio*, i.e. deputy to the decurion? A general feature is worth

---

5. One may note here that *caballus*, from the Celtic, discussed by Adams (1995, 124) as a possible vulgarism for horse, is used in a letter to Flavius Cerialis (Inv. 1246) in a clearly non-pejorative context ('ubi caballi belli sunt'). Further, Inv. 1575, two draft letters from a man called Florus, are full of spelling and grammatical errors (cf. below) of a kind scarcely found in the published items.

6. Several more *renuntia* have been found: Inv. 1250 *Can[didus optio]*; 1311; 1319; 1373; 1418, complete, cf. *Tab. Vindol.* II, p. 76; 1482A, the first to mention someone absent; 1552. Cf. also n. 2 above, on the unpublished Inv. 251.

emphasising: the accounts and some of the correspondence give the impression that the major task of the equestrian officers was supply.

c) Social history

The number of Flavii in the documents is of considerable importance. Before the discovery of the tablets there was scarcely more than a single equestrian officer called Flavius, i.e. a first or second generation new citizen, attested under Trajan. Now there are probably as many as six, first and foremost Flavius Cerialis.[7] A list may be useful, including information from unpublished texts:

1.Cerialis: *Tab. Vindol.* II, 166-171 (requests for *commeatus*), 225-8 (his handwriting), 229 (?), 230-2 (his handwriting), 233-245, 246? (from Brocchus), 247-280, 281-4?, (285-6??), 287-290?, 291-292 (Lepidina), (293-4: Lepidina), 347 (to his -?- slave Primigenius), 362 (from a slave of ?Cerialis), 373? (from or to *Cer[ialis?]*), 384? (from or to ?*[Ce]ria[lis]*), 430? (letter to Cerialis? - *Ceria[li]* not impossible), 462? (possibly beginning of draft by Cerialis); subsequent finds: Inv. 1223 (stylus)?, addressed *Flavio C..;* 1246 (mentioning *hospitium ubi caballi belli sunt*); 1329? (*a Broccho coll.*); 1351 (? - addressed *Flavio Ce[...] ab Arcano*); 1363 (?to Lepidina); 1371; 1376 (stylus address); 1378 (from Atticus); 1424; 1425A (from Pontius Festinus); 1443 (from Ingenuus, beginning *Vinoviae*); 1453? (draft by Cerialis, mentions Brocchus and *venatores mei*); 1454A, draft *Cerialis Casti[no]*; 1460A; 1474 (clearly his *expensa*: Bowman and Thomas 1996, 307ff.); 1496C (? - to a *praef. coh.* from [*?Septem*]*bre*); 1475A; (1488C, perhaps to Lepidina from Claudia Severa); 1498+1500 (from *[Cl]odius Super*); 1537, draft *a Ceriale pr*; 1544 (beer letter from Masclus: Bowman and Thomas 1996, 323ff); 1545, draft beginning *Flavius Cerialis*; 1563 (from Brocchus).
2. Conianus – *Tab. Vindol.* II, 296.
3. Genialis – *Tab. Vindol.* II, 217-224 (222 & 224?); 256; 301; 303?; Inv. 1337 from Proculus; 1379, from Haterius Nepos (known as *censitor Brittonum Anavionensium* and later prefect of Egypt - he asks G. to come to Coria); 1434 (to his freedman Cenosis).
4. Proculus – *Tab. Vindol.* II, 219 + Inv. 1337 to Genialis
5. Similis – *Tab. Vindol.* II, 254; 286a; 347c; cf. 235 (+186; 495?)

---

7. One should now delete 'Flavius Petrus', *Tab. Vindol.* II, 281 (??). Only *[ ]l Petri* is preserved - but this can now be restored as *[a]l(ae) Petri[anae]* —: cf. Inv. 1353, *a Veria[no?] dec. alae Petrianae.*

41

6. Vindex - Inv. 1477B; cf. (not specifically Flavius) *Tab. Vindol.* II, 260 (Vindex n · letter to Cerialis from Iustinus *coll.*); Inv. 1340 (Vindex in fragmentary letter); 1443.

These men probably came from the Rhineland, where stone inscriptions of equestrian officers from the area scarcely exist. Apart from the Flavii, the nomenclature offers a rich field for future study. One may note the following (unpublished examples marked *, those in the seven new tablets already published marked #):

previously unattested, presumably Celtic: Acranius; Andle[...]; #C.riaras; Cessaucius; *Ealtavirus; Gannallius (unless Germanic); Gav(v)o; Gramaseus (?); Ircucisso (or e.g. Irducisso, Proucisso?); Metto (or Melco, etc.?); #Ricarromaucus (?); Sattua (unless place-name); Sautenus; #Suasco (or Suasso); Tagamatis; Tagarminis; #Varcenus; Velbuteius; Veldedeius (unless Germanic). Note also *Russinius and *Sequentinius ('pseudo-*gentilicia*' typical for the Celtic area, formed from the Latin Russinus and Sequentinus).
previously unattested, presumably Germanic: Butimas; #Chnisso; Chrauttius; #Frissia[us?]; Gambax?; Huep[nus?]; Huete[ ]; Thuttena; Ucenius; [U]xperus.
Greek: *Alcimus; *Cenosis (*libertus*); Corinthus; Dio; Elpis; Gleuco; Hermes; #Onesimus; Paris; Trophimus.
names of Roman citizens (assumed equestrian officers, if not specified as such, marked +),
with three names: Sex. Attius Suburanus *cos.* 104; Marcus Cocceius Velox;
with two names (some of whom were not necessarily citizens): +Aelius Brocchus; Annius Equester *cent. reg.*; #Aspanius Comicianus; *Cacurius Montanus; +Caecilius September; Calpurnius Piso *cos.* 111; Cassius Saecularis; +Celonius Iustus; Cessaucius Nigrinus; Cessius Fin—(?); Claudia Severa; *Claudius Iustinus; Claudius Karus; Claudius Popa; [Cla]udius Verus *dec.*; [Cl]odius Super; Cluvius Faber; *Cluvius Florus; #Cocceiius Maritimus; Curtius Super; Felicius Victor; Flavius Cerialis *praef. coh. VIIII Batavorum*; +Flavius Conianus; Flavius Genialis *praef.*; +Flavius Proculus; Flavius Similis; *Flavius Vindex; Frontinius Julius; Furius Imber (?); *Gabinius Crescens (?); Grattius Crispinus; *Haterius Nepos; +Hostilius Flavianus; Julius Verecundus *praef. coh. I Tungrorum*; Licinius Asper; Macr[inius?] Iustus (?); N[eratiu]s Marcellus *consularis*; +Oppius Niger; *Pontius Festin[us]; Sulpicia Lepidina; *Valerius Maxi[mus] *praef.*; Valerius Niger; Vegetius (?) Genialis; Vettius Adiutor, *aquilifer leg. II Aug.*; Vettius Bolanus *cos.* 111;

Vettius Severus; Vocusius Africanus *praef.*; -rius In—; -scinius Nis[.]us; -stius Optatus;
-ius Fatalis; -ius Fontanus; -ius Vecetus;
other Roman citizens: Ferox *legatus*; +Flavianus; +Justinus; Priscinus *praef.*;
*Pacatus *praef.*; +Pastor; Rufinus *praef.*; Veranius *praef.*; ?Victor *[?praef.]*
eq.; -n...ul.i.[ ], *c.v.*

The number of women attested is of interest: Sulpicia Lepidina (*Tab. Vindol.*
II, 247, 257, 274, 288, 291, 292, 294 - and some unpublished items); Claudia
Severa (244, 291, 292, 293 - and some unpublished items); Pacata (320?,
353); Paterna (294?); Sattua (346 - unless place-name?); Thuttena (310);
Valatta (257); the unknown *contubernalis* of Tagamatis, if female (181). One
can now add Ingenua *v[e]stra filia*, daughter of Ealtavirus(?), wife or
concubine of Florus (Inv. 1575), and the wife(?) of Priscinus, Va[.]ia Priscini
(Inv. 1331R). (Note also Sponde (?), named on on the leather piece left by
Veldedeius in Cerialis' *praetorium*.) It hardly needs be repeated how delightful
is the birthday invitation from Severa to Lepidina (*Tab. Vindol.* II, 291).

Evidence for slaves is more limited: note Candidus, Severus (301), Rhenus,
Primigenius (347); plus perhaps Albiso (303), Allatus (?) (190) and Privatus
(190, 199, 448?), and ?an unnamed slave of Verecundus (302). Further
possible slaves and freedmen occur in the tablets found in the 1990s, and
one definite *libertus*, Cenosis, freedman of Flavius Genialis (Inv. 1379);
note also Optatus Aug. [*lib.*?] (Inv. 1220 - stylus), and the *Caesariani* in
Inv. 1022 cf. p. 38).

d) The addresses
One residual problem regarding the letters is the question of the address: a
number have a place-name in the locative at the top left of the address side.
This was initially taken to indicate the place at which the letter was written,
but the editors of *Tab. Vindol.* II, 42ff, strongly supported by Adams (1995,
109ff) and by Roger Tomlin (1996, 460), now argue that it represents the
destination, understanding (*dabis*), i.e. 'at Vindolanda (you will give the letter)
to x from y'. 'The oddity that six of the ten examples of letters found at
Vindolanda...record a place other than Vindolanda', viz. *Coris*, *Eburaci*,
Londini, *Vinovis*, is explained by the hypothesis that 'subsequently the
recipients came to Vindolanda bringing their correspondence with them'.
Note that they include in the ten examples several unpublished texts, including

Inv. 1022 (the Major letter) and some stylus tablets. Not all will find this satisfactory: the places named in further unpublished addresses again show non-Vindolanda locatives predominating: 1091B: VIARVLNI (?) (but this may be the recipient's name); 1110: VERTO...(?) (if place-name); ?1135III (if in fact part of address): P.....ACI S(?); 1145 (stylus): CATARAC ALBA[NO]; 1215 (*Martius Victori*): COR... (?=CORIS); 1220 (stylus): EBVRACO OPTATO AVG; 1359 (*Fideli su[o]*) MEDVMABI (?); 1520A: VINDOLANDE; 1581 (stylus): VINDOLANDA[E]. Given the examples of drafts written at Vindolanda by Flavius Cerialis (and now by Florus, Inv. 1575), one may surely still ask whether *Vindoland(a)e* in addresses found there do not mostly belong to drafts of letters written at Vindolanda. (Bowman and Thomas (1996, 326) note that 'the address on the back [*Vindolande*, on the Major letter, Inv. 1022] is upside down in relation to the writing on the front'. Might this not be confirmation that it was only a draft? It was after all written in bed, hence, perhaps, also the ink blotches.) At any rate, Michael A. Speidel has now joined the debate in his publication of the Vindonissa (stylus) tablets (Speidel 1996, 38f.), coming out firmly in favour of the locatives at both Vindolanda and Vindonissa representing the place of writing not the destination.[8] A definitive answer might perhaps come up if one found e.g. a letter to Flavius Cerialis or a draft of a letter from him, with *Vindoland(a)e* in the address. The question has some general importance. As for these letters, it clearly makes a difference to what was going on at Vindolanda, and who was actually there.

e) Other place-names in unpublished tablets

Several British place-names occur in the tablets in *Tab. Vindol.* II, in addresses and otherwise, both known - Bremetennacum, Cataractonium, Coria (not exactly already 'known', but now clearly identifiable, cf. *Tab. Vindol.*II, pp. 96f., as the place traditionally labelled by the corrupt form 'Corstopitum'), Eburacum, Lindum (?), Londinium, Luguvalium, Vindolanda itself and Vinovia; and unknown - Briga, Cordonovis, Ulucium,[9] and possibly Sattua,

---

8 In *Tab. Vindol.* II, 45 n. 27 the editors cite two Vindonissa texts to support their case. But *Vindoinsa* there is interpreted by Speidel (1996, nos. 42-3, with improved readings) not as a garbled form of *Vindonissa(e)* but as the name of a woman, the girl-friend of the soldier An(n)ius Lucianus: respectively *dabis Vindoinsae ab Anni[o] Luciano* and *dabis An(n)io Luciano qui est in gir(o) ece(stri) Vindoinsa*.

9 On *Tab. Vindol.* II, 184 the editors cite A. R. Birley (1991, 18) for the view that it might be 'a corruption of *Vividin*' in Ravennas. What was in fact meant was the opposite: that Ravennas' 'VIVIDIN' might be Ravennas' corruption of VLVCIVM, palaeographically quite plausible.

if this is not a personal name. In the unpublished tablets, as well as those mentioned above in the discussion of addresses, one may signal Inv. 1112 (stylus) *actum Londini*; 1215 (*Martius Victori*) - *Brem[etennacum? or enium?]* and *Cataract[onium]*; 1405 (?account) *Isurio*; 1409 (letter) *??castra Ar[.]atia*; 1379 (letter from Haterius Nepos to Flavius Genialis) *Coris*; 1443 (letter from Ingenuus to Cerialis) *Vinoviae*; 1471A *Lond[inium?];* 1475A (account) *Anavion[..]* (unless personal name); 1488D (scrap) *Vindolan[da];* 1503B (account) *a Londinio*; 1548 *Coris*; 1553 *Brocchus et postea a Ce/ [.]so reversus* - but probably a personal name, *Ce[l]so*.

f) Miscellaneous

There are a considerable number of <u>as yet unpublished accounts</u>: e.g. Inv. 1018; 1105; 1200 - *ratio*; 1210 - *ratio vestis*; 1298; 1299A; 1316 - *ratio Flori*; 1319; 1320A; 1322; 1326; 1350; 1405; 1435; 1451; 1472A; 1475A; 1476C; 1477C - *accepta*; 1477 (I) - *sumptus*; 1478B; 1480; 1482B; 1495 (I) - *recepta*, including *siliginis*; 1503B; 1507; 1522A - *[r]atio 7 Fe[licionis?];* 1528C-D-E; 1529; 1560; 1606R.

Further, one may mention <u>new letters with correspondents' names</u> (for those to or from Flavius Cerialis, see above): 822/3 (stylus), *a Cacurio Montano*; 1022 #*Major Cocceiio Maritimo*; 1110 ..... *.raviario (?)*; 1145 (stylus) *Alba[no];* 1146 (if addressees) *Passician[o] et L.[ ];* 1187 #*Mensori ab Aspanio Comiciano*; 1215 *Martius Victori [?praef.] eq.*; 1220 (stylus) *Optato Aug. [lib.?];* 1254 *Aemilianus Severin[o]*; 1279A *Priscino*; 1331 *Va.iae Priscini*; 1332 *Priscinus Cels[o];* 1337 *Flavius Proculus Genial[i];* 1353 *a Veri[ano?] dec alae Petrianae*; 1359 -*us Fideli*; 1361 *Cluvius Florus Quinto*; 1371 —*us Ceriali*; 1379 *Flavio Geniali praef. ab Haterio Nepot[e];* 1412 *Candido*; 1422 *[Pr]iscino*; 1425A+1426 *Pontius Festin[u]s Ceria[li];* 1434 *Cenosi liberto Flavi Genialis* ; 1449 (if from address*) a Vegetio (?) Geniale su[o]*; 1460A ....*usio (?)*; 1466A *a Valerio Maxi[mo] praef.* ; 1466BI ..*frilius (?);* 1466BII —*r[.]nus Ca.[...];* 1476B ...*uro ;* 1477A —*rio In—*; 1477B *Flavius Vindex*; 1481—*us Prisci[no suo];* 1575 (drafts) *Florus Ealtaviro* and *Florus Tito*; 1578 *Gabinio Crescenti ab Fidele coll. (?)*; 1602 *ab Att..io (?)*.

Some of the <u>other unpublished letters</u>, whose authors and recipients are unknown, and of which often only fragments are preserved, look interesting, sometimes only for a single phrase: 1197 and 1409 both have the same expression as in Major's letter, *scire te volui*, 'I want(ed) you to know'. 1491 is very personal, including *mater*, *consola* and *quid agas cum Priscinó tuó*. Cerialis, already known to be a keen huntsman, cf. his draft letter to Brocchus, *Tab. Vindol.* II, 233, refers in another draft, 1453, to *venatores mei*, 'my huntsmen', and a list, 1462, from the 'bonfire' site, includes hunting-nets 'left behind', one with a veteran (itself a point of interest), for catching duck, swans and thrushes. 1281 has *possimus lautius beneficio tuo ferias curare*, 'so that we can celebrate the holiday more elegantly thanks to your kindness'. 1340 contains the startling phrase *qui in causa fuerunt ex quibus unum in vinculis iussus est de provincia exportare*, 'of those involved in the case he has been ordered to deport one in chains from the province'. 1466A, from *Valerio Maxi[mo] praef.*, has the phrase *preses et familia*, 'the governor and family'. 1528, which includes several names of friends, has an emphatic statement that the writer is not going to withdraw from the *contibe[r]nio* or the *sc[o]la* and a reference to goldsmiths and silversmiths (or money-lenders?). 1197 has the phrase *diligenter muro* - it would be nice to take this as a reference to Hadrian's Wall... The already mentioned drafts (of letters to Ealtavirus (?) and Titus) by a man called Florus, 1575, have such misspellings and other solecisms as *qumque*, *signabet*, *benifeciario*, *frates*, *habea*, *dabes*, *dabet*, which are distinctly below the overall highly literate Vindolanda standard. At the other end of the literary and no doubt social scale there is part of a letter, 1606, which could have been written by the Younger Pliny on behalf of a protégé: *viri boni accedit etiam liberalium studiorum amor .[ ].e profectus morum denique te[m]peramentum et cla[ritudo? generis?]* - '...of a good man, added to which there is his marked enthusiasm for the liberal arts, finally his balanced character and ?distinguished family'.[10] One last comment on the unpublished tablets: 1215, from Martius to Victor, is in a script that looks much more like e.g. that of the Bath and Uley curse tablets or the Bu-Ngem ostraka than that in the other Vindolanda texts. It came from level VIA, certainly post-Hadrianic.

---

10. One can only speculate why such a letter was found at Vindolanda.

For Pilgrims, it may be a matter of regret that the tablets in general end just before the Wall began - but it may be registered that one, *Tab. Vindol.* II, 344 (from period IV, which could well go up to AD 122), can legitimately be taken to imply Hadrian's impending arrival at Vindolanda, a sensible place for him to stay when launching the start of the Wall. It is the appeal by the outraged victim of a centurion: *tuam maies[t]atem imploro ne patiaris me [i]nnocentem virgis cas[t]igatum esse ...[tu]am misericord[ia]m imploro ne patiaris me hominem trasmarinum et innocentem de cuius f[ide] inquiras virgis cruent[at]u]m] esse ac si aliquid sceler[i]s commississem* - 'I implore Your Majesty not to allow me, an innocent man, to have been beaten with rods...I implore Your Clemency not to allow me, a man from overseas and innocent, to have been beaten with rods till I bled, as if I had committed some crime.' The editors comment that the intended recipient of this draft 'can hardly be anyone of lower status than the provincial governor' - yes, but surely it was the emperor himself.[11] The stress by the writer on his 'overseas' origin, implying that for Britons to be arbitrarily flogged would have seemed perfectly acceptable, echoes the derisive attitude to the *Brittunculi*, a previously unattested word which must mean something like 'nasty little Brits', and the derogatory comments on the military qualities of the 'nu[di?] Brittones', in *Tab. Vindol.* II, 164. Interesting also is the discovery that Haterius Nepos was a correspondent of the Vindolanda prefect Flavius Genialis, and asked him to come to Coria (Inv. 1379). This man was known as '[p]raef. equit. censito[ri] Brittonum Anavion[ens.]' and later, after a rapid series of procuratorial appointments, prefect of Egypt under Hadrian. He was probably at Corbridge in his capacity as prefect of cavalry, also holding a census of the Britons in Annandale, and, no doubt, conscripting them into *numeri* for service on the Upper German *limes*. These items help to explain the revolt which flared up at Hadrian's accession, with heavy Roman casualties (of which the tombstone found at Vindolanda in 1997 of the centurion of the Tungrians, T. Ann[ius ...], 'in bell[o...inter]fectus' was probably one).[12] Roman attitudes to the Britons, the forced conscription and the ensuing revolt, was at least part of the reasons why he ordered the Wall to be built.

---

11. As argued in Birley 1997a and 1997b.

12. Cf. the items in the previous note, with further references. For the the new tombstone, see Birley 1998.

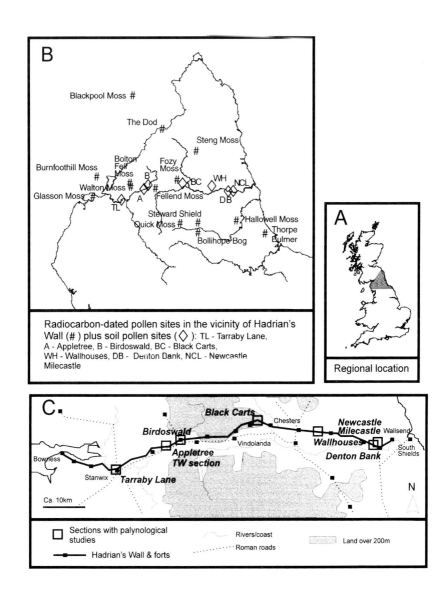

Figure 6. Pollen sites discussed in the text.

4. ENVIRONMENTAL EVIDENCE FROM HADRIAN'S WALL

J. P. Huntley

Introduction

Past Pilgrimages have concentrated very much upon structural remains, paying rather little attention to the landscape in which these remains lie and giving little consideration to the effect that the building of such structures, or indeed the tens of thousands of personnel, may have had upon that landscape and its associated economy. The last ten, indeed twenty, years have seen much work being done to redress this imbalance (Figs 6 and 7) and it is the aim of this paper to summarise, briefly, the evidence we now have regarding environmental matters along our Wall.

Therefore let us look, on this the Twelfth Pilgrimage, with a broader vision. Let us look at the landscape through which we pass and try to imagine how it might have been two thousand years ago.

Pollen evidence

Perhaps the prime method of investigating landscape changes is through the analysis of pollen obtained from stratified deposits. These are usually from natural sequences within bogs, mires or lakes laid down over many centuries or millennia although useful information can be obtained from stratified archaeological contexts in some instances. Pollen, which can be identified to varying degrees, is incorporated as sediments build up through time. By analysing the pollen grains in horizontal slices of these sediments it is possible to determine changes in the nature of the vegetation around the site. There are, of course, considerations such as level of pollen identification, its representation of the vegetation, the nature of sediment accumulation, type of basin (size of mire or lake, extent of tree cover around it) and so on to be taken into account but, nonetheless, a broad representation of vegetational change can be inferred. For a regional picture, basins of 100m or more diameter are required whereas if they less than about 30m diameter then they simply reflect the vegetation from immediately around them (Jacobson and Bradshaw 1981). Size of basin must therefore be considered before spatial questions are asked.

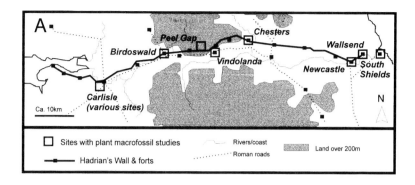

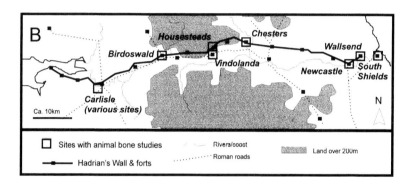

Figure 7. Sites with plant macrofossil and animal bone studies.

What pollen will not do, in many instances, is to date a particular deposit to any useful archaeological degree - hence the ongoing debate as to whether the local landscape had already been cleared of woodland by the time that the Romans arrived or whether it was the Romans who carried out the extensive clearance. Independent dating techniques using, for example, radiocarbon, are needed to provide anything more than a relative temporal framework but even here dates are not as precise as can often be achieved through literary references to the Wall due to the necessity for calibration of radiocarbon years to calendar dates (see, for example, Dumayne *et al.*1995). There is therefore a difference in perception between, on the one hand, Roman archaeologists where one or two years are not only important but distinguishable (when dendrochronological or documentary sources are

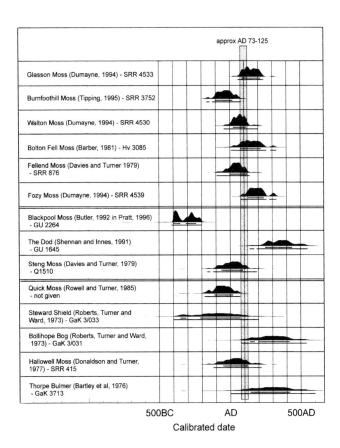

Figure 8. Probability plots of calibrated dates (2 σ) of major clearance of woodland in the Hadrian's Wall area.

available) and, on the other hand, the palaeo-environmentalists where that short a time-span is both less important in terms of vegetation dynamics and nigh on impossible to separate. As long as radiocarbon dates are used appropriately they can be of immense value but simply using the mid-point of a calibrated date is not appropriate, indeed it is mis-leading.

Almost twenty years ago Turner (1979) discussed the impact of the Roman army in northern England as evidenced from pollen analyses. Today we continue to debate its impact with as much energy as then. Figure 8 summarises the dates of major clearance of woodland and replacement by an open grass and herb-dominated vegetation, as determined by the original

51

authors, for radiocarbon dated sites relatively close to the Wall. The sites are arranged, broadly, west to east across the Wall. The dates (dating laboratory codes presented) have all been calibrated using Stuiver and Kra (1986) with the calibration program OxCal v2.18 used to calculate the probabilities. Each curve therefore represents the probable time over which that date spans, *i.e.* the start of that particular clearance episode. The thin lines under each plot represent the 1s (68% likelihood of the date falling within this range) and 2s (95% likelihood of the date falling within this range) age ranges. It is stressed that these are not necessarily the first clearances represented at the sites but simply the clearance dated as being broadly of late prehistoric times.

What is immediately clear is that there is no simple correlation between the Romans' arrival and the clearance of woodland, even for the five sites closest to the Wall (Glasson Moss, Walton Moss, Bolton Fell Moss, Fozy Moss and Fellend Moss: authors as on Fig. 8). Each site must be seen as distinct and, clearly, the reader should refer to the original papers for detailed discussion. In the west at Glasson Moss the most probable period for this clearance was after the Wall had been built whereas at Burnfoothill it was clearly an Iron Age event. Walton Moss and Fellend are probably late Iron Age but Bolton Fell Moss shows a clearance probably related to the arrival of the Romans. Fozy Moss remains largely uncleared probably until after the Wall has been built. The other sites lie rather further afield from the Wall and are of less relevance to this paper. Unfortunately there are no dated diagrams from natural sequences of deposits in the Tyne Lowlands and this would be an area to investigate for future research.

Whilst we have concentrated upon the dating of clearance events we have yet to discuss the nature of the vegetation itself. Pollen evidence suggests that the woodlands contained oak, alder, hazel and some ash, elm and pine, although it is unlikely that all were present in any one woodland. The alder values are often quite high from these pollen diagrams and it is reasonable to assume that this pollen originated from alder carr woodland growing locally to that site. This is almost certainly the case at Midgeholme Moss near to Birdoswald fort where alder stumps were scattered throughout the peat profile.

Pollen from sites such as those discussed briefly above therefore provide evidence for the regional vegetational changes: the broad nature of clearances, types of woodland and so on. Other types of deposit can be used for either more local or more specific questions. For example, one of the tantalising questions raised relates to soils lying immediately under the foundations of the Wall and its buildings. As before, radiocarbon dating of this material is not likely to tell us more than the fact that it's "Roman-ish", rather than "truncated and Bronze Age" for example. The *fact* is that these soils are buried under a feature whose date of construction is very precisely known. Pollen from such soils can be of use but interpretation needs to be cautious due to taphonomic factors: soils are biologically active and thus material can move around in them, they are not necessarily conducive to the survival of pollen, their surface may be truncated prior to building, etc. Nonetheless, pollen from such deposits (Fig. 6C) is proving informative and certainly further work looks promising.

To the east, soil deposits under the fort at Wallsend (Huntley 1995) and from adjacent to the Vallum mound and berm south of the Wall at Denton, just east of Newcastle upon Tyne were examined but no pollen survived. Buried soil from under the Westgate Road milecastle produced reasonable amounts of quite well preserved pollen with only 26% indeterminable grains (Huntley 1988). It was suggested that the pollen indicated a mixture of alder woodland and open grass/sedge dominated communities with a selection of herb taxa although none representative of arable cultivation or of Cereal-type. Balaam (1983) examined samples from under the north Vallum mound at Wallhouses. No pollen had been preserved although material from the Vallum itself was quite rich and indicated an essentially open landscape with a little woodland and cultivation. Unfortunately no data are presented. Black Carts is the next site moving westwards with palynological data, and lies on the eastern edge of the high ground. The main indications from its assessment pollen work (Huntley 1998a) suggest more open communities: heathland and wet grassland but few trees. There are strong differences between pollen data from under the south Vallum mound and from under the northern counterscarp bank which need addressing. The sites are too close to exhibit different pollen results if they really are contemporary and soil micro-morphological work is needed to determine whether the southern Vallum sample is a truncated profile.

Moving westwards again, Birdoswald lies in an equivalent situation to Black Carts but on the western side of the Pennine watershed and pollen from deposits under the original turf Wall and the stone fort rampart was interpreted as representing dense alder woodland in the immediate vicinity (Wiltshire 1997).

Samples from the uppermost organic layers (equivalent to LFH horizons) of a buried soil under the nearby Appletree Section of Wall, taken during the 11th Pilgrimage, produced evidence interpreted as "grazed moorland before Wall construction and this implies clearance by Iron Age peoples" (*op. cit.*). Those from the mineral layer immediately under the organic layers suggested a densely wooded environment. From Tarraby Lane in the lowlands of the west, Balaam (1978) published five profiles associated with both the Turf Wall and the Stone Wall including a soil under the counterscarp bank. All demonstrated an essentially wooded landscape.

With the exception of those by the author, none of any of the above reports on soil pollen indicates the levels of indeterminable grains which is unfortunate since such data can provide evidence of the burial environment.

There are apparently, therefore, strong differences between the east and the west of the high Pennines. The west seems to have remained wooded for longer and the Romans may, indeed, have undertaken significant clearance there in places. The east is the side where cleared, perhaps cultivated, ground with some woodland seems to have greeted the Romans and, indeed, ard marks have been found underlying Roman structures, for example at Wallsend (Griffiths 1993) and many other forts (see Wilmott 1997, 39 for other examples) suggesting that people had been cultivating the area prior to Roman invasions. Again, it is unfortunate that there are no radiocarbon dated pollen diagrams from natural sequences of deposits in the Tyne Lowlands with which to compare the soil pollen data.

A third type of deposit which can lend itself to pollen analytical work is that of specific contexts associated with archaeological features: ditch and pit fills, rampart turf etc. Dating will almost certainly derive from the archaeology. Few examples have been published and clearly further targeted work may be of use, for example in the determination of cereal straw frequently dumped into wells and pits. Whilst the straw itself cannot be characterised cereal pollen adheres to the straw and is at least recognisable into groups. Turves remain quite recognisable within some ramparts and, indeed, within the Turf Wall itself. Examination of pollen from these discrete entities can indicate the types of grassland resource available. Pollen, however, often has not survived to any extent due to the aerobic nature of the sediment. Associated soil micromorphological work is equally important as pollen in these cases.

Successful work has been done on turves from the Turf Wall at the Appletree section and at Birdoswald fort itself (Wiltshire 1997). She demonstrated that most of the turves could have been locally obtained from floors of woodland or from areas previously cleared and subsequently upon which developed a grassy heathland vegetation. High levels of microscopic charcoal fragments indicate that fire was used but the associated phosphate value confirms lack of long-term human intervention. In comparison, material from specific turves from the ramparts of the Annetwell Street fort at Carlisle produced minimal amounts of pollen and probably indicate that these turves were cut from areas with a highly biologically active soil. The macroscopic remains from these turves consisted of highly humified organic material with some roots, wood and stem fragments, all indicative of the organic horizons of an active soil (Huntley 1991).

Recent palynological work upon deposits within the fort ditches at Vindolanda provide further data contributing to the Roman clearance debate (Manning, Birley and Tipping 1997). The ditch fills have been dated tightly by archaeological convention, with pollen samples analysed from two monoliths: one dated c. AD 85-92 and the second c. AD 160-190. The authors interpret the data from the first monolith as predominantly indicating wet meadow or pasture habitats with minimal evidence for heathland. Tree pollen values, with the exception of alder, are low throughout the profile, hence little woodland remained in the vicinity. From the locality of the site it seems reasonable to suggest that alder trees probably grew along the stream valley to the east of the fort as they do today. The data from the late second century fills are likewise indicative of open grassland communities. The authors discuss the interpretational problems relating to pollen from this type of feature: namely inwash during erosion of ditch sides and pollen representation in such small deposits. In addition, the origin of the deposits needs consideration; not all of the pollen may have fallen onto the sediments as they accumulated but some may have been brought in with material deliberately dumped into such features. As the authors admit one such layer at least is present (units H/I) but their main interpretation is that these sequences do represent, by and large, accumulations of ponded silts.

Used appropriately it is clear that pollen can provide immensely useful information about the vegetation and landscape around "our Wall" but, as recent authors have commented (Dumayne-Peaty and Barber 1997; McCarthy

1997) it is only by considerably improved collaboration of palaeo-environmentalists, principally working with pollen from natural sequences, and environmental archaeologists, using archaeological contexts that we can hope to achieve our goal of determining the effects that the Romans did have upon the landscape.

Macrofossils

Moving to larger material and coming closer to the archaeological excavations, macrofossils (seeds, fruits, vegetative fragments and wood) provide further evidence for local vegetation but, in particular, often relate to cereal crop husbandry. Often the deposits are of mixed origin, for example an individual fill of a pit may represent several episodes of activity including material used in a building, swept into a corner (possibly over several days) and later gathered up and dumped into the pit along with some food debris. Hence interpret with caution. There is a huge body of data available, much collected over the last ten years (Fig. 7A). Much interpretation, however, remains site-specific and there is a strong need and opportunity to synthesise these data - looking for patterns across the Wall from east to west.

Charred remains generally relate to cereals and their associated weeds and are found on many sites, the nature of the preservation ensuring some survival. A few sites have produced excellent waterlogged material, for example Vindolanda and Carlisle, where information about wider habitats is found.

Across the Wall charred remains are dominated by grains of 6-row hulled barley except in specific contexts at South Shields. Here there was a major conflagration of a granary and it is clear that spelt wheat and bread wheat were being stored (van der Veen 1994). Interestingly the spelt was stored as grain rather than the more often quoted spikelets; it being a glume wheat means that the primary product after threshing (plus sieving etc.) is spikelets and not free grain plus intact, albeit battered, ears as in the free threshing cereals such as bread wheat. The glume wheats require further processing in the form of parching and pounding in order to release the grains for use; incidentally the parching is often the process in which the material is charred and hence we have a biased picture of cereal usage. There was discussion as to whether the South Shields bread wheat was local or imported but evidence was minimal either way and van der Veen concluded that source could not be determined.

Newcastle has produced a few Roman samples from excavations at the fort and, more recently, some have been taken from Bottle Bank in Gateshead. Both sites have been assessed and further analysis is underway although it seems likely that only small assemblages will be produced. At Chesters, samples from adjacent to the western Roman bridge abutment provided limited evidence of hulled barley and hexaploid wheat (probably spelt) plus some waterlogged material indicative of a flash flood episode (Huntley 1992a). Recently more excavation has been undertaken at Vindolanda, concentrating upon the *praetorium* of the third to fourth centuries. Bulk samples from within and around the commander's house have produced some large well preserved spelt grains although numbers were low. However, samples from the enigmatic circular features contained rather more barley grains leading Huntley (1998b) to speculate whether this might enhance the argument of the excavator, Robin Birley, that these features were native or even slave quarters (Birley, Blake and Birley 1998). More material was sampled during 1998 excavations but remains to be assessed. As yet any well preserved, deep, waterlogged deposits have not been reached and seem likely to remain untouched in this area of the fort.

Birdoswald was another fort whose granaries were extensively sampled although no catastrophic fires occurred there: hence concentrations of charred material were generally low. The granaries were kept reasonably clean although material did accumulate between the sleeper walls. The samples produced more or less equal amounts of barley and wheat, the latter a mixture of predominantly spelt with some bread wheat. Occasional samples contained large amounts of grassland taxa leading Huntley (1997) to suggest that perhaps hay was stored in these buildings too.

Many hundreds of waterlogged samples from excavations in and around the forts at Carlisle have been analysed but few contain more than the occasional charred remain. The few rich samples have produced large numbers of spelt glumes, perhaps the remains of chicken feed, or of cleaned hulled barley grain (Huntley 1989; 1992b). The latter were large, well formed and clean, similar to those from Peter Wilson's excavations at Thornbrough Farm, Catterick just outside the Antonine fort there. This led Huntley (1996) to suggest that barley may have been human food rather than the supposed animal fodder or punishment rations as documentary evidence suggests (Davies 1971). Clearly there was a demand for large quantities of beer, for which barley would have been used, as can be seen from several of the writing tablets recovered at Vindolanda. Indeed, one of them (*Tab. Vindol.* II, 4) records the procurement, for a week, of 46 litres wine, 68 plus litres Celtic beer, some vinegar/sour wine and over 178 litres barley. As Robin Birley (1994) says 'By any standards, this suggests a good party'. Further research is planned to investigate this aspect!

What has been preserved at Carlisle, in particular, are immense deposits of organic rubbish, in pits, wells and general layers. Much of this consists of cereal straw, bracken, grass and sedge remains plus weeds from associated herbs. Insect remains (Kenward *et al*. 1992) corroborate suggestions that this is stable waste (Kenward and Hall 1997) in abundance with the plants deriving from hay as well as bedding and from manure itself. Whilst conditions seem to have been 'ordurous' in and around the fort, parts of the edge of town, excavated within The Lanes, were kept much cleaner. Only in odd corners did debris accumulate. There is a similar difference between these areas in respect of the exotic taxa recovered, those that are not native to the British flora. Near the fort taxa such as figs and grapes (sometimes in their hundreds), olives, coriander, dill, kalange and even an apricot stone were found, but were quite rare elsewhere. Many are Mediterranean taxa and the author has suggested, on numerous occasions, that they represent an aspect of diet brought with the garrison from its homeland. Such taxa are likewise rare at Ribchester, garrisoned by Sarmatians who may have enjoyed a typical eastern European diet of cabbage and greens, and Birdoswald, an auxiliary unit.

Although the above macrofossils have all been recovered from excavations, providing insight to diet and economy as well as local vegetation, they can be recovered from peat bogs especially and here they can provide evidence for climate, a topic very much to the front of our minds today with Global Warming. *Sphagnum* species are bog mosses and different species have different requirements/tolerances of water levels in their habitat (Ratcliffe and Walker 1958). By fine resolution analysis of these remains plus associated radiocarbon dating, changes in surface wetness, by implication climatic wetness, can be determined. Elegant analyses by Barber, Chambers, Dumayne *et al.* (1993) and in particular Stoneman (1993) from Bolton Moss amongst others suggest that there was a generally wetter period from about 400 BC to AD 100. Here it is interesting to note that many of the Carlisle sites exhibit a very different level of preservation from early second century deposits and this could just reflect a climatic change although the change from timber to stone built structures at about the same time also has to be considered.

Woodland and its products are a further material resource of vast importance to the Romans , for structures, fuel, artefacts as well as needing clearing for strategic military reasons. Much discussion has ensued over woodland clearance as we have seen above but there is further evidence to extract from excavated material. Counting and identifying fragments of charcoal may be of little use in determining the proportions of specific taxa in woodlands (people are likely to have selectively chosen wood for its different burning qualities) but analysis of size and age structure of roundwood can provide indications of formal woodland management practices. Caution, of course, is needed in interpretation of these data especially when they have been obtained from massive dumps of fragmentary wattles rather than from a discrete wattle hurdle for example.

Carlisle, again, has provided an excellent resource for such studies (Huntley 1987; 1989b; 1992b). At the Annetwell Street and Castle Street sites, both military, the initial timber used was alder as well as the expected oak for structural work. Nonetheless some of the alders formed significant posts. A wide range of ages was encountered but diameters clustered around two or three sizes suggesting that the wood was chosen for a specific job but probably from areas of poorly and well grown stands of trees. The interpretation was that alder was abundant in the adjacent river valley, needed clearing for strategic reasons and was then put to further use. By the second century the pattern had changed to one of hazel and birch with some alder. The hazel, in particular, was from quite a narrow age range suggesting that there may have been some woodland management in the form of coppicing. This is a practice which ensures a regular supply of specific size (age) roundwood. This may not have reached the formal heights of medieval woodmanship since deciduous trees naturally re-grow if cut a short way above the ground and the Romans may just have taken advantage of nature. Late second-century material utilised a far wider selection of species perhaps reflecting the need to move further afield to obtain supplies. This would suggest that formal management was not occurring. The Lanes sites were "edge of town" and again used quantities of hazel. Much of their material, though, reflected either conversion of oak to timber or craft working. Wood-working debris, off cuts, broken joints, chips from axing and working surfaces, therefore dominated the assemblage. Craft working included use of both yew and probable re-use of silver fir barrels.

Animal remains

The most obvious remains of animals on archaeological sites are their bones and these are predominantly from domesticated species. As with the plant remains an enormous body of data has accumulated over the last ten or more years and synthesis is required. One of the principal questions to address is that of size (Stallibrass in Huntley and Stallibrass 1995). Most of the cattle represented on these sites were quite small but, through time, there are indications that larger animals were present. Whether these were specific ritual beasts or an improved breed is unclear. Arguments regarding data from the south of England suggest that the Romans did indeed undertake breeding programmes leading to larger animals and hence more beef per beast (King 1978). This does not appear to be the case at Carlisle (Stallibrass 1991, 1993; Connell and Davis, submitted) although data from the third and fourth centuries are very limited.

Cattle bones are by far the most common on all sites investigated in Carlisle and there are indications that animals were slaughtered on-site since all elements of the body are represented. In addition, it seems that shoulders of beef, probably preserved through salting and/or smoking were brought into Carlisle since there are far more animals represented by shoulder blades than by the other skeletal elements (Stallibrass 1991). This seems to be quite a common phenomenon throughout the Roman north although, as yet, no-one has found a site with the equivalent 'missing' scapulae! From the ages of the cattle at slaughter the military personnel seem to have enjoyed more meat from younger animals than did the civilians and also than did the auxiliary troops stationed up at Birdoswald. Here too the botanical data give the same conclusion: Birdoswald soldiers did not partake of the figs and olives favoured by the Carlisle garrison.

Whilst prime beef could indicate a high status diet there are arguments that it may represent meat from sacrificial animals as discussed by Gidney for Wallsend material (Gidney 1998). The sacrifice for the Eternity of Rome required two bulls, two oxen and three steers (Henig 1984) and Henig also notes that for the event, *Ambarvalia*, the sacrifices of young healthy specimens of pig, sheep and bull were required. Rituals such as these may, therefore, be implied especially if bones from such young animals are otherwise rare. A combination of the proportions of young bones in an assemblage plus the associated archaeological context must therefore be considered.

What is lacking from Carlisle and many other forts is evidence that the military used local wild resources to any extent. Most fish bones are too small to recover by hand excavation and even for sites with extensive sampling strategies fish remains are rare. For example, Thornbrough Farm, Catterick, on the River Swale, produced only 14 fish bones from about 150 bulk (30 litre) samples (Stallibrass 1997). It is well recognised that the Romans used their fish liquid (*liquamen*) in which to steep some of their food (Edwards 1984); this must have been somewhat akin to the Thai 'delicacy' of rotting shrimp paste or fish sauce today. Presumably this was principally a traded commodity and not produced at each fort by fermenting locally procured fish despite the fact that the finest *liquamen* was made from the gills, intestines and blood of mackerel, easily available around the British coasts. According to Edwards (*op. cit.*) this mixture was saturated with salt and vinegar, parsley, wine and sweet herbs added after which it was left to seethe in the sun until the fish parts liquified to a thick sauce. Maybe the British sun was inadequate for this fermentation process. Interestingly more fish bones, but still rather few and all from flat fish, have been obtained from the Lancaster Mitchell's Brewery site currently being analysed by the author and Sue Stallibrass.

Antler, a craft commodity hence easily traded, is often present but post cranial material from red or roe deer is rare. Wild fowl, geese and so on, are rare although the Solway marshes would seem an obvious hunting\wild-fowling ground in the west. The nature and extent of these marshes during the Roman period needs addressing in relation to the Roman occupation. There are suggestions of such hunting expeditions from recent work at Vindolanda. The *praetorium* produced numerous bones from black grouse; although the sample was small they equalled the number of chicken bones which is highly unusual (Stallibrass 1998). No doubt the black grouse would have been abundant on the local grassy moorlands and would have provided a relatively easy target when involved in their elaborate mating 'dances' at their lecks.

Moving across to Chesters a small assemblage from near the west bridge abutments (Stokes 1993) gave an indication of everyday life. Cattle bones predominated as usual but many of the metapodials exhibited splayed ends, characteristic of heavy stress during life. This is generally attributed to the animals being draught animals and pulling carts or ploughs. This was not generally a character of note in the Carlisle material.

The fort of South Shields is a well known supply base and, unusually, sheep/goat bones were slightly more abundant than cattle in one study (Phillips 1995) from between the later Roman courtyard house and the fort's rampart. Material from the courtyard house, on the other hand, demonstrated rather higher status food including numerous chickens and geese (Stokes 1992). He noted that pigs were more common than usual too, as at Vindolanda (Stallibrass 1998) where many were from juvenile animals, suggesting that the commanding officers, and their guests, enjoyed roast suckling pig.

Besides cattle, sheep and pigs, bones of cat and dog occur in low numbers at most sites. Dogs varied in size from large hunting type animals, similar to the modern Irish wolfhound to more stocky Labrador type animals to much smaller terrier and lap dog types. Horse bones generally are not common even in assemblages from cavalry forts.

Leather has been preserved in the excellent anaerobic conditions at Vindolanda and Carlisle. At the former there is a huge amount of tentage most of which was made from goat skins (van Driel-Murray *et al.* 1993). Whilst the majority of goat bones are indistinguishable from those of sheep some are distinct. Few definitive goat bones have ever been recovered from Roman sites in the north, so these skins must represent imports. Van Driel-Murray (1990) suggests that it is to do with weight that goat skins are used, a goatskin tent weighing 18-20 kg whilst a calf skin one of the same size weighs in at 30 kg or more, clearly an important factor to consider when there items are being carried by men. The preservation of leather is so good that immensely detailed work upon the techniques of shoe manufacture has been carried out by van Driel Murray (*op. cit.*) and she has produced elegant patterns of the changing "fashions" in foot wear for what might otherwise be seen as a rather remote northern fort.

Bones from smaller species, mammals, birds and fish, are mostly obtained from sieving samples since they are too small to reliably collect during hand recovery. Our knowledge of these species is thus only recently being enhanced, at the same time as our knowledge of plant remains.

Rodents are common on some sites but large samples need taking and analysing for them to be of value. South Shields has, so far, provided the most results in respect of small mammals where Younger (1994) found bones from an estimated 340 dead rodents in one context alone. The most common were from house mouse and field mouse (both grain feeders) but field voles, black rats, water voles and bank voles were all recorded. They were all associated with the active storage phase of the granary where perhaps they were well fed! Another, comparable sized, sample was taken from the area after the granaries had fallen into disuse and principally field voles were recorded, as well as two black rats and six house mice. The voles are mainly a grassland species and therefore provide evidence for conditions around the fort at this time. In addition to these British native rodents, Younger (*op. cit.*) also identified bones from the European garden dormouse (*Eliomys quercinus*) which is not British. Whilst the Roman climate may have enabled it to survive there is no other supporting evidence for this hypothesis. Likewise it may have been an accidental import with grain. Although its natural habitat is woodland it will readily invade buildings (Corbet and Harris 1991). The third possibility is that it was imported as specific food or as a pet. Dormice were a delicacy for the Roman elite although whether they ate this species or the fat dormouse (*Glis glis*) is unclear.

Summary

Over the last ten to twenty years a vast amount of information has been gleaned from analyses of a wide variety of biological remains, from both excavated material and from natural deposits. We have a better inkling of what the landscape was like when the Romans came: they saw some woodland, more so probably in the west, but also found well established arable cultivation almost certainly growing barley and spelt wheat - but there are plenty more details still waiting to be investigated. Charred plant remains from sites provide evidence for local crop husbandry whilst waterlogged material shows us trade and imports plus production of hay amongst other commodities. Animal bones show a military preference for beef but hints of status and religion can be inferred. Small mammal bones show that they caused problems in granaries and maybe in dwellings too and waterlogged deposits in some sites suggest that life was fetid and menial at times. These interpretations are further enhanced by documentary evidence from writing tablets and, in all instances, by an increased collaboration between the so-called specialists and the archaeologists who provide all this material for study.

An example of how various materials can be brought together to provide a graphic picture of life during the Roman times comes from a hedged bank and ditch boundary surrounding a property of a simple wooden building at The Lanes, Carlisle. Bones in sieved samples from this area contained numerous small, acid etched fragments, probably resulting from passage through a gut (Stallibrass 1993) whilst plant remains indicated cereal bran and edible plants. Parasite eggs from human whipworms (*Trichuris trichura*) were abundant. Coins of low denomination (small change?) were found in the same deposits. No latrine pits were found on this property and it was concluded that the local populace perhaps had a rather more lax attitude towards sanitation then elsewhere within the town (Huntley and Stallibrass 1995).

It is only through collaboration of all specialists, whether trench- or laboratory-based, that we can enhance our interpretations of what life was like for the Romans when they came, saw and built "our Wall".

Acknowledgement : I am grateful to English Heritage for allowing me to undertake this publication.

5. THE MANAGEMENT OF HADRIAN'S WALL

C. J. Young

Ever since it was abandoned by the Romans around AD 400, Hadrian's Wall has been subject to a variety of pressures. Apart from natural decay, stone robbing had begun by the eighth century, while there have long been damaging impacts from agriculture and from development.

All these pressures have intensified enormously since the early nineteenth century. Acquisition for preservation began in the mid-nineteenth century while legislative protection has increased markedly over the last century. Nonetheless, it was clear by the early 1970s that Hadrian's Wall was suffering pressures leading to damage and that existing arrangements were not adequate to cope with this. There were several reasons for this. First, the existing pressures were increasing. Major proposals for development came forward in a number of areas. The radical changes in agriculture during and after the Second World War increased the amount of land under arable cultivation while in upland areas there were moves to increase stocking levels and also to improve grassland. The numbers of tourists also increased greatly, leading to considerable damage between Steel Rigg and Housesteads, the repair of which required a major programme of grant-aided work by the National Trust, grant-aided by English Heritage.

Alongside this increased pressure there has been increased recognition by archaeologists that the archaeological significance of the Wall extended beyond the structures themselves to encompass the surrounding landscape. Even in the least promising circumstances the quality of survival of archaeological evidence has been shown to be very high. This was one of the major lessons from Charles Daniels's work at Segedunum where he was able to recover a high level of detail about the fort even though the site had been covered by Victorian housing.

Attempts to address the issues of visitor management were made in the Dart Report of 1976 and the Hadrian's Wall Consultative Committee Report of 1984. Both contained many excellent recommendations, few of which were

Figure 9. Turret 44B, Mucklebank, photo by J. P. Gibson. The Management Plan
aims to safeguard the spectacular setting of the Wall.

implemented, principally because no body had overall responsibility for doing
so.

The inscription of Hadrian's Wall as a World Heritage Site in 1987, shortly
before the last Pilgrimage, at first sight did little to alter this position. At first,
inscription felt more like a gold star for excellence than a status with obligations
and responsibilities, while it was made clear from the outset that there were no
additional powers or funds available for the protection of World Heritage Sites.
It was only slowly that it became apparent that inscription could be a real
factor in aiding the wider conservation of the Wall. Recognition by UNESCO
of the site as being of universal significance to the peoples of the world helped
to raise its profile and the sense of its importance locally and among decision
makers. It also helped to build among the wider public a sense of the Wall and

its associated features being a whole rather than a series of isolated sites. The public inquiries in the early 1990s into the proposals for open-cast coal mining test-drilling for hydrocarbons north of Corbridge demonstrated that the existence of the World Heritage Site was the significant factor leading to the refusal of planning permission by the Secretary of State.

Coupled to this recognition was increasing advice from UNESCO and from ICOMOS (the International Council on Monuments and Sites) that management of World Heritage Sites should be co-ordinated through the production of management plans. This became official government advice in Planning Policy Guidance Note 15 (PPG 15) in 1994. This stated that World Heritage Sites and their settings were key material factors in determining planning applications and invited local authorities to work with owners and others to produce management plans.

The recognition of the need for a management plan led to the announcement by (now Sir) Jocelyn Stevens, its Chairman, that English Heritage would lead the preparation of the management plan. The announcement was made, appropriately, in July 1993 at the ceremony in Cawfields Quarry to mark the inscription of Hadrian's Wall as a World Heritage Site.

Developing a Plan posed considerable problems. The size of the Hadrian's Wall World Heritage Site means that many different bodies are involved with it. Around ten per cent of the Site is managed by some eight bodies for conservation and public access. While this includes some of the most important parts, the remaining 90 per cent is owned by other bodies, public and private, for other purposes. The vast bulk of the World Heritage Site outside the urban areas is in fact owned as agricultural land; and the primary interest of the owners and occupiers is agricultural, though most are well aware of the significance of the Site, and respect it as far as possible.

Apart from ownership, numerous other bodies are involved. On the planning side, there are twelve local Planning authorities. Some are also involved in economic regeneration, primarily through tourism promotion and in some cases site management, and five of these are highway authorities. Central government planning and transport powers are exercised mainly through Government Regional Offices, two of which cover the World Heritage Site. Government

Regional Offices are also major players in decisions on both government and European funding. The Heritage Lottery Fund is also now a major funder of work in the World Heritage Site.

There are also a large number of specialist government agencies dealing with specific aspects of conservation, tourism or economic regeneration. These include English Heritage, English Nature, the Countryside Commission, two regional tourist boards, the Rural Development Commission and the Environment Agency. The new Regional Development Agencies will be powerful new players in the economic field. The Ministry of Agriculture, Fisheries and Food and the Forestry Authority are also very significant players since the major land use is agriculture which is largely outside the local planning system and is heavily influenced by grant-aid regimes administered by MAFF.

The interests of the owners and other bodies are clearly very diverse and sometimes in conflict with each other. Behind the multitudes of bodies is an equally wide range of different systems of legislation and government regulations dealing with various aspects of conservation, economic regeneration and agricultural support.

A holistic approach to the management of the World Heritage is clearly desirable but is difficult to achieve without considerable effort and a willingness to work together on the part of the many individuals involved. The Management Plan provided a vehicle for achieving this, though it has no statutory basis. Its success therefore depends on the willingness of individual organisations to implement aspects of it which impinge on them. Only by involving bodies other than English Heritage will the Plan gain acceptance.

This means that process is all important, possibly more than the Plan document itself, since this was the method by which a consensus was achieved. Essentially there were three stages. First there was the process of drafting the Plan. Secondly came the publication of the Plan itself. Thirdly there is its implementation which also has to be done through partnership and has to be planned and resourced.

The plan was therefore drafted through a series of working parties on local plans, landscapes, the urban areas, and tourism and visitors. When views on policies had begun to crystallise, an invited seminar tested those ideas which then led to the production of the first consultation draft. There was a considerable response, much of it concerned. As a consequence the consultation period was lengthened and a great deal of time was spent in negotiation and discussion, with the eventual, changed, Plan being published in July 1996, a year after the consultation draft. Essentially the Management Plan aims to achieve a balance between four major needs. These are conservation of the archaeological sites and their characteristic landscape, the interests of the local community, access to Hadrian's Wall, and the contribution made by the World Heritage Site to the regional and national economy.

The Plan is essentially a strategic document setting out principles to achieve an appropriate balance between the four areas discussed above. It does so by discussing the issues and making specific policy recommendations within the context of objectives set out for the next five years and of guiding principles intended to last for thirty years. It also recommends a mapped definition for the World Heritage Site and of its Setting which has now been adopted by UNESCO's World Heritage Committee. Also, very importantly, the Plan establishes a mechanism for its implementation by establishing a small Co-ordination Unit.

The Co-ordination Unit has been provided by English Heritage. Its role is to be the first point of contact with English Heritage on all matters concerning the World Heritage Site, to carry out English Heritage's day-to-day casework and recording on all parts of the World Heritage Site not in its direct care (less than 5% of the Site is directly managed by us) and to implement the Management Plan in partnership with others, as well as to record the standing remains of the Wall. The Unit also now provides advice on World Heritage issues within England as a whole.

The significance of both casework and recording is considerable. Making an accurate drawn record of the standing remains of the Wall provides the basic information for its future conservation, maintenance and interpretation. Through casework, there is daily contact with a variety of bodies and individuals managing parts of the World Heritage Site. It is thus possible to raise awareness of its significance as well as to deal with issues of consent for works to the protected monument, give advice on particular issues and occasionally offer financial assistance.

English Heritage on its own has the power to prevent actions which would damage the protected monument. We can give advice to owners on how they should manage parts of the Site and we can sometimes offer financial assistance for conservation work. We can manage our own sites as exemplars of good practice to the best of our ability, and we can use our other activities, such as marketing, to support the objectives of the Plan. Nonetheless our abilities to implement the Plan on our own are limited by our own statutory powers and by our comparatively modest resources.

Some areas of the Plan, for example the transport strategy, fall within the responsibilities of other bodies. Only by working through partnerships have we any chance of carrying forward the objectives of the Management Plan. In addition to particular projects, we work closely with the Hadrian's Wall Tourism Partnerships which exists to develop sustainable tourism in the World Heritage Site.

The Plan is now at about the mid-point of its first five years. Given the number of bodies involved, the size of the World Heritage Site, and the shortage of resources, it has not been possible to move as quickly as we had hoped. The biggest gap is that there is not yet a research strategy for the whole World Heritage Site and the database to support it. This remains a crucial objective since accurate information is fundamental to the proper management of the Site. In the meantime much valuable new information is being produced by excavations and fieldwork at a number of sites.

Another major gap is that there is not yet an overall conservation strategy for the Wall zone and particularly for the management of change in the landscape. Steps have been taken towards this. A study of the eleven milecastles under plough is underway as a pilot to working out the methodology, treatments and funding for those parts of the World Heritage Site under cultivation and perhaps suffering damage. A post-graduate student has begun a study of the options for improved management of the twenty-five kilometre stretch of the Wall where this problem is greatest. A European Heritage Laboratory project under the EU Raphael Programme is about to begin the study of wear on earthworks by visitors and produce definitive advice on their proactive management.

Substantial inroads are being made into the backlog of conservation of standing remains. At Vindolanda and South Shields, the site managers are planning substantial programmes of reconsolidation of buildings last consolidated over twenty years ago. Elsewhere, the National Park (in one case) and English Heritage (in two) are planning the conservation of the only major exposed structures in the World Heritage Site which have never been treated.

There has been substantial progress in raising awareness of the significance of Hadrian's Wall and the need for an integrated approach to its management. This has been done through the process of developing the Management Plan, through the media, through meetings, lectures to a wide variety of audiences and through publications, including a regular newsletter, *News from Hadrian's Wall,* which appears three times annually and is circulated widely. The *Hadrian's Wall Visitors Guide* provides information on all the sites open to the public and helps visitors to be aware of the Site as a whole.

These moves have been coupled with the development of an Interpretative Strategy, produced jointly by the Tourism Partnership and the Unit. This takes the principles in the Management Plan and develops them into coherent guidelines and policies for orientation, telling people what there is to see and guiding them around the Site. These policies are then developed in Local Interpretative Plans for specific stretches of the Wall which adapt the policies to local conditions. Four of these have now been produced and adopted.

Most recently, work has begun on a Transport Strategy to address another major policy area identified in the Plan. This study is being funded by a partnership of local authorities, government agencies and non-government organisations, led by English Heritage.

On the ground, a number of major initiatives are being developed for visitors. The National Trail will be completed by the Countryside Commission in 2001. At Wallsend, North Tyneside Council and Tyne and Wear Museums have re-excavated the fort of Segedunum and are now conserving it for display with a new museum. It will provide a new focus for visitors at the eastern end of the Wall and help to emphasise its linearity. It should also help the economy of a depressed area of Tyneside. At Birdoswald, towards the western end of the Wall, a new residential study centre has just been completed by Cumbria County Council. This has adapted historic farm buildings on top of a Roman fort and given them a new use. This will develop the educational role of the Wall as well as providing better displays for visitors to this site. None of these last three initiatives has been led by English Heritage but all have been supported by us as meeting the objectives of the Plan.

A final area in which the Plan has had considerable success is in supporting applications for funding. Successful examples of funding from EU programmes have already been quoted. Funding has also come from the European Regional Development Fund. Another major source of funding has been the UK Heritage Lottery Fund which has committed over £10 million to projects connected with Hadrian's Wall. The Plan seems to have been a major factor in persuading the Lottery Fund to contribute funds, because it provided a secure framework of priorities within which the Fund could commit resources. Organisations directly connected with the development of the Plan have also committed additional resources. English Heritage has committed itself to maintain the Co-ordination Unit for five years and has also provided grant support to some schemes. The Countryside Commission has also supported particular initiatives and many other bodies have contributed towards particular studies commissioned under the aegis of the Plan or towards the running costs of the Hadrian's Wall Tourism Partnership.

At this half-way point of the Plan's life, there is clearly much that still needs to be done. Nonetheless, the solid achievements of the Plan are obvious. The existence of the Plan has also encouraged a wide number of organisations to focus activities on the World Heritage Site. Underpinning all this is a much greater sense of the significance of the military zone as a whole. It is now necessary to build on these achievements to develop the Management Plan for its next quinquennium, from 2001 to 2006.

6. SURVEY AND EXCAVATIONS ON HADRIAN'S WALL, 1989-1999

Introduction

These summaries are arranged in the same order as sites appear in the *Handbook to the Roman Wall*, running from South Shields in the east to Ravenglass on the Cumbrian coast with a final section on the outpost forts. A few post-Roman features or sites have been noted, mainly for the benefit of Pilgrims. The site summaries include references to relevant publications which have appeared in the last decade; the main references to older work are given in the thirteenth edition of the *Handbook* (Daniels 1978) and, for publications appearing between 1979 and 1988, in *The Eleventh Pilgrimage of Hadrian's Wall* (Daniels 1989a). Annual entries for sites in the 'Roman Britain in 19XX' section in *Britannia*, which are usually published in the volume for the year following that in which the work was carried out, are not cited; however, where a report has been held over to a later volume, a reference is given.

SOUTH SHIELDS – *Arbeia*

Excavations have taken place at South Shields every year since the 1989 Pilgrimage (continuously 1989-1991; in summer seasons 1992-1998). The work has been financed by South Tyneside Council, Training for Work, and, since 1993, the Earthwatch Institute. A grant from The British Academy assisted the 1994 season. From 1998 work will once again be year round, with the inception of a Heritage Lottery funded scheme to re-excavate and re-display deteriorating remains (exposed since the Victorian period) in the central part of the fort.

The earlier monograph publications of excavations at the site are now augmented, and in part superseded, by P. Bidwell and S. Speak, *Excavations at South Shields Roman Fort* vol. 1 (1994). This reported on excavations in the central *principia* (1984-6) and on the south-west gate, ditches and approach road (1985-9), and provided a new history of the fort.

Work inside the fort 1989-1998 has concentrated on an area of some 1,500 sq.m in the eastern quadrant. Overall direction of the work inside the fort since 1989 has been by Paul Bidwell and Nick Hodgson.

The fort

Complete excavation to natural in the eastern quadrant has produced the first

73

structural evidence for prehistoric occupation, a well-preserved round house of mid-Iron Age date (400-100 BC cal.). This overlay earlier prehistoric features. The house itself was burnt down at least two centuries before the arrival of the Roman army. Ard-marks sealed by the earliest Roman horizon suggest that there must have been an immediately pre-Roman settlement, but no structural trace of it has yet been found.

The prehistoric remains were well-preserved through having been sealed by a raft of clay and cobbles forming a foundation for a rammed gravel area measuring 35 by 30m. This, the earliest substantial Roman structure in this area, is tentatively identified as a parade-ground. As it is cut by the defensive ditches of the first stone fort, the parade-ground must pre-date the mid-second century, and is presumably associated with an as yet undiscovered early fort on a different site. Beneath the central area of the known fort, further structures probably lying outside an early fort (or forts) were described to the 1989 Pilgrimage.

Of the first (mid-Antonine) stone fort, little has been learned from excavation since 1989. One of the barracks appearing on the plan in the 1989 Pilgrimage handbook, however, is now thought to be a pre-stone fort building. Its removal suggests that the fort plan bore a striking resemblance to that of Hadrianic Wallsend (compare Figs 10 and 14), which can now be shown with near certainty to have housed a *cohors quingenaria equitata*.

The parade-ground described above remained open for a while after the construction of the stone fort. A track with wheel ruts ran from the *porta decumana* of the stone fort, diagonally across the parade-ground towards higher ground to the east; this might indicate the location of the earlier fort. Eventually the parade-ground was covered with an accumulation of sand, in which traces of flimsy timber *vicus* buildings were discovered. These extended to at least 30m beyond the south-east defences of the fort.

With the enlargement of the fort in order to create the well-known supply-base, the whole of the area of investigation in the east quadrant was for the first time drawn within the defensive circuit. In the last decade no evidence has emerged which refines the late-second to early-third century date provided by stratified finds for the conversion to a supply-base. All that is certain is that the supply-base developed in two phases (Figs 11 and 12), the second

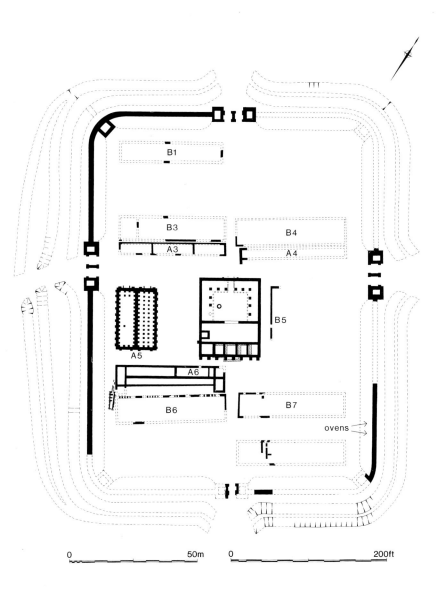

B1

B3
B4
A3
A4

B5

A5

A6

B6
B7

ovens

0   50m   0   200ft

Figure 10. The mid-Antonine fort at South Shields (Period 4). Scale 1:1500.

witnessing an increase in capacity from 15 to 24 granaries, and that the second phase was in use until at least *c*. 270. On the other hand, finds from the site, notably the series of lead sealings bearing portraits of Septimius Severus and his two sons, and datable to the period 198-209, leave little doubt that the supply-base saw intensive use during the Scottish campaigns of 208-11. Three more of these sealings have been discovered in the last three years (unfortunately in residual contexts), the first Imperial examples to be discovered since the great series found in 1877-80. A fourth, undated Imperial sealing has been found in a context probably dated later than the 230s. At present it seems most likely, when all of the meagre dating evidence is taken into account, that the supply-base originated in connection with either the renovation of the frontier under Alfenus Senecio in *c*. 205-7 or the great Scottish campaign itself, *c*. 208-9, and that its enlargement dates to the period 222-235.

Our ignorance of the exact historical circumstances of the two periods of supply-base is compensated for by the wealth of detailed knowledge of the barracks housing its garrison obtained in the last 10 years.

In the first supply-base period the supply-base occupied the northern half of the fort, while a dividing wall separated this from the area for a unit in the southern half. Four barracks, 22m in length, aligned along the long axis of the fort, lay in the east corner. Rear walls and most end walls were of stone, frontages and most interior partitions of timber. The *contubernia* were entered from passages running along one side of the front room (*arma*); in one block (IX) pairs of *contubernia* shared a common extra-wide passage. Each block contained four *contubernia* and an officer's apartment, the last usually separated from the *contubernia* by a stone partition.

A lead sealing of *cohors V Gallorum* (first epigraphically attested at South Shields in 213) found in 1991 in the demolition levels of these barracks strongly suggests that the unit was present in the first supply-base period. The four-*contubernium* barracks at first seem puzzling, but it is possible that the four buildings represent two complete barracks split into two and placed back to back. In this case two of the officers' houses would be for centurions, two for junior officers. This would result in a more usual nine *contubernia* arrangement for the complete barracks (cf. Wallsend, where the barracks have nine *contubernia*). It is tempting to reconstruct two further rows of similar buildings to the north-west (where the space running up to the dividing wall separating

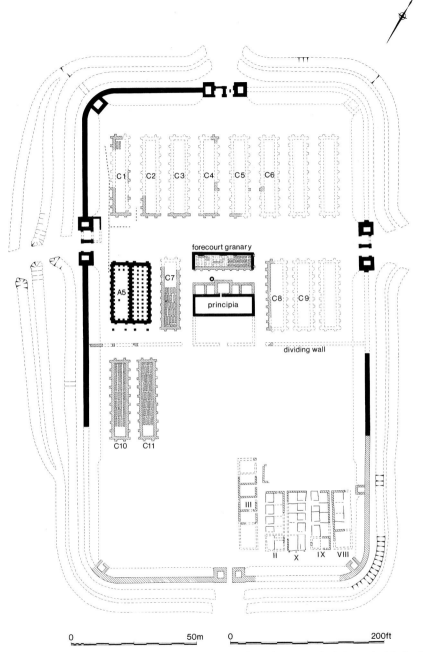

Figure 11. The supply-base at South Shields, first phase (Period 5), probably built in *c* 205-7/208-9 and incorporating parts of the mid-Antonine fort (shown in black). Scale 1:1500

the accommodation area from the granaries is of exactly the right length). This would give twelve buildings in all or accommodation for the six centuries of an auxiliary cohort. But this must be highly speculative until the area to the north-west is excavated. A further building (III), (probably one of two) of uncertain purpose, backed on to the *via praetoria*; it was not a cavalry barrack.

In the second supply-base period (presently thought to begin *c*. 222-235) these barracks were demolished and replaced by a series of five or six running south-west to north-east, confined to the investigated area. To the north there was now nothing but granaries, the supply-base now having expanded south of the now demolished dividing wall. Evidence for dividing walls closing off the south-eastern ends of the streets between the new granaries has recently been discovered. This rebuilding episode also saw the transfer of the *principia* to this southern end of the fort. Thus the basic idea of the re-planning was to segregate rigorously the area of troop accommodation and administration from the enlarged supply-base to the north-west.

Constructed of clay-bonded external walls standing to full height in stone (as demonstrated by a well-preserved wall collapse), with timber partitions, the new barracks were also entered through side passages. Each contained five *contubernia*, yet each was a complete barrack in itself: the centurions' houses were of equal size and present in each case. This suggests that by the 230s the centuries had been reduced in size to no more than 40 men (cf. p. 27).

A remarkable amount of detailed evidence regarding the day-to-day life of the occupants of these barracks has been recovered. Hearths for cooking and heating lay in regular positions in the rear rooms. Small ovens, probably for the communal preparation of bread on a *contubernium* basis, were regularly placed in the front rooms. A milling stone in position on the floor of one front room also illustrates that food preparation had devolved to *contubernium* level. A series of complete buried pots was sunk into the floors, perhaps for storage. Although one or two *contubernia* had been turned over to craft activities (such as bone-working), the bulk of the barracks seems to have been normally constituted and occupied at the time of their destruction.

At some date between *c*. 273 and *c*. 318 these barracks were destroyed in a fire. The buildings seem to have been separately and systematically fired from their north-east ends, and yet had not been completely cleared of valuable

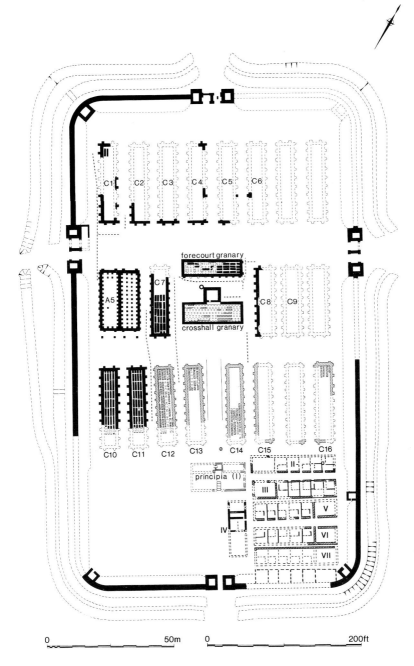

Figure 12. The enlarged supply-base at South Shields (Period 6), probably built *c.* 222-235 (new buildings with hatched outlines). Scale 1:1500

possessions: 1997 saw the discovery of a complete suit of ring-mail armour in barrack II (now on permanent display), and more than one object of gold has been recovered. This combination of circumstances suggests that the fire was a result of enemy action.

The fire was followed by the reconstruction of the entire south-eastern half of the fort (the other half probably being retained as a reduced supply-base) (Fig. 13). The arrangement of a new *principia*, ten barracks and a courtyard house was described to the last Pilgrimage, but since 1989 it has been recognised that the plan is of a recognisable late-Roman type (p. 28). The re-planning of the fort was almost certainly connected with the arrival of a new and larger unit (possibly the *numerus barcariorum Tigrisiensium* of the *Notitia Dignitatum*) to replace *cohors V Gallorum*.

As in the preceding period, the fourth-century barracks contained five *contubernia*, each designed to accommodate at least six men. As the complete complement of ten barracks is known, this allows the intended strength of the late-Roman unit to be calculated as at least 300, divided into 10 operational sub-units. Apart from the lesser number of *contubernia*, the barracks were as formally organised as examples from the second and third centuries; the *contubernia* were still entered by side-passages and each barrack possessed an officer's house with brick mortar floor and channelled hypocaust.

Now completely excavated, the courtyard house occupying the east quadrant, almost certainly the commanding officer's residence, stands revealed as an architecturally ambitious peristyle house whose closest parallels occur in town houses in Mediterranean contexts as diverse as Ostia, North Africa and Syria (Hodgson 1996). The function of the rooms is well understood, with residential areas, two *triclinia* (dining/reception rooms), an entrance court and porter's lodge, kitchen and stables all identified. The discovery of the courtyard house (which flourished as an aristocratic residence until the period 350-380) is of great interest because it demonstrates the high social status, Mediterranean affinities, and very probable Mediterranean origins, of a fourth-century unit commander on the northern frontier of Britain.

There was no further general re-planning of the fort, although much alteration has been traced in buildings excavated in recent years. There is no evidence that the barracks were not still functioning as barracks throughout the second half of the fourth century. After *c*. 350-380 the courtyard house was no longer

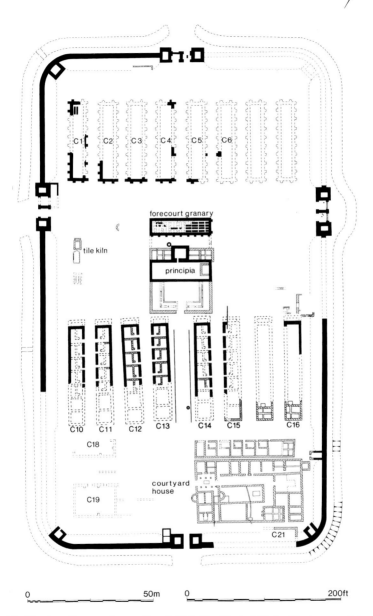

Figure 13. The late Roman fort at South Shields (Period 7), built at some date between *c*.273 and *c*.318 (new buildings in hatched outlines). Scale 1:1500.

maintained to its former Mediterranean standards, but a nucleus of rooms in the house was retained as a residential area, which, on the evidence of coins running down to the Theodosian period, was occupied until at least the early fifth century.

Evidence has been cited in previous publications for the continuation of occupation well into the fifth century and perhaps beyond, but the excavations in the east quadrant have provided evidence for dislocation rather that continuity in the fifth century. The sequence in the courtyard building was closed by the notable burial of two young adult skeletons in the centre of the courtyard. The skeletons, exhibiting identical injuries and therefore of identical date, have been radiocarbon dated to 140-430 AD cal and 340-660 AD cal, indicating an earlier fifth-century date. The pair had been put violently to death, and some time had elapsed between death and burial. Their disposal within the ruins of the fort would seem to mark the end of a community living in Roman fashion.

Outside the fort

Outside the walls of the fort a single important excavation has taken place since 1989, at the nineteenth-century find-spot of one of the fragments of the Victor tombstone (*RIB* 1064). In 1993, 240m south of the fort in an area of modern housing, cremations and inhumations belonging to one of the Roman cemeteries were found, extending in date from the second to the fourth centuries. No skeletal material was preserved, owing to acidic soil conditions, but one of the graves yielded an assemblage of late-Roman grave-goods (Snape 1994a, 1995).

Despite a number of archaeological interventions in advance of development at various points between the Mill Dam and River Drive, on the river frontage west of the fort, the whereabouts of the Roman port remains unknown. A single sherd of Roman pottery was recovered in 1990 in a trench cut through late-medieval foreshore reclamation at a point 400m west of the fort, immediately to the west of the In Sand.

N.Hodgson

Note also: Croom 1995, on a hoard of military equipment; Croom and Snape 1996, on small finds recorded from the Victorian excavations and now lost.

WALLSEND - *Segedunum*

The 1989 Pilgrimage closed at Wallsend (Segedunum). By then the fort site had again been backfilled following its almost complete clearance in rescue excavations by Charles Daniels in 1975-84, and of the excavated Roman fabric only the consolidated *principia* was visible to Pilgrims.

Since the last Pilgrimage extensive excavation has taken place inside and outside the fort at Wallsend. Work was given a particular impetus in 1997 with the beginning of an £8 million project to create an archaeological park. When opened to the public in 2000, Segedunum will include a new museum, observation tower and study centre, a reconstructed baths, the displayed remains of the fort, and a length of Hadrian's Wall - accompanied by a reconstructed portion - running away from the fort to the west.

The requirements of conservation and display of Roman remains in an urban context have led to outstanding opportunities for archaeological research. Salient results to date are outlined here, starting with work inside the fort and then moving to areas outside the walls. Archaeological work has been carried out by Tyne and Wear Museums Archaeology Department on behalf of North Tyneside Metropolitan Borough Council, the principal funders being the Heritage Lottery Fund, European Regional Development Fund, Northumbrian Water Kick-Start Fund, National Heritage Arts Sponsorship Scheme, Bellway Urban Renewal and North Tyneside City Challenge.

The Fort

In 1997-8 the whole of the fort interior south of Buddle Street was revealed once again, to prepare it for display. In selected areas re-excavation has been undertaken, in order to explore deposits unexcavated in 1975-84 and to allow display of original Roman remains (in areas not re-excavated in detail, the outlines of the building discovered in 1975-84 are to be marked out in modern materials). The following account describes the provisional results of this new work in a chronological narrative which differs in significant respects from the structural history of the fort offered by Charles Daniels in the 1989 Pilgrimage Handbook (1989, 77-83). The Daniels excavations are currently being prepared for definitive publication by the Archaeological Practice, University of Newcastle upon Tyne. The finds from those excavations are being studied and prepared for publication by Tyne and Wear Museums.

Pre-Roman

Excavation in several areas has revealed the pre-Roman cultivation reported by Daniels. Beneath the Roman forehall and in the area south of the granary, the clay sub-soil was sampled and found to be scored with intersecting ard marks. In the overlying soil horizon was a series of north-south running rigs, on average 1.10m apart, separated by furrows 50-200mm in depth. This 'cord rig' was observed under the Roman *principia* forehall, granaries and hospital, running, without apparent break, as far south as Building IX. This implies a field or cultivation area measuring at least 60m north-south by at least 60m east-west. This cultivated surface was heavily burnt, and then cut by a secondary series of spade dug slots (on the same alignment), still open when work began on the construction of the fort: their clay fill was homogeneous with that of the construction trenches and foundations of the primary Roman buildings. This sequence demonstrates that agricultural activities were continuous up to the time when the army selected the site for the fort.

The Hadrianic Fort (Fig. 14)

The excavations of 1997-8 necessitate some revision of the plan of the Hadrianic fort which was the pioneering and outstanding achievement of Charles Daniels' work at Wallsend. In the central range, fragments of a primary timber building were located beneath the area of the hospital (itself now known not to be part of the original plan). The timber building measured 16m east-west, with the wall that faced onto the *via quintana* being *c.* 2.5m south of the south wall of the *principia*. A return in the west wall suggested that the building might have been square rather than extending all the way to the *via principalis*. This raises difficulties in identifying it as one of the long corridor buildings found in central ranges and variously interpreted as hospitals, workshops or stores (although an almost square version of such a building can be found at Oberstimm in Raetia).

Re-excavation in the great *principia* forehall cast no new light on the date or function of that structure, but revealed a previously unseen series of pier bases for a primary portico at the north end of the granary, identical to that already recorded at the south end of the building. The northern granary portico had been demolished and superseded by the forehall, constructed originally of timber, and subsequently stone. Two buildings in the *retentura* were re-excavated in their entirety: IX (a barrack) and XII (interpreted by Daniels as

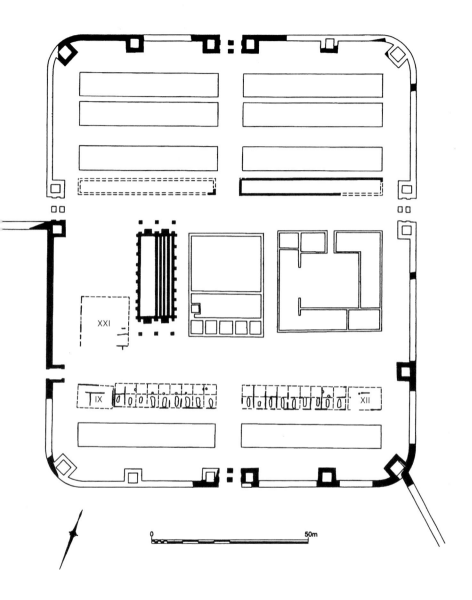

Figure 14. The Hadrianic fort at Wallsend, showing timber cavalry barracks (IX and XII), timber building on site of Antonine hospital (XXI) and stone double granary. Buildings not re-excavated in 1997-8 shown in outline. Scale 1:1250.

85

a stable in its earliest form). It was found that in fact both had been barracks in the Hadrianic period. What is more, each had originally been constructed of timber throughout. This must strongly suggest that all of the barracks were timber in the Hadrianic fort. Each timber barrack measured 45m by 7.20m, and consisted of nine *contubernia* and a detached officer's house at the rampart end. Each 3.60m wide *contubernium* possessed, in its front room, a centrally placed elongated pit, running north-south, on average 3m long and 0.80m wide. Corresponding with each front room pit was a hearth in the rear room, set up against the longitudinal partition. The results of environmental analysis of samples from the pits are awaited.

This disposition of features resembles exactly that found in certain Roman fort buildings on the Continent (notably at Dormagen in Lower Germany and Ladenburg in Upper Germany, but also at several other sites). There, environmental evidence and finds of equestrian equipment proved that horses were accommodated, and that the pits were for the collection of waste from the stalled animals. The continental buildings were of first- and second-century date and only fragments of their plans were recovered. Hitherto these have generally been seen as the best evidence to date for the existence of stables in Roman forts. At Wallsend, where for the first time whole building plans are available, it is clear that these features occur in the context of regular barracks. Thus the perspicacious suggestion made by C. Sebastian Sommer (1995), that buildings of this type represent not stables, but cavalry barracks shared by troopers and mounts, stands triumphantly confirmed by the Wallsend discoveries. The commonest layman's question: 'where did they keep the horses?' and the long-standing difficulty in identifying stabling in Roman forts, are simultaneously resolved.

The officers' houses of these barracks, most clearly in the subsequent stone phase, contained elaborate stone-lined pits and drainage systems, evidently serving the stabling areas for the complement of horses which a decurion is known to have possessed. There is thus no question of the buildings being stables with accommodation merely for grooms or servants; the living space is typical of a barrack and reflects the normal hierarchy of the Roman army.

Each *contubernium* would have been capable of accommodating three troopers (with relatively luxurious space provision) and three mounts (in cramped conditions by modern standards, but paralleled in the Roman world, as for

86

example at Tebessa in North Africa). Thus each Wallsend cavalry barrack would theoretically have held 27 troopers and an officer. This is close enough to the figure of approximately 30 attested for the strength of a cavalry troop, or *turma*, to suggest that each barrack accommodated a *turma* and its commanding decurion.

The Hadrianic garrison of Wallsend is unknown, but given the fact that there are ten barracks, including some cavalry barracks, in a fort too small for an *ala quingenaria* (which would contain 16 *turmae*), it seems almost certain that Wallsend was built for a *cohors quingenaria equitata*. Indeed we can go further. Four *turmae* are usually believed to have made up the cavalry contingent of a quingenary part-mounted . At Hadrianic Wallsend the *turmae* were almost certainly accommodated in the four barracks in the *retentura*, while six barracks in the *praetentura* will have housed the expected six centuries of infantry. The presence of the four *turmae* may explain the

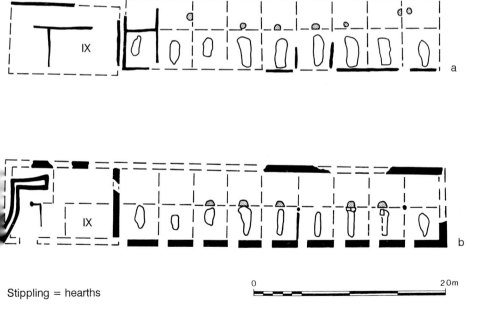

Stippling = hearths

0   2 0m

Figure 15. Cavalry Barracks, Building IX; a: Hadrianic, timber; b:Antonine, stone.

unusually wide space immediately south of the central range, perhaps intended for the movement and exercise of horses.

The Antonine period (Fig. 16)

The date of the conversion of the barracks to stone is uncertain, but likely to fall in the Antonine period. As we have seen, this made little difference to the internal arrangements of the two excavated examples, which still contained nine *contubernia*, with their regular pits and rear room hearths. The officer's accommodation, with its own stabling arrangements readily apparent, was now part of a continuous block, but separated by the only stone partition in each barrack. Other internal partitions were of timber, as in the Hadrianic period. The stone cavalry barracks, whose life did not extend beyond the mid-third century, were presumably occupied (if not from the beginning) by the *turmae* of the known third-century garrison of Wallsend, *cohors IV Lingonum equitata* (which on analogy with other sites may have been stationed here by the 180s).

A more significant change to the plan occurring in the Antonine period was the building of the hospital, a well-constructed stone courtyard building which encroached upon the open area to the south of the central range. During the re excavation of 1997-8 BB2 pottery, which is dated to no earlier than the Antonine period on Hadrian's Wall, was found in the construction levels of this building. The identification as a hospital remains a hypothesis, if a strong one.

The large drain running at the back of the west rampart was not constructed until some time after the hospital, as it was associated with an *intervallum* street of higher level than the original entrance to the building. The drain may therefore have been supplied in the later second century. It is tempting to associate it with a large drainage gully leading from the area of the south-west angle of the fort located in excavations in the *vicus*, where the earliest datable material was late-second/early-third century.

In 1997 the *porta quintana sinistra* was revealed in its entirety, having only been seen in a single trench in 1977. All the stone was robbed, but a sequence of street surfaces was excavated, showing that this had remained a main thoroughfare into the fort throughout the Roman period. Attached to the south side of the tower accommodating the minor gate was a stone building, 3.20m

88

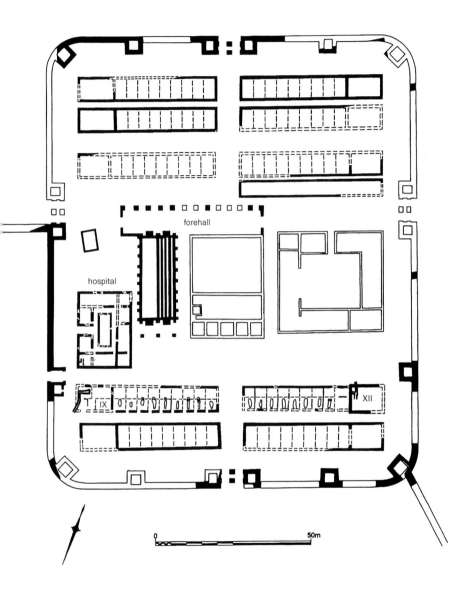

forehall

hospital

T IX XII

0   50m

Figure 16. The fort at Wallsend, following the rebuilding of timber buildings in stone which probably took place in the Antonine period. Scale 1:1250.

square overall. This was later demolished and covered by a reinstated rampart. Similarly there was evidence for industrial activity in the rampart area just north of the minor gate, sealed by a rampart reinstated in the late-Roman period.

The third and fourth centuries (Fig. 17)
The re-excavation of Building IX has shown that it was not replaced in the earlier third century by a narrow building ('stable') as shown on Charles Daniels' sequence of plans. It is clear that the south wall of the 'stable' was in fact a longitudinal spine wall, running through, and contemporary with, a series of accommodation units (the so-called chalets). This could be interpreted as a back-to-back pair of barracks of the type excavated at Vindolanda in 1980 (Bidwell 1985), or as a single very wide barrack. In either case the number of *contubernia* was five.

In Building XII, also re-excavated, there was no spine wall; the second-century cavalry barrack was replaced by five free-standing units (as recorded by Charles Daniels) and a larger accommodation area at the rampart end.

The regularity of provision of five *contubernia* and an officer's house strongly suggests that the new buildings were formally arranged barracks. The transition to this late-Roman barrack type now seems to have been earlier than previously assumed: the first detailed study of the pottery from the 1978-9 excavation of Buildings IX and XII suggests that the new-style barracks here were constructed before the middle of the third century (cf. p. 27).

The presence of stone-lined drains in at least four of the rooms fronting onto the *via quintana* suggests the possibility that cavalry were still accommodated in these barracks. It is easy to see how in Building IX the spine wall might have divided men's quarters (south) from the horses (north). In the spine wall one doorway survived to demonstrate communication between front and rear rooms. A similar division might have been made in the *contubernia* of Building XII by means of timber partitions, no longer extant. This view is supported by the officer's house of Building XII, in which a double wall separated a room on the northern side containing drains from an accommodation area on the south side of the complex.

The area available for horses in the front rooms ranged from *c*. 21 sq. m. in

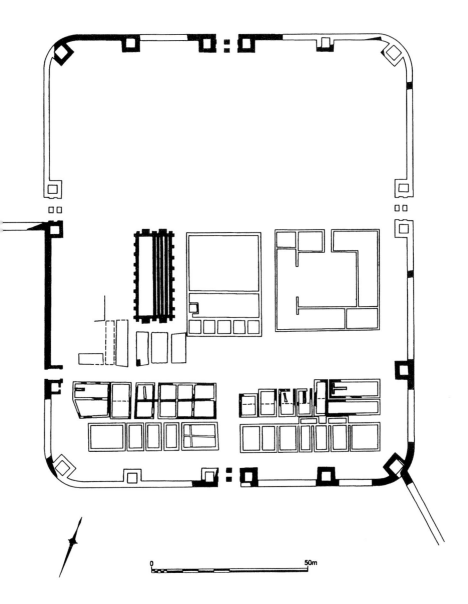

Figure 17. The fort at Wallsend in the third and fourth centuries. Mid- or late-Roman structures in the northern part of the fort not shown. Scale 1:1250.

Building XII to 23 sq. m. in Building IX. Compared with the space for three horses is the second-century barracks, which ranged from 11-12 sq. m., this is almost twice as much. If each of the five late-Roman *contubernia* contained six troopers and their mounts, the individual cavalry troops would have been 30 strong. Presumably the other 'chalet rows' represent a third-century conversion to new barrack types, some no doubt for infantry.

A further change which presumably dates to the later-second or third century was the demolition of the east range of the hospital. Heavy rutting in the street surface overlying the demolished range shows that traffic was accustomed to enter the *porta quintana sinistra* and sweep around the corner of the reduced hospital to gain access to the northern part of the fort. This change in plan cannot be of very late date, as the new street had seen considerable use before it was in turn covered by timber constructions probably representing a barrack (see below). Daniels associated the reduction of the hospital with the insertion of a building south of the granary. The only evidence for this building seems to have been floor surfaces which correspond exactly with the interiors of two of the *contubernia* of a timber barrack, constructed before the end of the third century.

The actual building, or series of timber buildings, was inserted on the north side of the *via quintana* south of the granary and extended west from the *principia* over the site of the now wholly demolished hospital. The structures were recorded in part by Charles Daniels, who described them as 'strip houses'. Now more fully revealed, this series of buildings has the aspect of a timber barrack of five detached *contubernia* and an officer's house. The circumstances in which a barrack might come to be added in this way cannot be known. It could have been inserted at the same time as the third-century rebuilding of the stone barracks in the *retentura*: at present no material later than the mid-third century is known from the levels preceding the timber barrack. Once built, the barrack enjoyed several phases of occupation and rebuilding.

The identification of this timber building as a barrack must ultimately remain a hypothesis. Significantly, however, in one of the '*contubernia*' there survived a hearth in the rear portion and a stone-lined drain in the portion fronting onto the *via quintana*, suggesting that once again a cavalry barrack may be in question. Whatever the true nature of the building, it is notable that in the third and perhaps the fourth century there was such a pressure on accommodation space that a formerly open area had to be encroached upon. This must lead us to wonder whether the apparently open spaces in the northern half of the fourth century fort (as currently known) really reflect a lack of buildings, or merely poor preservation of the later levels.

Building IX had seen much modification (later walls unrelated to the original third-century plan, etc.) but too little survived, either in 1979 or in 1998, for overall sense to be made of these. A number of post holes hinted that at some late period the building might have been entirely replaced in timber.

The major additions to our knowledge of the fourth century fort since Charles Daniels reported to the last Pilgrimage are largely confined to the area of barracks in the *retentura*. Few late Roman levels remained to be excavated in other parts of the fort re-examined. Observations in a trench across the western rampart (just north of the minor gate) suggested that the fort wall, standing on a west-facing slope, collapsed and was rebuilt in antiquity. Found unstratified in this area in 1998 was an inscription of probable early-third century date recording building work on a baths (*'balineum'*).

Damage to the latest levels has made it impossible to trace the history of the fort into the post-Roman period. Some material found unstratified in the older excavations has been recognised as being of Anglo-Saxon date, including a fragment of a pottery vessel, probably of the sixth century, which may have been used in a funerary context. The fort may therefore have been a focus of interest for the first Anglian communities to arrive in this area of the Tyne valley.

The *vicus* and fort ditches

An area of 580 sq. m (the intended site of the reconstructed baths), 25m south of the fort, was totally excavated in 1997. Poorly preserved Roman structures, damaged by ploughing, were discovered. The northern part of the area contained part of a timber strip building 6m wide and at least 15m long, running parallel to the southern defences of the fort. The head of a child had been deliberately deposited in one of the construction trenches. A stone foundation 5m further south represented the western end of a substantial building, at least 12m wide. This was in turn replaced by a series of wall foundations and timber wall slots belonging to a building of uncertain form. These buildings probably fronted onto a road swinging south-west from the south gate of the fort. On pottery evidence the whole sequence of buildings here was confined to the third and early fourth centuries. There was no evidence for later-fourth century activity on the site.

An area immediately north of Hadrian's Wall and immediately west of the fort was investigated. The Wall ditch was not seen, being obscured by the unexpectedly well-preserved remains of the eighteenth-century Wallsend colliery 'B-Pit'. The central and outer ditches (their centres at 12 and 20m from the fort wall) of a triple ditch system belonging to the fort were located. Both were 1.10m deep and about 5m wide.

Outside the east gate an area of 650 sq.m (the site of a new museum building) was excavated on the outer edge of the ditch system. In the second century a defensive ditch lay 19m east of the fort; this was only seen in a small trench. East of the ditch, probably by the south side of a road leading to the east gate, lay a rectangular timber building, surely the first to be recorded north of the Wall at a Hadrian's Wall fort. This structure was subsequently demolished to make way for a new road running east from the gate, which on the evidence of pottery from a roadside gully was certainly in use in the earlier third century. Later in the third century an outer ditch, 1m deep, was added, 30m from the fort, with a 1.50m wide causeway. At the beginning of the fourth century this causeway was enlarged and another substantial road surface laid running east.

N. Hodgson

Note also: Snape and Bidwell 1994, on the extent of the *vicus*; Griffiths 1993, on excavations north-east of the fort; Griffiths 1995, on the reinstatement of a length of the Branch Wall.

With the unexpected discovery of a milecastle at the Arts Centre, Westgate Road, in 1985 (Harbottle et al*. 1988), what many had suspected became certain: the postulated positions of turrets and milecastles from Wallsend to turret 7B, relying on unsatisfactory antiquarian accounts, cannot be accepted. Bennett (1998, 30-2) has attempted to deduce a new scheme of spacing, but this involves accepting that there was only one turret rather than two between the milecastles at the eastern end of the Wall. Until new evidence emerges, it is convenient to cite the old system in inverted commas.*

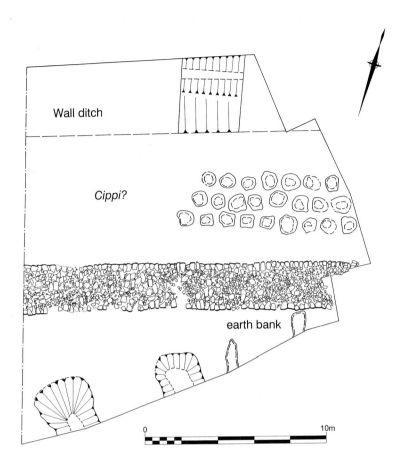

Figure 18. The Wall at Buddle Street, Wallsend, with *vicus* or annex defences to south and possible *cippi* on berm north of Wall.

'Wall Mile 1'
The Wall at Buddle Street. Following trial excavations in 1988 (Bidwell and Watson 1989), Tyne and Wear Museums on behalf of North Tyneside Council have exposed a stretch of the Wall 83m in length, work in 1991-2 having been funded by the Inner Areas Programme; excavations renewed in 1998 and still in progress are part of the Segedunum Project (funding bodies as for the fort excavations, see above).

The excavated length of the Wall lies 50m west of the fort (Fig. 18). Despite the survival of pre-Roman soils, no evidence of cultivation was found on the Buddle Street site. The Wall was built to Narrow gauge with foundations of clay and rubble 2.5m in width. For a length of 35m at the eastern end of the site, the Wall had been reduced to its foundations. On the south side of this length of the Wall, the terminals of three defensive ditches were found and to the east were traces of an earth bank possibly fronted by a timber revetment. They represent the defences of an annex to the fort or of the *vicus*, running at right angles away from the Wall towards the river. North of the Wall on the berm south of the Wall ditch were three rows of large post-holes extending eastwards from a point opposite the front of the earth bank on the other side of the Wall. The post-holes had been dug in a quincunx pattern, recalling Caesar's description (*de Bello Gallico*, VII, 73) of branches with sharpened ends (*cippi*) set in staggered rows to form an impenetrable entanglement. The system at Buddle Street strengthened the Wall line where it formed the northern side of a defensive circuit attached to the east side of the fort. An irregular series of post-holes showed that at some stage the system had been extended westwards. The defences on both sides of the Wall had been demolished by the 260s or 270s.

To the west the Wall crossed a depression which was probably the head of a small valley running down to the river and defining the west side of the fort platform. Much still remains to be excavated at the time of writing, but at the lowest point in the depression the Wall has been cut through by a nineteenth-century pit and can be seen to stand to a height of eight courses; it has been built entirely without mortar, its core of rubble and clay and the facing stones bonded with clay. At present an opening through the Wall is being revealed which possibly represents a large culvert. To the west there has been a minor landslip, presumably caused by the collapse of the side of the valley to the south. The north face of the Wall is lying at an angle of about 45 degrees and a new face seems to have been supplied at a higher level. The south face shows at least two episodes of repair. The first consists of a new face 32m in length, built to project beyond the original Wall face. Reused in its fabric were part of a stone relief showing a hound and architectural fragments, probably from a demolished shrine. Pottery associated with the repair suggests that it took place after the mid-third century. A second, later repair was cut back behind the original Wall face.

Although work on the site is far from complete, two general observations can be made. As has already been noted in the Denton report (Bidwell and Watson 1996, 30), the repairs on the south side of the Wall resemble the insets and outsets visible in the south face of the Wall west of Housesteads. Secondly, the landslip caused the foundations of the Wall to move apart so that at one point the distance between the surviving Wall faces is in excess of 4m. It has been claimed that the width of 3.10m recorded for the Wall at the former St Francis' Church (now the Ray Gray Community Centre), 650m to the west of Buddle Street, means that construction was to Broad gauge and that thus from the very first the Wall was intended to run as far east as Wallsend (Bidwell and Watson 1989, 26; Bennett 1998, 25-6). But there were clear signs of subsidence at St Francis' and, in the light of the Buddle Street discoveries, it seems quite possible that the Wall had been built to Narrow gauge, its foundations having subsequently moved out of position (further excavations are intended on this site and should resolve the matter).

P. Bidwell and W. Griffiths

The Avenue. In 1999, some 350m west of the fort at Wallsend, the robber trench for the Wall was exposed and the Wall ditch was sectioned; the latter was largely filled with Victorian debris, having remained open until the 1890s.

Near 'Wall Mile 1'. Allason-Jones 1994, on a stone head from Walker Dene.

'Wall Miles 2/3'. The course of the Wall is lost from the top of Byker Hill, along Shields Road and across the Ouseburn valley to the top of Stepney Bank, a distance of 1.3km. Numerous small excavations and observations of building works over the last decade have yielded no positive results.

'Wall Mile 3'. Excavations on the Wall at St Dominic's Priory in 1981 have been published by Bennett (1998, 22, fig.4).
Fragments of the Wall were recorded at Garth Heads in 1994.

NEWCASTLE UPON TYNE – *Pons Aelius* (Fig. 19)
Excavations by J. Nolan for Newcastle City Council in 1990 and 1992 revealed more of the east granary and three buildings to the north; in 1992 excavations also took place on the northern defences. In 1996 rescue excavations in the cellar of the Bridge Hotel uncovered layers of metalling bounded to the north by buildings of at least two phases; the metalling probably represents the south *intervallum* street, suggesting that the line of the southern defences of

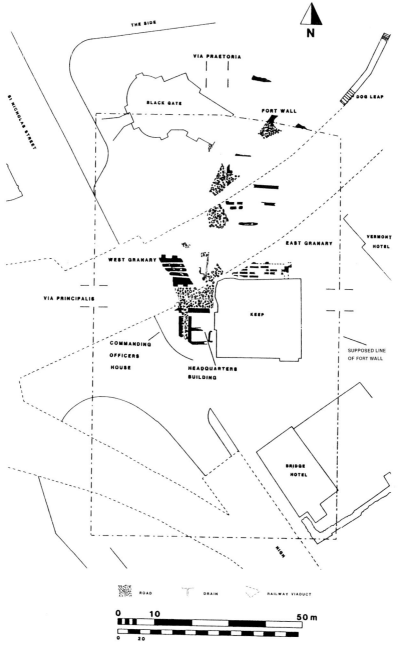

Figure 19. The fort at Newcastle upon Tyne. The dot-and-dash outline is an attempt to impose a conventional rectangular plan on the known remains. It is more probable that the fort defenses followed an irregular polygonal plan.

98

the fort was followed by the castle wall. Indeed, the irregular plan of the fort buildings and the north defences would best fit a polygonal fort, as at Bewcastle, its defences extending around the top of the spur above the Tyne. Post-excavation work on the series of excavations undertaken for Newcastle City Council between 1976 and 1992 is now in progress. The fort was established in the mid-Antonine period; features underlying the fort levels seem to be associated with cultivation in the ealier Roman period.

Riverside
Immediately to the east of Castle Stairs Roman levelling deposits were found over the foreshore (Passmore *et al*. 1991).

Settlement at the southern bridgehead in Gateshead
The pier identified by Bruce as part of the *Pons Aelius* has been shown to have been one of the medieval bridge-piers (Bidwell and Holbrook 1989, 99-100). Although the exact position of the Roman bridge remains uncertain, finds of inscriptions on the river bed indicate that it was not far from the medieval bridge. On a site to the west of Bottle Bank, a medieval road leading down to the riverside, test excavations in 1994 and 1997 encountered an extensive spread of Roman deposits, including pits, gullies and a stone-lined drain. The associated pottery was mainly of later second- and third-century date with a few earlier sherds. The excavated features are presumably associated with a bridgehead settlement on the south bank of the Tyne, but the possibility remains that there was an earlier fort at the southern end of the bridge which was replaced by the Newcastle fort following the abandonment of the Antonine Wall.

The cathedral of St Nicholas, a parish church until 1882, for the most part displays fourteenth- and fifteenth-century work. It contains a monument by George Simmonds to John Collingwood Bruce in the form of 'a marble sarcophagus supporting a draped bier, on which rests the recumbent figure of Dr Bruce in his doctor's gown', which was unveiled by the Earl of Ravensworth on Ocober 6th, 1896 (Bruce 1905, 398). At the feet of Bruce's effigy lies a copy of the third edition of The Roman Wall *(1867), inscribed with the last paragraph of the Preface. Nearby is a memorial window for Bruce's wife Charlotte, designed by C. E. Kempe and dated 1896; it shows the holy women at the sepulchre, and three early saints with northern connections: St Helena,*

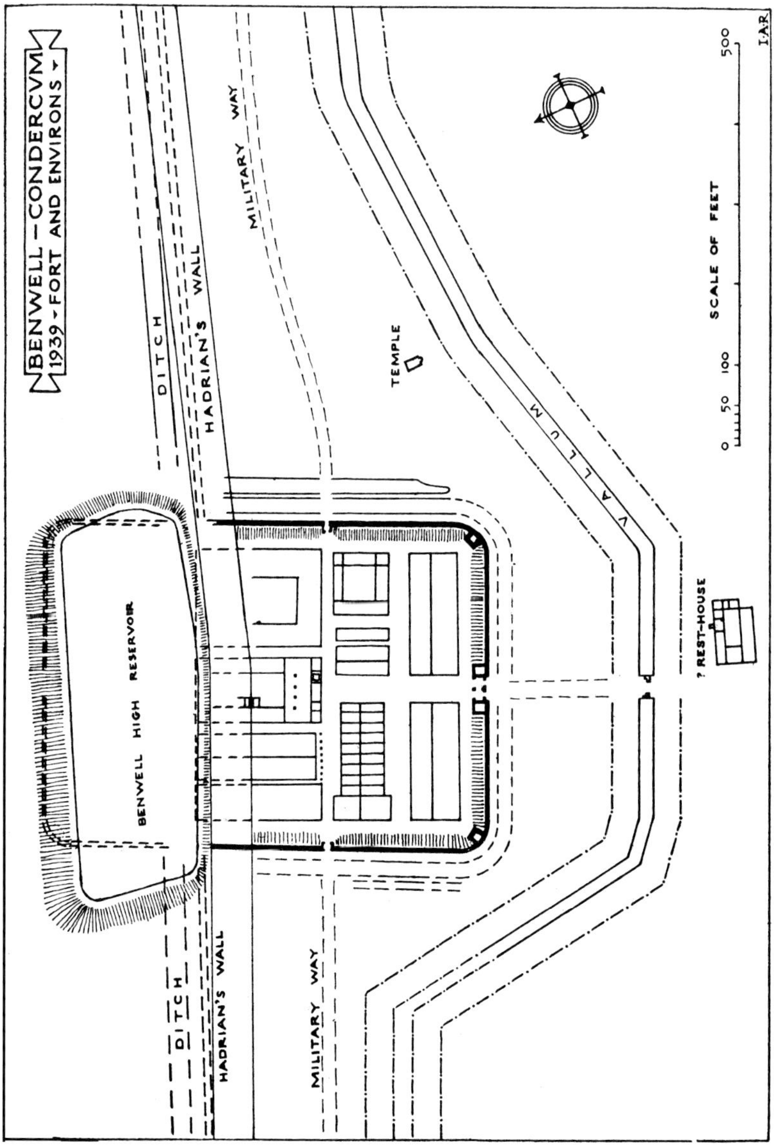

Figure 20. The fort at Benwell.

DENTON HALL TURRET

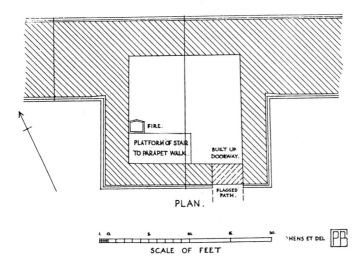

Figure 21. Turret 7B, Denton Hall.

wife of the emperor Constantius who died in York in 306, St Hilda and St Ethelburga.

'Wall Mile 4' (west of the Westgate Road milecastle): three excavations have fixed the position of the Wall ditch which lies almost entirely under Westgate Road. Indeed, the road seems to have developed as a hollow way running along the partly-filled ditch; possible revetting walls of medieval date were seen along the northern lip of the ditch.

'Wall Mile 6'. The Wall ditch, cut through sandstone, was sectioned 200m to the east of the fort at Benwell in 1992, and was found to lie under the southern edge of Rutherford School playing field.

BENWELL - *Condercum* (Fig. 20)

In 1990 a trench for a new gas main cut through the eastern half of the double granary excavated by Simpson and Richmond in 1937, which proved to have been divided into two bays by a transverse wall. The raised floor of the northern bay had been supported on closely-spaced sleeper walls running across the width of the granary; at some stage this part of the building had been demolished and metalled over. The southern bay had a flagged floor overlying levelling deposits 0.35m in depth (Holbrook 1991).

Taylor (1997) has reviewed the conflicting dimensions given in various sources for the size of the fort at Benwell. He concluded that the measurements made by Robert Shaftoe in 1751 or 1752, 560ft (170.69m) north-south and 396ft (120.70m) east-west, should still be accepted.

Turret 7B (Fig. 21). Records of consolidation work in 1939 mention 'splayed stones', possibly window voussoirs, reused in the blocking of the turret door (Bidwell and Watson 1996, 5).

Denton (Fig. 22). Excavations carried out in 1987-9 and reported in the Eleventh Pilgrimage Handbook have been published (Bidwell and Watson 1996).

Figure 22. The Vallum ditch at Denton, excavated in 1987.

Culvert just to the west of the probable site of milecastle 8. See the publication of a water-colour painted when this culvert over the Sugley Burn was briefly exposed a little before September 1864 (Bidwell 1997).

Wall Mile 11. For a survey of the extent and state of preservation of the Wall at Heddon-on-the-Wall, see Rushworth and Lucas 1997.

RUDCHESTER – *Vindobala* (Figs 23-4)

An analytical field survey of the fort and its environs was carried out in 1990 by RCHME (Bowden and Blood 1991). The line of the fort walls and part of the ditch on the west side are visible, but in the interior most features are of recent date, mainly ridge-and-furrow and old excavation trenches. Terracing extending westward from the fort to the Mithraeum appears to be of Roman date and associated with the civilian settlement. The course of the Vallum was established by geophysical survey (see also Goulty *et al.* 1990). It makes a single dog-leg west of the fort, then runs on a new alignment south of the fort without deviation for 2.5km to Heddon-on-the-Wall, where both Wall and Vallum change course. This was taken to suggest that the Vallum was under construction to the west when the site of the fort was selected and, rather than making the usual diversion, the line of the Vallum was shifted southwards to allow space for the fort.

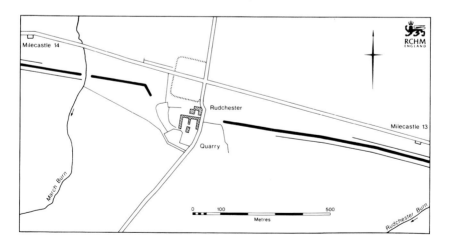

Figure 23. The fort at Rudchester and the course of the Vallum (ditch shown as heavy black line). © *Crown copyright. RCHME*

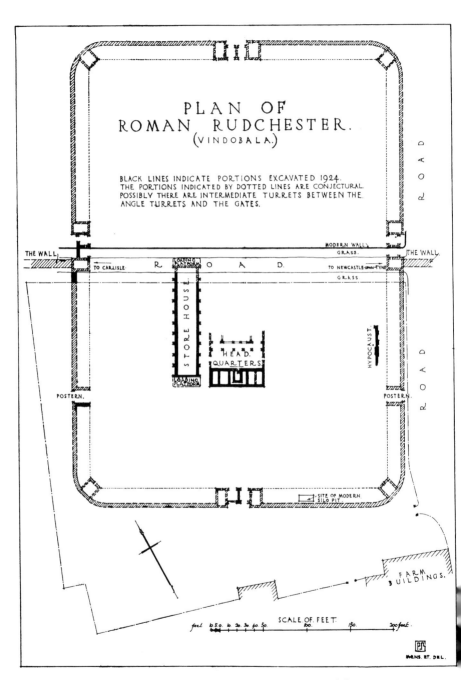

Figure 24. Plan of the 1924 excavations at Rudchester.

104

HALTON CHESTERS - *Onnum*

A geophysical survey of the fort was carried out in July 1995 (Taylor and Berry 1997, 51-60) and is interpreted as follows. The fort is situated astride the Wall, with the *via principalis* being overlaid by the modern road, the B6318. The curtain wall can clearly be seen to all sides together with the ditches to the north-west and south-east (3). The inner ditch is particularly wide to the north and north-west, and makes a return up against the east guardchamber of the north gate. The general street pattern followed the traditional pattern for a Hadrianic fort. The later alterations to the buildings to the north-east of the *praetentura,* fronting the *via praetoria* (Simpson and Richmond 1937, 166), project into the eastern side of the original line of the street (8), reducing its width, so reflecting the blocking of the east portals of the north gate.

To either side of the *praetentura* can be seen evidence of double barrack blocks (12,13) with officers' quarters positioned adjacent to the *intervallum* road. To the west is the third-century bath house (16) planned in the nineteenth century by John Dobson (Daniels 1978, 87). A strongly defined building is situated adjacent to the *via praetoria* (17), and may be contemporary with the later buildings to the east of the *via praetoria.*

Little can be seen in the northern part of the *latera praetorii,* and nothing can be seen of the forehall (20) spanning the *via principalis* (Simpson and Richmond 1937, 168-170). The greater part of the *praetorium* (15) can be identified, together with the rear range and part of the courtyard of the *principia* (14).

Two double barrack blocks (23,24) can be seen in the *retentura* ranged symmetrically to either side of the *via decumana;* both these blocks would seem to comprise two sets of eight *contubernia.* It is probable that a latrine (25) was sited in the south-east corner, the lowest part of the fort. The buildings in the extension to the south-west are complex.

The drain (26) from the latrines runs out of the fort to the south-west. The road leading up to the fort from the south has buildings built up to its edge on the western side (27). To the east of the road on the line of the drain can be seen two buildings. The western building (29) is almost certainly a bath house with a hot room to the north with its apsidal projection, and the *apodyterium* and latrine to the south. The use of the building to the east (30) is harder to

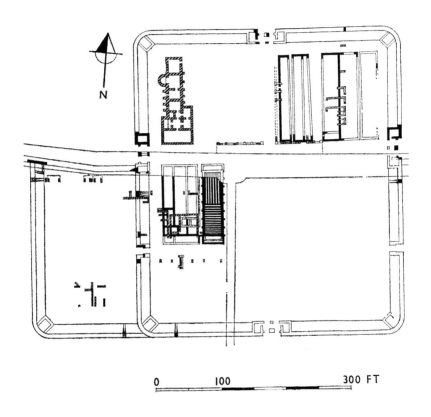

N

0   100   300 FT

Figure 25. The fort at Halton Chesters: excavated features.

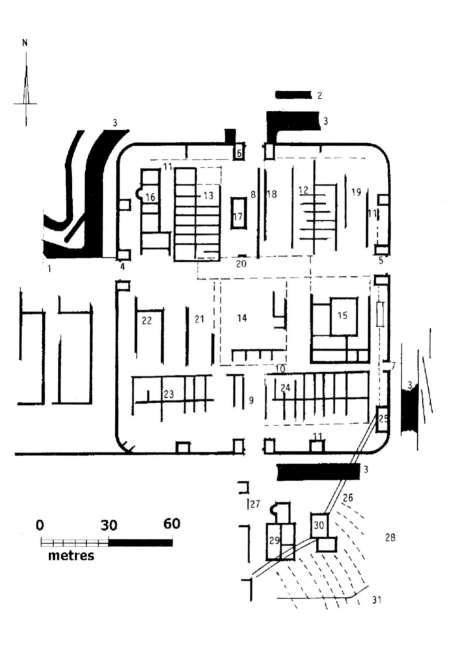

Figure 26. The fort at Halton Chesters: interpretation of the processed
magnetometer results.

107

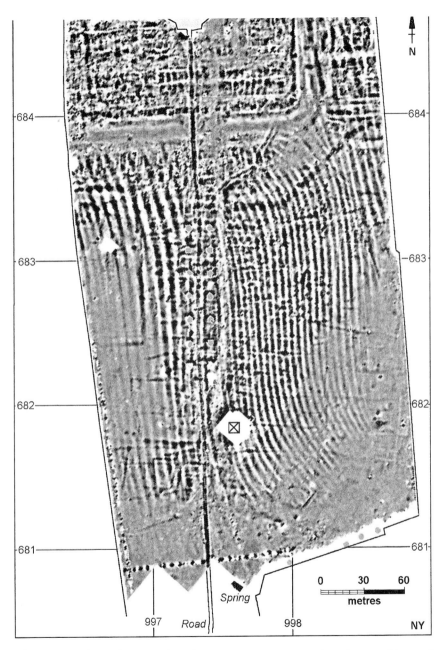

Figure 27. Halton Chesters: plot of magnetometer survey of south part of fort and *vicus*.

deduce; what is clear, however, is that the drain changes direction to pass through the length of the building and out at its south-west comer. It is possible that the building was an additional latrine, perhaps built for the use of the extension to the fort.

J. Berry and D. J. A. Taylor

The following contribution has been included in the final stages of editing. No interpretative plot was available, but the quality and importance of the survey warrant the inclusion of this preliminary account.

The settlement outside the fort at Halton Chesters

A survey of the fort and part of the *vicus* was carried out in May 1999 by Alan Biggins and Julia Robinson of Timescape Archaeological Surveys in association with David Taylor. The extent of the survey, covering some 9ha, included the area directly south and slightly to the east of the fort. The ground has been under pasture for some time with the remains of well preserved medieval ridge and furrow, up to 40cm in depth, covering most of the archaeological features. The survey, which also included the southern portion of the fort, confirmed the findings of Berry and Taylor (1997 and above) and the use of improved computer software produced enhanced images of the fort interior. East of the road leading south from the fort to Halton Castle, the line of the Vallum was well defined and diverted south of the fort and its associated ditches. This highly defined response suggests that Vallum functioned for some considerable time before it was backfilled. West of the road it is less well characterised, implying that it was backfilled earlier than the eastern section; there is also evidence of a ditch to the north of its line.

North of the Vallum and east of the fort, ranges of buildings are sited between the Vallum and Hadrian's Wall. These buildings are located on either side of a wide road leading from the *porta quintana dextra*. An auxiliary interconnected road appears to run to the north of a series of smaller buildings set close to the northern margin of the Vallum. The substantial stone buildings might represent more than one constructional phase. Similar substantial buildings lie between the southern ditches of the fort and the Vallum to the east of the road leading south out of the fort.

To either side of the road leading south from the *porta decumana* are a series of substantial stone buildings, including some which may be of timber construction. Plot boundaries may be associated with many of these buildings, some of which especially to the east extend for a considerable distance. Some of the buildings within these plots could be of timber. To the east of the area surveyed are a series of enclosures, which might relate to paddocks, possibly for the horses. In the south-east of the survey area, a linear stone building was observed which was over 60 m in length and of unknown purpose. Elements possibly associated with this structure appear to cross beneath the nineteenth-century field enclosure boundaries into the adjacent field. Surrounding boundary features were observed west of this building and may be associated with its use. The area to the rear of the buildings bounding the road to the west does not seem to contain as many features as the comparable area to the east. This could, however, be due to obscuring of the significant magnetic anomalies by the prominent ridge and furrow.

The extent of the survey clearly does not include a major portion of the settlement, which probably extends to all sides of the present survey area. It is possible that the main civilian settlement lies within the scheduled areas to the west. This would place the settlement in a more sheltered position, closer to water supply from the Stagshaw Burn and with access to the major arterial route of Dere Street. The buildings within the survey area bear the imprint of military planning with those within the boundaries delineated by the Wall and Vallum possibly reflecting an overspill development outside the fort. This development could relate to the extension of the fort at the beginning of the third century. The buildings to the east of the road are suggestive of burgage plots with the enclosed plots to the rear. The low density of this building development, would seem to indicate the high status domain of the settlement and reflect overall military controlling influence.

The initial survey has left many questions unanswered and it hoped that these can be resolved when it resumes in future. What is clear at this stage is that the overall scale and structure of the settlement will form a distinct contrast to that observed at Birdoswald (Fig.52).

D.J.A. Taylor, J. Robinson and J.A. Biggins

Note also: Blood and Bowden 1990, an RCHME survey of the fort and its environs, including observations of the courses of the Vallum and Military Way, and a suggested site for the Hadrianic baths.

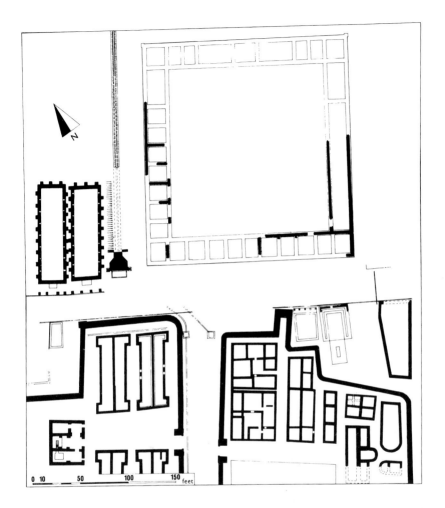

Figure 28. Central area of Corbridge with east and west compounds, courtyard building and granaries.

Milecastle 22 (Halton Shields). A small excavation in advance of an extension to 'Sunny Brae' in 1992 found the eastern length of the south wall of the milecastle surviving up to five course in height (P. Austen).

CORBRIDGE – *Coria* (Fig.28)
The fort and town
Excavations down to 1980 have been published by Bishop and Dore (1988); there has been no further work on the site. Bishop (1988) has identified the

baths on Site17, excavated in 1909, as those of the secondary fort of c. 105. The excavation in 1974 of a cremation cemetery dating from the late first or early second century, north of the main site, has been published by Casey and Hoffmann (1995). For a large selection of photographs of the early excavations, some hitherto unpublished, see Bishop 1994.

The Roman bridge (Fig.29)

The bridge over the Tyne was surveyed by Bourne in 1963-6 and previous descriptions were summarised by Bidwell and Holbrook (1989, 103-7, fig. 74). In recent years erosion of the south bank has exposed more stonework behind the abutment of the bridge. In 1995 excavations by Tyne and Wear Museums, funded by Northumberland County Council and English Heritage, examined the eroded area, revealing what appears to be part of a road ramp approaching the abutment from the east, that is at right angles to the bridge. Four courses of large blocks, originally held together with bar clamps, represented the partly collapsed wall revetting the core of the ramp, which, as at Chesters, consisted of sandstone rubble. Tumbled stones beyond the remains of the revetting wall included blocks with mouldings on their upper edges and slots in their upper surfaces, presumably to secure the uprights of a parapet, and an elaborately moulded octagonal base1.2m in width, possibly a plinth to support an octagonal altar or statue base.

These architectural fragments suggest that the bridge at Corbridge was as elaborately decorated as the Chesters bridge; the two bridges appear to have formed part of the same building programme, which, following new discoveries at Chesters (p.120), can be dated to no later than the mid-Antonine period.

Work in 1995 also included the survey of a timber and stone structure in the river bed by the north bank, which incorporates blocks reused from the Roman bridge (*ibid.*, 106-7, fig. 75). The remains can now be recognised as those of a wheel-house forming the basement of a large horizontal-wheel mill; its Anglo-Saxon date was established by C14 dates obtained on its timbers by R. Selkirk.

Note also: Bishop 1995a, on a tile stamp of *legio IX Hispana*, shown elsewhere to have been from Carlisle (*Britannia*, **25** (1995), 389); Dixon 1989, on an openwork buckle; Snape and Speak 1995, on a section through Dere Street at Riding Mill.

Figure 29. Collapsed revetting wall of south road ramp of the Roman bridge at Corbridge.

Hexham. Antiquaries, Horsley and Bruce amongst them, inclined to think that there had been a Roman fort or town at Hexham. Long discounted, the possibility of Roman occupation has recently been revived but is a forlorn hope as Corfe (1997b) has amply demonstrated. Settlement probably began when Wilfrid built a church in *c*. 675-80, said to have had no match north of the Alps. All that remains is the crypt, constructed entirely of Roman blocks, the majority of which probably came from the Roman bridge at Corbridge.

St Oswald's Church, Heavenfield (Wall Mile 25). The wooden cross by the road was erected in 1927 to mark the site of the battle in 634 where Cadwallon was defeated by St Oswald, King of Northumbria. It now seems that Heavenfield was the rallying point for Oswald's forces, from where they advanced to a battle site south of the Tyne (Corfe 1997a).

Wall Mile 26. Of all the elements of the frontier, the Military Way has received the least attention in the past, and it has been possible for RCHME to locate

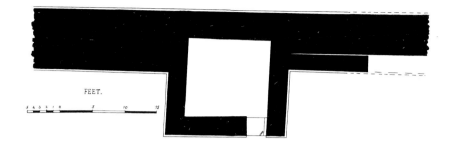

Figure 30.Turret 26B at Brunton.

and survey it accurately for the first time in many places, as part of the Hadrian's Wall Project (see also **Wall Miles 43/44**). It has been understood since Horsley's survey in the early eighteenth century that for most of the way from a point just west of Portgate westwards for about 16km the Military Way occupied the north mound of the Vallum, with a number of minor deviations at some milecastles, at Chesters fort and elsewhere. A departure of the road from the north mound, not previously noted, occurs at NY 927 696. Here, where the Vallum descends a steep west-facing slope, a turf-covered trackway leaves the line of the north mound to run down the side of a dry valley north of the Vallum, apparently to rejoin it some 180m to the west, though the actual junction is destroyed by ploughing. This diversion effectively eases the gradient. To the east it is an indistinct terrace partly destroyed by surface quarrying, but as the valley opens out it becomes an agger, 0.2m high and about 7m wide.

K. Blood, RCHME

Note also: Rushworth and Lucas 1997 for a survey of the extent and state of preservation of the Wall at Planetrees and turret 26B at Brunton (Fig.30).

CHESTERS – *Cilurnum* (Figs 31-2)
The fort and *vicus*
There have been no excavations in the fort since 1960, when Harper carried out some small-scale work in the *praetorium*. In the last decade, however, a

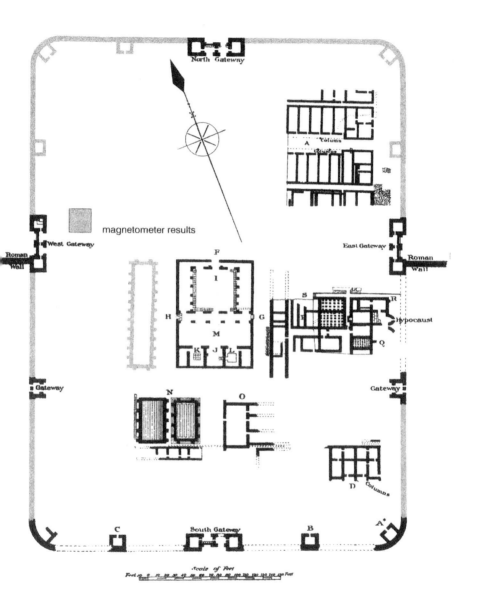

Figure 31. The fort at Chesters with some of the results of the magnetometer survey (1992). There is no accurate published plan of this fort showing all the known structures and a version of the earlier *Handbook* plan, which is the most reliable, is used here.

115

Figure 32. The fort and *vicus* at Chesters: fort, visible remains; *vicus*, plot from aerial photographs, rigs shown as dashed lines. © *Crown copyright. RCHME*

116

series of surveys, unpublished in detail, have yielded much information. Geophysical survey by English Heritage in 1992 established that there were two granaries in their expected position west of the *principia*; in the western half of the *praetentura* were indications of barracks matching the position of those exposed to the east; two interval towers were seen midway between the *portae principales* and the northern corners of the fort; in the *retentura* the outline of buildings excavated in the nineteenth century were recorded. A documentary survey by Bidwell and Snape (1993) has disentangled the very complicated sequence of excavations which began in 1840 and continued until the end of the century. Contemporary drawings, particularly Robert Blair's, record in detail the appearance of the buildings as excavated.

Aerial photographs of the *vicus* were plotted by RCHME in 1992-3, amplifying the version by Salway. Buildings extend as far west as the gardens of Chesters; buildings were also seen on both sides of the road running from the eastern *porta quintana* to the bridge, those to the north of the road extending right up to the back of the Wall. Walls of *vicus* buildings are now visible in the river bank and are gradually being washed away as the river erodes the base of the bank.

A remarkable discovery on the northern coast of Spain attaches new meaning to the name of the fort (Fernandez Ochoa and Morillo Cerdán 1996). *Cilurnum* was supposed to have been derived from the Celtic for 'cauldron-pool' or the like, referring to some natural feature in the North Tyne, perhaps the Boat Pool downstream from the fort, or to the Ingle Pool, a natural pool west of the fort. Excavations at Gijón in modern Asturias have recovered a tombstone which mentions the *gens Cilurnigorum*, an otherwise unknown division of the *conventus Asturum*. By 178 or a little later the unit at Chesters was the *ala II Asturum*; derivation of the name *Cilurnum* from the *Cilurnigi*, a people of the *Astures,* seems highly probable.

P. Bidwell

The baths

Survey at Chesters baths in July 1997 produced a new ground plan and recorded the heights of surviving walls. The aim was to provide data useful for the Roman baths reconstruction at Wallsend; however, the results also produced significant new insights into the remains at Chesters.

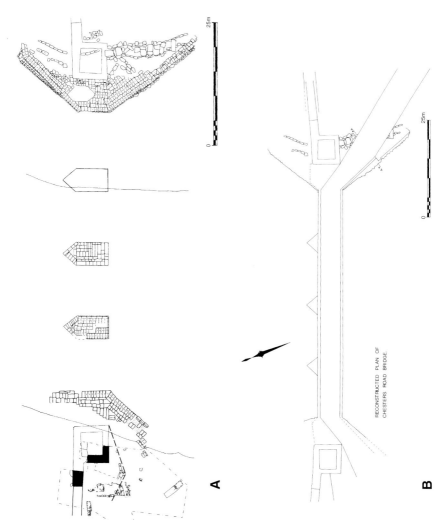

Figure 33. The road bridge at Chesters. A. Excavated remains. Scale 1:750.
B. Reconstruction of carriageway and approach ramps. Scale 1:1000.

RECONSTRUCTED PLAN OF
CHESTERS ROAD BRIDGE.

A

B

118

Study of the metrology of the building showed it had been laid out in modules of 10 or 20 Roman feet (using a *pes Monetalis* of 287mm), with walls 3 Roman feet thick. Computerised analysis was carried out in conjunction with architects of the David Ash Partnership, to elucidate the likely design of the original barrel-vaulted ceilings and the roof. This process indicated that the west wall of the baths probably survives to the height of the springing point of the vault. The irregular ground plan of the *laconicum* suite can now be seen as the result of difficulties encountered by the Roman builders when attempting to carry the roof-line over this addition to the original building. Inspection of the fabric of the building confirmed the projecting apse of the *caldarium* as a secondary feature, probably replacing an original rectangular plunge bath.

M. Snape

The bridge (Fig.33)
Further work on the bridge at Chesters was carried out in 1990 and 1991 by Tyne and Wear Museums for English Heritage (for previous excavations, see Bidwell and Holbrook 1989). Erosion of the west bank of the River North Tyne had exposed masonry which, following limited excavation, was either consolidated for display or re-buried; the bank was then reinforced with rubble-filled gabions.

Hadrian's Wall had been robbed down to its clay-and-cobble foundations for a distance of 11m westwards from the river bank, but beyond that point the Wall, Broad gauge and with a clay and rubble core, stood to a height of *c.* 2.6m. Nothing associated with the original bridge that carried the Wall-top walk across the river was seen.

When the Wall bridge was replaced by the road bridge, a huge ramp of sandstone rubble was built to carry the road approaching from the west up to the level of the carriageway, some 9m above the river bed. Within the excavated area the maximum width of the ramp at its base was 12m and its estimated height was 6m. Its north side was revetted with a wall of large blocks; its southern side appears to have consisted of a sloping wall, each course of blocks stepped back from that below. A tower at the western end of the bridge was represented by its western wall; the remainder had been destroyed by the river. The area to the west of the tower between the road ramp and the Wall soon became covered with rubbish including shoes, pottery and animal bones.

The pottery established a mid-Antonine *terminus ante quem* for the building of the road bridge. It had previously been argued that the bridge was Severan, although the dating evidence was described as 'far from satisfactory because none of it can be indisputably linked with … construction [of the bridge]' (*ibid.*, 28).

A second revision of the account of the bridge published in 1989 is also required. On the eastern bank the road ramp was thought to have run along the rear of the Wall, an upper storey of the tower serving as a gate-house through which the road passed onto the carriageway of the bridge. The work in 1990-91 showed clearly that the ramp approaching the west end of the bridge ran along the south side of the west tower (Fig. 33B). Certain features associated with the eastern abutment seem best explained if the position of the eastern road ramp mirrored the arrangements on the west bank.

The area between the western road ramp and the Wall was filled not long after the bridge was built and several layers of metalling were recorded on the widened ramp, the northern side of which was formed by the Wall. A building was put up west of the tower but appears to have been demolished by the end of the third century. Coins running down to the House of Valentinian were found above the latest metalling of the ramp, which suggests that the bridge continued in use down to the end of the Roman period (for a partial rebuilding of the west abutment, see Griffiths 1992).

P. Bidwell

Note also: Lewis 1995, interpreting the barrel-shaped stone from the west abutment as a pile-driver (*festuca*).

Wall Mile 29.
Turret 29A. For a survey of the extent and preservation of this turret and adjacent lengths of Wall, see Rushworth and Lucas 1997.

Black Carts. During June and July 1998 a project was mounted by English Heritage to characterise the state of preservation and archaeological potential of the earthworks of the Wall in this area, with particular emphasis on the recovery of samples for environmental analysis, the establishment of the original profiles of the earthworks, and whether the Wall itself survived at all

120

in an area where it was marked only by the spoil banks of stone robbers. The project took the form of a staggered transect through all of the works excluding the north Vallum mound, along which the modern road runs. To the north of the road, a trench near the site of turret 29B covered the Wall, ditch and counterscarp bank, while to the south, a trench nearer to turret 29A examined the Vallum.

In the northern trench, excavation of the spoil banks showed the history of dereliction and collapse, followed by two phases of stone robbing. Of the Wall fabric, a single course of split, whin boulders survived; enough to show the classic pattern of Narrow Wall built upon Broad Wall footings. To the north, the Wall ditch was only 3.5m wide and 800mm deep, contrasting with the more usual profile which is 8m wide and 2.5m deep. Though cut through Whinstone bedrock, it contrasts sharply with the impressive rock-cut profile less than 1km further west at Limestone Corner. The lack of anything but recent silting, together with the waterworn condition of the natural bedrock, suggests that it was, until recently, little more than a gully down which to channel run-off water. The implications of the contrast between the ditch here and at Limestone Corner remain to be considered, but will be significant in the study of the sequence and planning of this part of the frontier. The counterscarp bank to the north of the Wall ditch consisted here of a bank on the northern lip of the ditch and a series of low mounds further to the north.

Excavation showed that all of these were formed of piles of split whin boulders and stone chips. Conventionally these are regarded as ditch upcast, but the ditch is far too slight to have produced this quantity of material. It is possible that the counterscarp consists of waste from the quarrying of wall material further north, possibly by splitting surface rock over a wide area, rather than by deep quarrying. The bank on the ditch edge appeared to be roughly, but deliberately constructed in the manner of a linear cairn. It seems possible that this construction was an attempt to make the slight ditch appear to be a more substantial barrier than it really was.

Beneath the counterscarp lay a substantial, intact sealed buried soil horizon. This was sampled in order to recover pollen data. Although the deposit was initially considered unpromising, somewhat surprisingly pollen proved to be present. It indicated a heathland landscape, followed by a more sedge-dominated vegetation immediately prior to the erection of the counterscarp.

The southern trench too produced pollen, this time indicating a more open grassy environment. This difference between the two trenches in terms of pre-Roman landscape opens up an exciting field for future research. The south Vallum mound, and the marginal mound both sealed the ard marks which attest to early ploughing. Immediately before the mound was thrown up, the ard marks were cut by the hoof prints of what appears to be a large number of beasts, though whether cattle or horses was not established. Ard marks are now found on virtually every excavated site between Wallsend and Carrawburgh, and open up the possibility that much of the frontier was built over requisitioned arable land, with all that might imply for the Roman/native relationship. It is, however, also possible that the ard marks are earlier, perhaps even bronze age, or that they are not all contemporary.

The Vallum ditch showed a classic profile. It was 2.8m deep from contemporary ground level, and 6m wide. It was uncompromisingly vertical sided and flat bottomed, despite the fact that the bottom 1.3m were cut through the solid whinstone bedrock. The contrast between the depth and size of the Wall ditch and the Vallum ditch invites questions on perceptions of the relative function and importance of the two features.

As always on the Wall, this excavation has opened up a series of new questions, and the ongoing analysis work should allow certain details to be looked at in new ways.

T.Wilmott

CARRAWBURGH – *Brocolitia* (Fig.34)
There has been no recent excavation at Carrawburgh. A survey of the extent and preservation of the archaeological remains has been compiled by Snape (1994b).

Wall Mile 34. Excavations in 1978 and 1979 on Hadrian's Wall to the east of milecastle 35, including the discovery of a long cist burial, are reported in Crow and Jackson 1997. For a documentary survey of the area in the guardianship of English Heritage, including milecastle 35, see Rushworth and Lucas 1997.

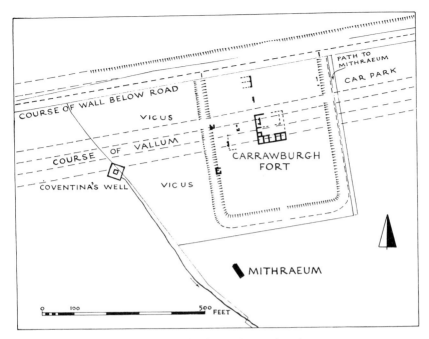

Figure 34. The fort at Carrawburgh.

HOUSESTEADS - *Vercovicium* (Fig.35)

Housesteads is the best known and most visited of all the forts along Hadrian's Wall. Excavations over the past century and a half have revealed the well-preserved remains of the circuit wall and gates as well as all the major internal buildings, including the headquarters, the commanding officer's house, the granaries, 'the hospital', two of the ten barracks, the latrines, bakehouses and a large, late-Roman store building (XV). The last major excavation took place in 1984 (Crow 1988) and since then work has been progressing on the publication of the excavations of the north-east quarter of the fort (1974-81) directed by the late John Gillam and Charles Daniels. The final editing by Alan Rushworth is nearly finished and it is anticipated that this text, which also incorporates a study by the RCHME of the remarkable relict landscape around the fort, will be completed by 1999. Despite the lack of fieldwork over the past decade Housesteads remains central to the study of the forts and garrisons of Hadrian's Wall. A new study of Housesteads from Roman times until the present day by Crow (1995) provides the first general review of the archaeological and epigraphic evidence from the fort since Bosanquet's excavation report published in 1904. Crow has considered the history of the fort from the construction of Hadrian's Wall to the final phases of Roman

123

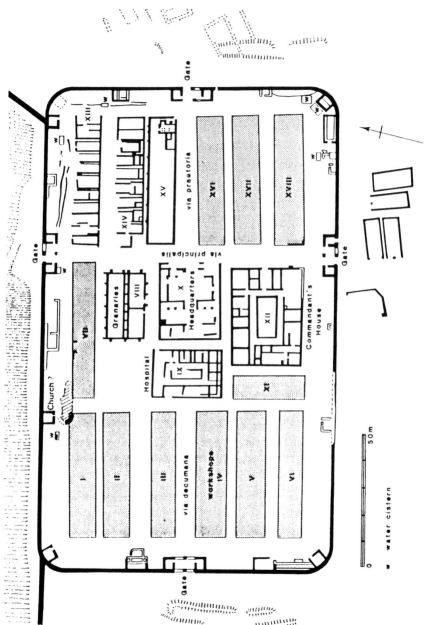

Figure 35 . Plan of the fort at Housesteads including the cist burial and possible late Roman church.

rule. Past studies often saw the history of a fort and its garrisons as part of wider narrative determined by military events and disasters as recorded by Roman historians like Cassius Dio or Ammianus Marcellinus. More recent scholarship on the Wall has questioned this approach and Crow's study of Housesteads attempts to create a narrative based on the structural and epigraphic evidence from the fort itself rather than one imposed from outside. He suggests, for example, on the basis of a small reused inscription recently found in the granaries (Crow 1995, 52), that the *cohors I Tungrorum* which is known to have been based at Vindolanda in the period before the construction of the Wall may have moved to Housesteads possibly during Hadrian's reign and certainly during the second century. The Tungrians appear to have remained in garrison until the end of the Roman occupation, with a possible exception during the Antonine advance in to Scotland. The other main units attested at Housesteads were the *cuneus Frisiorum* and the *numerus Hnaudifridi* (probably the same regiment); examples of the additional irregular units found along the Wall in the third century. Many of the main structures, such as the commanding officer's house, appear to undergone major rebuilding in the early third century but it is often difficult to directly associate fragmentary inscriptions with specific building phases. The extra-mural settlement (*vicus*) seems to have flourished during the third century and in addition to the substantial stone buildings located south of the south gate, normally interpreted as shops and bars, it is likely that the German irregulars were stationed outside the fort on the basis of specific finds of Frisian-type pottery, the so-called 'Housesteads Ware' (Crow 1995, 72-73; Jobey 1979).

A new study of the coins from the fort and *vicus* (Rushworth *et al.* forthcoming) indicates that the occupation of the settlement outside the walls declined significantly from the early fourth century, but that at the same time there were extensive rebuilding and modifications within the fort. These works began around 300 and can be associated with a fragmentary inscription of the Tetrarchs (Crow 1995, 77). The largest new building at this period was the very substantial stone structure known as building XV. It was probably a store building for the collection and distribution of the *annona militaris*, a late-Roman system of taxation-in-kind. The existing granaries continued in use, although they were reduced in size. Other new work included repairs to the fort wall and the construction of additional interval towers along the curtain. The west and north gates were probably finally blocked at this period and it would appear that the fort was being placed on a more defensive posture than in earlier centuries.

Housesteads is one of the critical sites for the archaeological study of the garrisons of the late-Roman army in Britain. How the army changed during the final century and a half of Roman rule still remains a matter of debate with some scholars suggesting a massive and radical reduction in the effective strength of the Wall-garrisons, while others see a limited scaling down of both the size and status of the frontier forces. Excavations at Housesteads during the 1960s and 1970s revealed a specific type of late-Roman barrack composed of structurally distinct units, termed 'chalets'. These and other examples of this type of building were discussed by Daniels (1980), who argued that they represented 'married quarters' for a greatly reduced garrison, at a time when the civilian settlement was all but abandoned. He proposed that the late garrisons were reduced to as little as 10% of their former size and these conclusions have been rapidly accepted as significant evidence for the reduction and decline of the garrisons in the late-Roman frontier on Hadrian's Wall (cf. Esmonde Cleary 1989, 59).

More recently Daniels' interpretation of the chalet-barrack has been challenged by Bidwell who does not recognise a radical change in the planning of barracks and suggests that the chalet-type construction was present in some British forts from the mid-third century and that they are not necessarily to be associated with soldiers and their families (Bidwell 1991, 12-14; see also the discussion of *vici* and soldiers' dependants by Snape 1991, and the recent review of the archaeological evidence for unit-size in the late-Roman army by Coello 1996, 52-56). Crow's discussion of the late barracks (1995, 85-93) forms part of a wider assessment of the history of the fort in the fourth century. While questioning Daniels' association of chalet-barracks with 'married-quarters', he also argues that the changes in the structure of the chalets was different from the comparative evidence from Vindolanda and South Shields advanced by Bidwell. More especially, unlike those two sites, the individual 'chalets' at Housesteads underwent a distinct structural history showing that rather than forming part of a single, uniform barrack that groups of individuals were responsible for each chalet.

Elsewhere in the fort it is apparent that the principal buildings continued to be maintained and that this in turn must reflect the overall status of the garrison of the time. Particularly significant is the evidence which shows the continuing use of the commanding officer's house, including the rebuilding of a heated dining room in the north range (Crow 1995, 78-79). At Housesteads these structures were uncovered in the last century, but it is significant that recent excavations at both South Shields and Vindolanda have shown continuing concern for the commanding officers' accommodation throughout the fourth century.

As with most forts on Hadrian's Wall the final phases of Roman occupation remain obscure. However Crow noted the cist-burial located in a water tank behind the north curtain and its association with the late, apsidal structure recorded in Bosanquet's excavations (*ibid.,* 95-97). The proximity of the two structures further strengthens the likelihood that there is a very late-Roman church at Housesteads, comparable in size and orientation with the newly-excavated building from within the *praetorium* at Vindolanda (p.135).

J.Crow.

Note also: Crow and Rushworth 1994, a survey and analysis of archaeological deposits in the area of the fort and its environs; Mann 1989a, discussing the Housesteads latrine.

Milecastle 37 (Housesteads) and the Central Sector of Hadrian's Wall
The main programme of excavations from Steel Rigg to Housesteads was completed in 1989 (see Crow 1991a and 1991b) and the final excavation report is in preparation. Excavation at milecastle 37 continued in the summer of 1990 when the blocking of the north gate of the milecastle was removed. This revealed the passage walls of the gateway largely unweathered (see Fig. 36) with excellent survival of the original tooling. It is quite clear that the north arch of the gate collapsed soon after its construction and that this can be attributed to poor building by the Romans rather than to 'enemy action' as has been suggested. A gate stop was found *in situ*, but significantly there was no metalling within or outside the gate. It was blocked with a clay bonded wall to the full thickness of the two arches and probably led a walkway across the site of the former gate. Later a narrow gateway was inserted at a higher level to provide access to the north (Crow 1989, 30-33). As part of the consolidation of the south arch of the gate three fallen voussoirs were replaced close to their original position to provide the visitor with a clearer impression

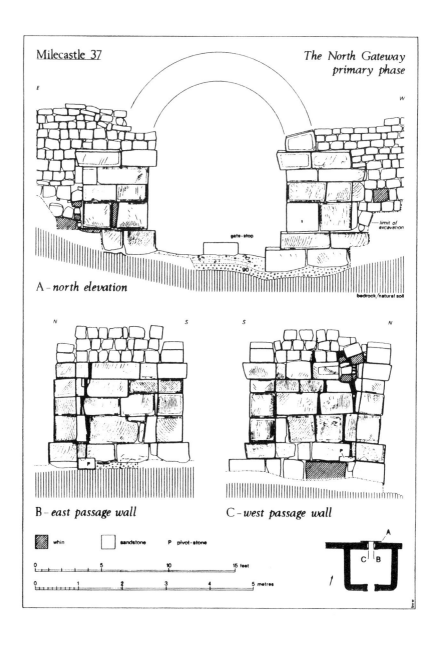

Figure 36. Elevation drawings of the primary stonework of the north gate at milecastle 37.

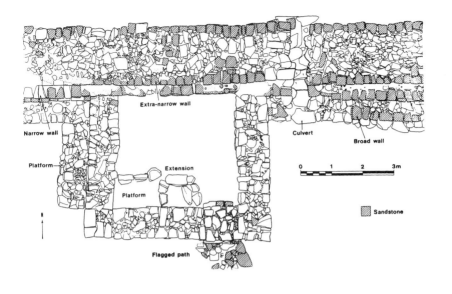

Figure 37. The tower at Peel Gap.

of the scale of the original Hadrianic archway.

A major concern over the past decade has been the long-distance footpath and the creation of the National Trail. Very little new archaeological evidence has emerged during this work, the only exception being a length of Broad Wall foundation at the west end of Housesteads Crags. Like the isolated length on Mons Fabricius (Crow 1991b, fig.1) this is further evidence for the lack of co-ordination between the laying of the Broad foundations and the construction of the Narrow curtain wall. As part of the increasing awareness of archaeology within the National Trust's properties a detailed inventory of the Hadrian's Wall Estate was completed by Robert Woodside in 1995 and this will be published as an illustrated landscape history of the Estate by Woodside and Crow in time for the 1999 Pilgrimage (forthcoming). This sets the Roman remains into their local and regional context and considers the history of the Estate from prehistoric times up to the twentieth century.

Although a number of tombstones survive from forts and other locations close to Hadrian's Wall, there is very little evidence for cemeteries and other burials associated with the Wall garrisons. A stone-lined cist was located abutting the south side of Hadrian's Wall at Sewingshields in 1976-77 as part of the excavation of the curtain wall. Crow and Jackson (1997) have now published the results of the excavation with a discussion of other burials found in the immediate vicinity of the Wall, turrets and milecastles.

Another initiative within the Central Sector which remains largely unpublished is an important programme of air photography carried out by Tim Gates under the auspices of the RCHME and Northumberland National Park Authority. This covers a wide sector of the central uplands both north and south of Hadrian's Wall and the results are very significant for our understanding of native settlements from the Roman period in the central part of the Wall zone. Contrary to most people's expectations, the line of the Whin Sill in the central part of Hadrian's Wall (excepting the major forts) is poorly represented as part of the air photographic cover of the uplands of northern England and south Scotland. New and extremely well-preserved native settlements together with extensive areas of cord-rigg have been identified within 1-2km south and north of Housesteads. One near Crindledykes Farm, close to the Stanegate (Crow in *Archaeology in Northumberland* 1994-95, 29), incorporates a complex of circular houses, yards and small fields including cord-rigg. Another east of Queen's Crags and only 700m north of Sewingshields Crags represents a classic, rectalinear enclosure with a circular house. The presence of this and other settlements just north of Hadrian's Wall is of particular importance for future studies of Roman and native interaction especially when this is considered in relation to recent studies of the vegetational history of the Central Sector (see Chapter 4).

J.Crow

VINDOLANDA (Figs 38-40)

A substantial amount of work has taken place at Vindolanda since the last Pilgrimage, with the continuation of the programme devoted to the early wooden forts (1988-89, 1991-94), and the excavation of the *praetorium* of Stone Fort 2 (1997-98), followed by its consolidation for permanent display. The Museum at Chesterholm has been expanded, to provide two large research and storage areas, and one of them bears the name of 'The Eric Birley Research Building'. Eric Birley died in October, 1995, in his ninetieth year, and his ashes are buried in the Museum gardens. On the west bank of the stream the first phase of an Open Air Museum has been constructed, with full scale replicas of a number of Roman civilian buildings and other features.

The excavations between 1988 and 1994, in the area immediately to the west of the west wall of Stone Fort 2, produced more detailed information about the occupation of the site before the construction of the *vicus* in the second decade of the third century (Fig. 38). A 40m length of the western ditch of the primary fort on the eastern part of the plateau was excavated, and produced a large quantity of La Graufesenque samian ware broadly dateable to the middle years of the 80s. It was significant that Dragendorff 29s were scarce. It may be that traces of a possible fort site, visible in aerial photographs, on the north side of the Stanegate road, to the north-west of the main site, may represent an Agricolan fort.

The western ditch of the primary fort, currently labelled Period I, had been efficiently back-filled with turf from the rampart mound, a large quantity of whin boulders and lengths of wattle fencing and other timbers (for a report on the timber forts, see Birley, R., 1994). The latter included one complete and one fragmentary wagon axle. The four successive timber forts constructed between *c*. 90 and *c*.120 were substantially larger than the primary fort. The plan, Figure 38, shows their approximate position in relation to the later third- and fourth-century stone fort and third-century *vicus*. Apart from a re-examination of the Periods II and III south gate in 1993, which located the major bonfire site where the Cerialis archive, amongst other materials, had been burned, the bulk of the work between 1988 and 1994 lay to the north of the *praetorium* site. In this area the construction of two western ditches for the first stone fort had severely damaged the earlier wooden buildings, and the presence of substantial later stone structures made it impossible to examine sufficient of the structures to obtain meaningful plans.

It is, however, now possible to provide a provisional chronology for the wooden forts. On the basis of the pottery from the ditch, the Period I fort, perhaps occupied by *cohors I Tungrorum*, was replaced *c*. 90 by a fort of some 7 acres, occupied by *cohors VIIII Batavorum* (and perhaps a detachment from *cohors III Batavorum*). Some ten years later the fort buildings were replaced with new and more substantial structures, for the same garrison, which was at one time commanded by Flavius Cerialis. Material from his archive proved occupation within the governorship of Neratius Marcellus, continuing until at least the late spring of 105. There was plentiful evidence to suggest that

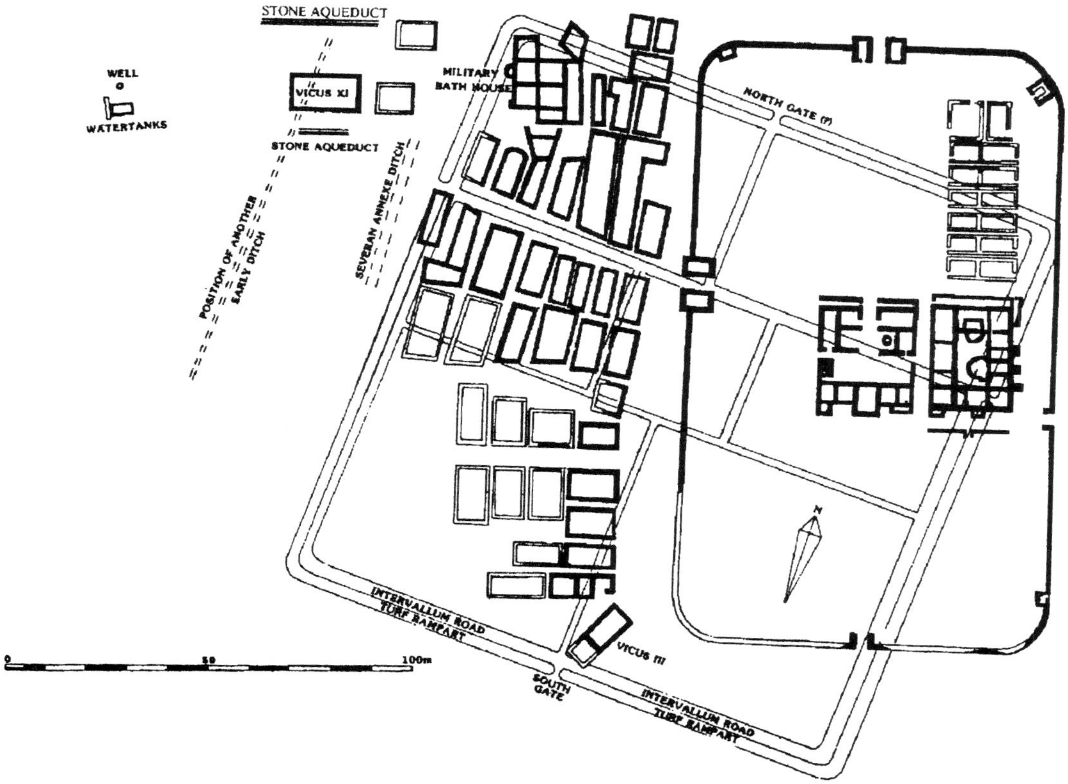

Figure 38. Vindolanda: Stone Fort 2, with the outline of the larger early timber fort.

STONE AQUEDUCT

STONE AQUEDUCT

SEVERAN ANNEXE DITCH

POSITION OF ANOTHER EARLY DITCH

VICUS XI

WELL

WATERTANKS

MILITARY BATH HOUSE

NORTH GATE (?)

INTERVALLUM ROAD TURF RAMPART

INTERVALLUM ROAD TURF RAMPART

VICUS III

SOUTH GATE

N

0   50   100m

the Batavian cohort abandoned its fort in some haste that summer, probably because of a posting to the Danubian theatre of war. The large quantity of ink writing tablets recovered from a bonfire site in 1993 (the bulk of them from the Cerialis archive), will form the bulk of a further Vindolanda Tablets volume by A. P. Bowman and J. D. Thomas in the near future.

A new Period IV fort was constructed soon after 105, probably for the return of *cohors I Tungrorum*. The old south gate was blocked and the site of the Cerialis *praetorium* became a barracks. It is assumed, but not yet proved, that the new fort was extended by some 40m to the west, where an early ditch was located by E. Birley in 1930. Dated material from this occupation included a stores list naming the consuls for 111, and plentiful Trajanic coinage, including the *Via Nova* issue of 112. Early in Hadrian's reign, the wooden fort was reconstructed once more. Two early but worn coins of Hadrian were recovered from its floors, which, where flagged with stone, exhibited considerable traces of patching and wear. An exceptionally well appointed structure of this period, lying just south-west of the later stone fort's western gateway, was partially examined in 1992, revealing *opus signinum* floors and traces of painted wall plaster. It was not unreasonable to suggest that it may have been erected to house Hadrian when he visited the area in 122, to inspect progress on his new Wall.

The Period V wooden fort was demolished when Vindolanda's first stone fort was constructed on the eastern side of the plateau. The precise date of that building work has yet to be determined, but it must have fallen somewhere between the mid-120s and the 160s. The new fort possessed two substantial western ditches, later filled with a variety of domestic rubbish and sealed, to make way for a large timber annex. The orderly plans of the large buildings suggested occupation by the military, rather than civilians. In the northern part of the site, these annex buildings were later demolished to make way for a stone-built unorthodox, military complex, surrounded by a broad clay rampart. These stone buildings, once thought to represent an early *vicus,* were certainly of Severan date, on the evidence of coins, and they appear to have extended to the east, onto the site of the stone forts. It is argued (Birley *et al.* 1998) that they were contemporary with the stone-built circular huts which briefly occupied the site of Stone Fort I after its military buildings had been demolished.

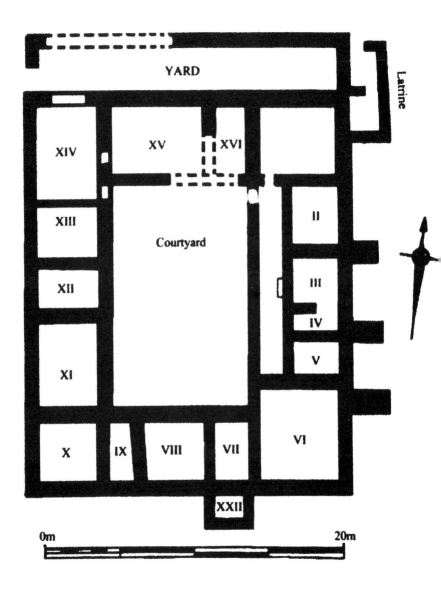

Figure 39. Plan of *praetorium* at Vindolanda.

134

The last phase of occupation to the west of the stone fort site saw the construction of the civilian settlement, now to be dated to the end of the second decade of the third century. There has been no further evidence to refute the suggestion that this *vicus* was probably abandoned before the 280s.

The *praetorium* site in Stone Fort 2

Birley *et al.* 1998 and 1999 provide Interim Reports on the work undertaken on the site of the *praetorium* of Stone Fort 2 (Fig. 39). The site of Anthony Hedley's 1831 work was located and compared with Hodgson's 1840 and manuscript accounts. It was evident that the remains uncovered by Hedley had been those of a late baths suite, probably constructed *c.* 370, which extended further to the north, beyond the site of the original *praetorium*. There had been extensive stone robbing after Hodgson drew his sketch plan in 1832, almost certainly during the back-filling process.

The original *praetorium* of Stone Fort 2 was presumably constructed in the second or early in the third decade of the third century, to accommodate the prefect of the incoming *cohors IV Gallorum*, as suggested by *RIB* 1686, the Petronius Urbicus altar found by Hedley. The building had been comprehensively reconstructed around 300, after a period of disuse. During the fourth century there were a series of further alterations to the structure, most notably the erection of a new baths suite at the northern end, and finally, after the eastern wing had been demolished, the erection of a small church-like apsidal structure in the former courtyard.

Nearly three hundred coins were recovered from the site, with a heavy concentration of mid fourth-century issues of Constantius II, Constans and Magnentius, together with some thirteen of the House of Valentinian. But in line with the findings of Bidwell (1985), it was evident that occupation of at least a part of the site had continued beyond 400. The apsidal building in the courtyard had been constructed some years after the courtyard had been flagged in 370, and there were traces of an even later structure on the roadway to the south. But there was evidence of early medieval ploughing in many areas, which, combined with the activities of stone robbers, had removed the bulk of the evidence for the last period of occupation.

Two important inscriptions were recovered in the course of the excavations

Figure 40. Tombstone of Titus Annius.

(Fig.40). The Titus Annius tombstone is reported in the most recent edition of *Britannia* (Birley, A., 1988 and see pp.15-17 and 47), and another large altar, in the style of the Petronius Urbicus example, is discussed in the 1998 Interim Report (Birley, R. *et al.* 1988). Both can be seen in Chesterholm Museum.

R.Birley

Note also: various studies of finds, Birley, A., 1997 (keys and locks), Birley, R., 1996 (weapons) and 1997 (writing materials), Funari 1991 (Dressel 20 amphora inscriptions), van Driel-Murray *et al.* 1993 (leather, textiles, environmental evidence and dendrochronology); for additional studies of the writing-tablets, see Birley, A. R., 1995 and 1997a, Nouwen 1995 (on *cohors I Tungrorum*) and Tomlin 1996. For a possible signal-tower at the southern end of Barcombe Hill, see Woolliscroft *et al.* 1992.

Wall Miles 40-42 and 45. For a survey of the extent and state of preservation of the archaeological remains in the guardianship of English Heritage at

Winshield Crags, Cawfield Crags and Walltown Crags, see Rushworth and Barker 1997.

Wall Miles 40/41. The course of the Military Way approaching milecastle 40 from the east is clear but immediately to the south of the milecastle it is lost in a small marsh. It re-emerges as a slight agger and is thereafter visible intermittently, sometimes only as a strip of ground cleared of rocks, as it climbs towards the crest of the hill. Just short of the crest at NY 7427 6756 the Military Way has to cross a gully. This it does by means of a causeway, 0.8m high on the north side and as much as 1.7m high to the south. The roadway is constricted at this point to a width of only 2m.

There is no definite trace of the Military Way going west from this point until it passes to the south of the triangulation pillar. Here a narrow terraceway, though much eroded, probably represents the route. The Military Way then seems to continue parallel to the Wall towards Green Slack. Before reaching the Slack, however, its line is blocked by a large rock outcrop, which it seems to bypass to the south before swinging back through a rocky declivity which leads the road into the Slack. This is somewhat further north than the line suggested by the Ordnance Survey. The route across the bottom of the Slack is marked by two lines of stones 2.5m apart but there is no agger and no sign of the road on the west side of the Slack. This, together with a slight vertical drop from the declivity on the east side, suggests the possibility that the Military Way crossed the Slack in a raised position, perhaps on some form of timber bridge.

The agger is visible a few metres to the west of Green Slack and can be traced easily to the lip of Lodhams Slack. The Military Way descends the precipitous east side of Lodhams Slack by a terraceway, now much reduced by erosion, and crosses the bottom on a substantial agger which has been subsequently modified to carry traffic through the line of the Wall. Another terraceway leads up the west side of Lodhams Slack. At the top of this slope a shieling, the walls of which survive as turf-covered stony mounds, has been built over the Military Way at NY 7367 6724.

Thereafter the route of the Military Way can be followed with less certainty as a vague vegetation mark with intermittent signs of a scarp on the south side until NY 7339 6718 where a line of stones in one such scarp almost certainly marks the course of the road. The scarp here is approximately 0.3m high.

Westwards from this point the route is very uncertain for the next 200m. The line given by the Ordnance Survey is probably correct but there is a possible alternative route further to the south which would lead the Military Way into the natural gully at NY 7320 6707 from the south side rather than the north. From the foot of this gully the agger is clearly visible passing to the south of milecastle 41 (Shield-on-the-Wall). Here it is up to 0.7m high to the south and has some revetting stones in the south side, but has been disturbed by later activity.

The agger fades rapidly, however, to the west and the line becomes uncertain again. The Ordnance Survey line continues across Bogle Hole and descends by a sharp zig-zag down the crags to its known position in Caw Gap. While this is the most direct route it may be doubted on the grounds that the descent is too steep. Unfortunately this section has largely been destroyed by quarrying but the short remaining length of the suggested line over the crags has a gradient of nearly 1:2. Nowhere else along this section, including the sides of Lodhams Slack and the causeway over the gully at NY 7427 6756, does the Military Way have a gradient steeper than 1:3. An alternative route is suggested: from the agger below milecastle 41 the road continues to the east lip of Bogle Hole before turning sharply to the south and running through a slight gap to take the gentlest gradient to the lower ground. A number of hollow ways, perhaps associated with the deserted farm on the site of milecastle 41, as well as a modern tractor track, follow this line. The route would then turn west and run close to the Vallum to the existing fragment of agger to the east of the modern road in Caw Gap. This is a longer route than the Ordnance Survey line but the gradients involved are much less formidable. Beyond Caw Gap the route of the Military Way is well known.

A detailed study of the Military Way over one of the most hostile stretches of terrain that it has to negotiate raises the question of what purpose the road was intended to serve. Given that a number of spur roads linking the Military Way to turrets and milecastles have now been identified, its role is clearly connected with these installations for the movement of troops and/or supplies.

Two points emerge regarding constraints on the use of the road: steepness of gradients and narrowness of the roadway. Although the road surveyors and builders have tried to avoid the steepest of slopes in this very broken terrain, gradients of 1:4 or even 1:3 are found over short stretches. Similarly, though generally the road is up to 4 or 5m wide there are places where it is reduced to as little as 2m. Both these factors, though particularly the first, make it doubtful whether the Military Way, in this sector, was ever intended to carry wheeled transport, a point suggested by Collingwood Bruce (1867,76).

The use of a timber structure to facilitate the passage of the Military Way has been postulated at Green Slack. Similar obstacles on the line of the road could have been negotiated more easily by the use of such bridges but no evidence for this has been recovered by field observation. In some places, such as the gully at NY 7427 6756, the use of solid stone-and-earth causeways has been preferred.

M. Bowden, RCHME

GREATCHESTERS – *Aesica* (Fig.41)

There have no recent excavations at this fort. Note: Allason-Jones 1996, on small finds from the fort; Mackay 1990, on the course of the aqueduct; Whitworth 1997b, on carved stones and an architectural fragment.

Wall Mile 43. At Cockmount Hill another example of an unfinished length of Wall Ditch, as at Limestone Corner, occurs from NY 6926 6685 to NY 6947 6688; here the ditch becomes increasingly shallow from west to east with a number of dolerite boulders on the line, which would need to be moved to finish the ditch. It is unclear why the ditch should not have been completed here, as the natural slope to the north is relatively shallow. Possibly the intractability of the dolerite was responsible for the abandonment of ditch digging (K. Blood, RCHME).

Wall Mile 43/44. Of particular interest is the stretch of Military Way between Cockmount Hill at NY 696 668 and Walltown at NY 680 665 (1.8km) which, though well-preserved as a terrace or agger, had never been positioned accurately until the Hadrian's Wall Project was undertaken (K. Blood, RCHME).

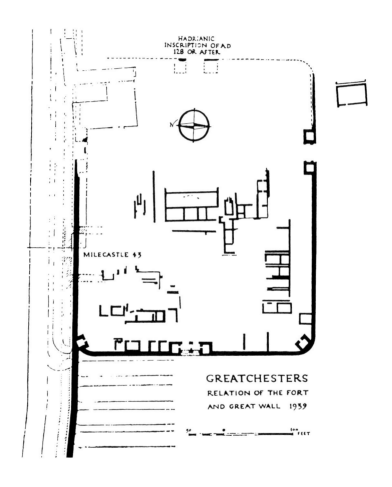

Figure 41. The fort at Greatchesters.

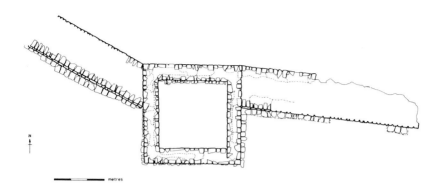

Figure 42. Turret 45A, Walltown Crags.

Turret 45A, Walltown Crags. Crow (1991, 62-3) has argued that this turret, rather than originating as a free-standing tower, is associated with the construction of the Narrow Wall.

CARVORAN – *Magna* (Fig. 43)
There have been no recent excavations.

Wall Mile 48. A section was cut across the Wall at Willowford Farm, west of turret 48b (Whitworth 1997a). For a survey of the extent and state of preservation of the Wall (including milecastle 48 (Fig. 44) and turrets 48A and B) in the guardianship of English Heritage, see Snape, Bidwell and Croom 1995.

Willowford Bridge Abutment (Fig. 45)
There has been no further work on the remains of the eastern bridge abutment since its re-excavation in 1984-5 (Bidwell and Holbrook 1989, 50-98), but two later discoveries throw some new light on the history of the bridge. First, revision of the date for the construction of the road bridge at Chesters, now to be placed in the mid-Antonine period or possibly earlier (p.120), partly

141

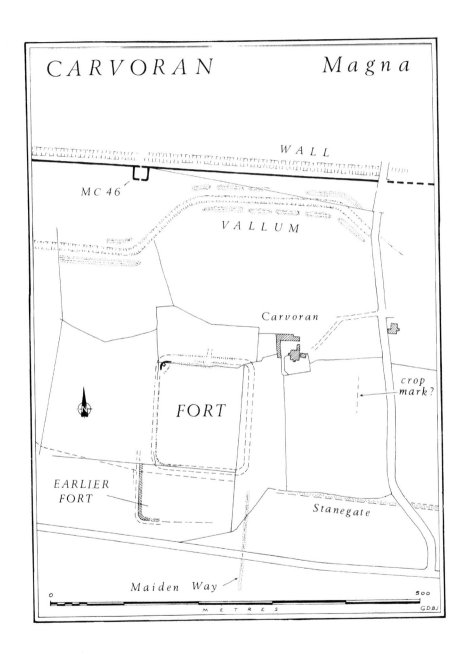

Figure 43. The fort at Carvoran.

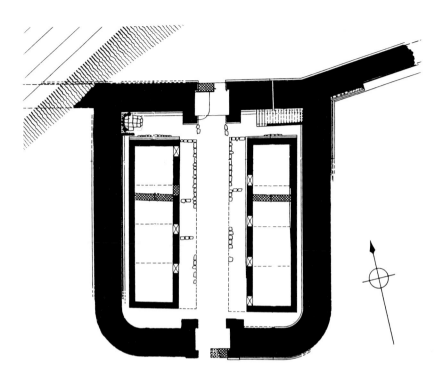

Figure 44. Milecastle 48, Poltross Burn, restored plan.

undermines the dating proposed for Bridges 2 and 3 at Willowford. It was argued that Bridge 3 (the road bridge) would have been built at the same time as the road bridge at Chesters, as part of a general programme of improvements made to the road system in the Wall zone. But at Willowford there are some stratified finds which, although small in quantity, certainly indicate that Bridge 3 was not built before the late second or early third century.

The other discovery bearing on the history of the bridge was made at Birdoswald where blocks from the bridge were found built into a repair of the east fort wall (p. 152). Their reuse in the third century, the date suggested for the repair, probably results from a repetition of the destruction by flood that took place in the mid-second century. Whether the bridge was rebuilt

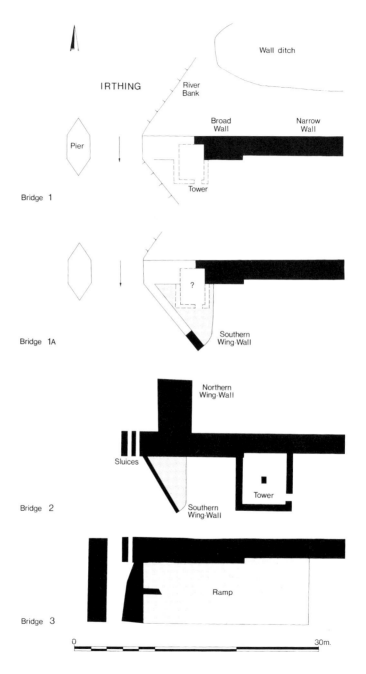

Figure 45. Sequence of rebuildings, east abutment of bridge at Willowford.

144

after this later destruction is uncertain.

P.Bidwell

BIRDOSWALD - Banna (Figs 46-50)

The last ten years have been extraordinarily productive of new information at Birdoswald. The 1989 pilgrims visited the site during the third year of a five year programme of excavation on the principal west gate, the external ditch and berm, the granaries, *via principalis*, and buildings in the *praetentura* which ended in 1991. Further excavation on the minor east gate and adjoining curtain wall took place in 1992, prior to consolidation. All of these works have now been fully analysed and published (Wilmott 1997b). In 1996, advancing erosion on the river spur upon which the fort is built prompted excavation to evaluate the survival of the archaeology which had been previously excavated between 1928-33 by Simpson and Richmond, to confirm the plan, and to assess the causes of erosion. The success of Cumbria County Council in securing Heritage Lottery funding for the development of a new residential study centre for Hadrian's Wall within the buildings of the former Birdoswald farm prompted excavations within the farm buildings and yards in 1997-8; an area equivalent to 9.6% of the fort interior. As a result, Birdoswald may now claim to be the third most excavated fort on the line of the Wall (in terms of modern excavation), after Wallsend and Housesteads. In addition, also in 1997-8, the geophysical survey described elsewhere (pp.157-61) was carried out. All of the excavation work was undertaken by the Central Archaeology Service of English Heritage. The net result of the excavations has been to recover a sequence of development for the site from the second to the twentieth century, and to establish the character and histories of all of the buildings in the western *praetentura*, together with the granaries in the *latera praetorii*.

Hadrianic site development (Fig. 46)

The development of the site during the Hadrianic period was extremely complex, and evidence for a series of starts, checks, and changes in plan, was discovered. There is no doubt that the Turf Wall (which the 1989 Pilgrims saw *in situ*) was the earliest Roman feature, as it sealed undisturbed pollen assemblages which demonstrated that the site was under 95% tree cover before the Wall was built. Clearance was rapid, and immediately followed by the Wall's construction. A construction camp for this operation may be represented

145

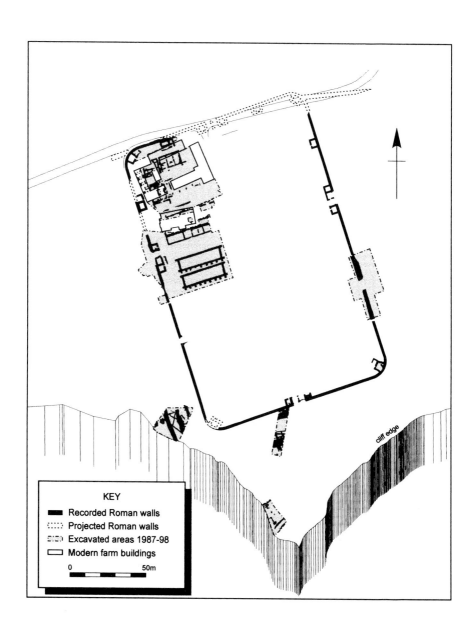

KEY
▬ Recorded Roman walls
⋯ Projected Roman walls
⊐⊏⊐ Excavated areas 1987-98
☐ Modern farm buildings

0   50m

cliff edge

Figure 46. Birdoswald fort showing areas excavated 1987-98.

by a polygonal ditched and palisaded enclosure on the cliff edge, the ditches of which produced tent leather in 1932 and in 1996. This had been interpreted previously as a prehistoric settlement (Birley 1961, 143). Turret 49A was found beneath the fort in 1945, and must have been demolished when the first fort was constructed. There is slim, but growing evidence for the existence of a timber predecessor to the stone fort. This early fort was associated with the Turf Wall, though there is no evidence for its exact dimensions and position. The latest indicative evidence to emerge was the discovery, in 1998, of pits containing leather shoes and military metalwork beneath the stratigraphy of the stone fort. These were found to the north of the Turf Wall, and begin to suggest that the early establishment was a projecting fort (*contra* Wilmott 1997b, 54).

The Vallum appears to have been constructed to the south of the primary fort, and to be related functionally with it. This association makes sense of the odd relationship between the Vallum and the stone fort, where the Vallum is extremely close to the south west corner of the fort. This can no longer be explained by limited space between the river cliff and the corner of the fort, as it can now be shown that a great deal of the hillside has been lost (and continues to be lost) by river erosion since the Roman period. The Vallum seems to have been very short lived. Certainly the ditch was deliberately backfilled before any primary silt was deposited, and the ditch fill seems to have been capped by material from the mound. All of the pottery from the fill of the ditch fits into a Hadrianic milieu. It is probable that the Vallum was dismantled to allow space for the construction of a larger stone fort. The construction of the stone fort began with the defences and the lower courses of the gate piers. A variety of indications, from the analysis of soils, stratigraphy and stonemasonry, shows that there was a long pause in the building of the fort, and that the defences remained incomplete for long enough for scrub vegetation to generate within the walls. This was eventually burnt off, and the defences, drainage and internal buildings completed in a quick and concentrated burst of activity. The original build of the fort included two single-portal subsidiary gates to the east and west, indicating that the stone fort had initially projected to the north of the Turf Wall. The construction of the Stone Wall, which adjoined the north corners of the stone fort, however, rendered these gates redundant, and they were walled up, the gate towers dismantled, and the earth rampart raised against the blocking.

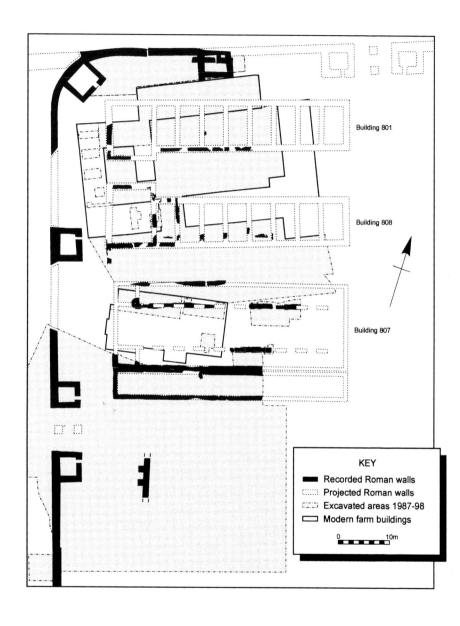

KEY

▬ Recorded Roman walls
⋯ Projected Roman walls
⋯ Excavated areas 1987-98
▭ Modern farm buildings

0 ▬▬▬▬ 10m

Building 801

Building 808

Building 807

Figure 47. The north-west quarter of the stone fort at Birdoswald showing primary structures.

It has long been held that the Turf Wall was replaced in stone from Harrow's Scar to milecastle 51 in the later Hadrianic period. The evidence for this remains the presence of Hadrianic material in occupation deposits within both Turf Wall and Stone Wall installations, notably the two milecastle 50s (see most recently Welsby 1985, 75). This is important, as it provides a *terminus ante quem* for the sequence outlined above, and it must be concluded that all of these operations took place between 122 and *c*. 140.

The Hadrianic fort plan (Fig. 47)
The initial plan of the stone fort within the excavated area is difficult enough to reconstruct, and it is not possible with any certainty to derive primary building plans from geophysics. With one notable exception, all primary buildings were radically altered in later centuries, emphasising the fact that this early period can only be understood through excavation

An important element discovered in 1996 was a third external ditch, augmenting the known pair. This ditch clearly continued around the south-west corner of the fort, and its existence affords positive proof of substantial post-Roman erosion.

In the north-west *praetentura* four buildings have now been identified. On the frontage of the *via principalis* was a long, narrow structure, 5.6m wide, undivided, and with a flagstone floor. To the north of this, with the narrowest gap between the two structures, lay a building of basilican plan, 16.05m wide, which is mathematically calculated at 42.78m in length. This building, so far unique in any Roman auxiliary fort throughout the Empire, is interpreted as a *basilica exercitatoria*, or drill and exercise hall of the type described by Vegetius (Wilmott 1997a). An alley 6.27m wide separated the basilica from the next building northwards, which appears to have been a barrack block, with officer's quarters at the western end, facing north. The barrack had eight *contubernia*, averaging 3.91m in width. Unusually, the *contubernia* appear to have had narrow rooms at the rear (unless the dividing wall is really a later rebuild). A primary wall projecting to the south from the western end of the officer's quarter suggests further accommodation existed to the rear of the building, though it is not possible to suggest what form this took. The northernmost building was probably another barrack. It was altered in the late second or early third century, but remained a barrack throughout its life.

149

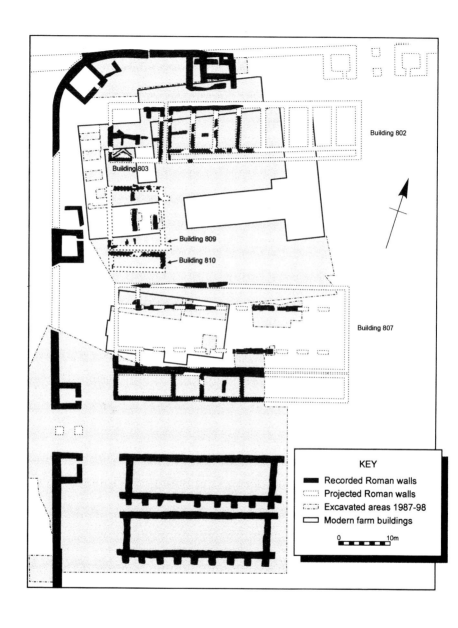

Figure 48. The north-west quarter of the stone fort at Birdoswald showing
structures of the early third century.

150

It should be noted that the 1929 excavation of the eastern *praetentura* revealed a long narrow road-front building, mirroring that to the west, and that this building backed onto a barrack block.

To the south of the *via principalis*, beneath the existing granaries, was a partial foundation trench for an unfinished, buttressed building, which may have been preparatory to the construction of north-south aligned granaries. There was, however, no evidence to suggest that the granaries were completed in this primary phase. The Hadrianic garrison of Birdoswald is unknown, though the presence of a samian ware vessel inscribed with the name of the *decurio* Martinus may suggest that a part-mounted cohort was present.

The later second and third centuries (Figs 48-9)
There is no sign that the fort was deserted during the Antonine period; on the contrary, it appears to have been maintained in use, and both numismatic evidence and the evidence of samian ware suggest continued occupation. However, the failure to provide the fort with granaries might suggest that this occupation was, in fact, limited. From this time onward only the inner ditch around the fort was open and maintained, and the fort drainage discharged into it.

During the later second and early third centuries a number of changes took place. The most important of these was the construction of the granaries during the governorship of Alfenus Senecio (205-8), as recorded in *RIB* 1909. Building work is also recorded at the east gate in 219 (*RIB* 1914), while *RIB* 1910 and 1911 attest building under Severus and Caracalla respectively. It is at this time too that the first garrison title known from Birdoswald appears, *cohors I Aelia Dacorum*. Inscriptions relating to this unit occur in large numbers throughout the third century, and the unit is listed for Birdoswald in the *Notitia Dignitatum*.

Physical changes were made to a number of buildings in the western *praetentura*, and it is clear that several of these were part of a general re-planning. A small building was inserted into the western end of the alley between the basilica and the southern barrack, which was rebuilt with slightly larger officer's accommodation. The north barrack was substantially changed, with the officer's quarters becoming a separate square building. This was extremely well appointed, with a private latrine in the north-east corner, and at least one heated room, with a saltire-pattern channel hypocaust in the south west corner. The barrack, though substantially rebuilt, appears to have retained eight *contubernia*, and acquired a verandah to the south. At the same time as this rebuilding was carried out, the interval tower on the north wall, between the north gate and the north-west corner, was demolished and replaced with a rampart building containing a pair of ovens.

The basilica itself remained unaltered, while the long narrow building to the south was remodelled twice. The first change was the provision of separate rooms, after which the western end was demolished, and a new end wall inserted. It seems likely that some kind of craft or industrial process took place within this building. The demolished west end was replaced by a lean-to structure, with an open eastern side. This was used for smithing, as attested by the discovery of a large amount of hammer scale, the alteration of clay floors through firing, and the construction of stone boxes, thought to be for quenching and carburising.

The south tower of the west gate was dismantled and rebuilt, with a plinth constructed with true ashlar masonry of fine quality, which may have been resused from elsewhere. This is dated to the earlier third century period by association with a fine and little worn intaglio depicting either Caracalla or Geta. Rebuilding of the eastern curtain wall seems to have incorporated stones reused from the demolition of Bridge 2 at Willowford (p.143). The towers of both the east and west gates were used for industrial activity during the third century, and the north tower of the west gate was certainly used for smithing. Also during this century, one portal of each of these gates was blocked, and the surviving, inner, fort ditch was recut to respect the single surviving portal. In the west gate the blocked portal, south tower, and an internal annexe functioned as a small industrial premises, again with evidence of smithing. Industry, probably ironworking was also practised in the open, on the intervallum road to the north of the northern barrack.

Ever since the discovery of *RIB* 1912, there has been speculation as to whether the fort was deserted at the end of the third century. This now seems very likely. The cessation of industrial activity, the collapse of the lean-to roadside industrial building, and the silting of the fort ditch to the point that silts washed over the berm and against the fort wall, are associated with coins of the Gallic

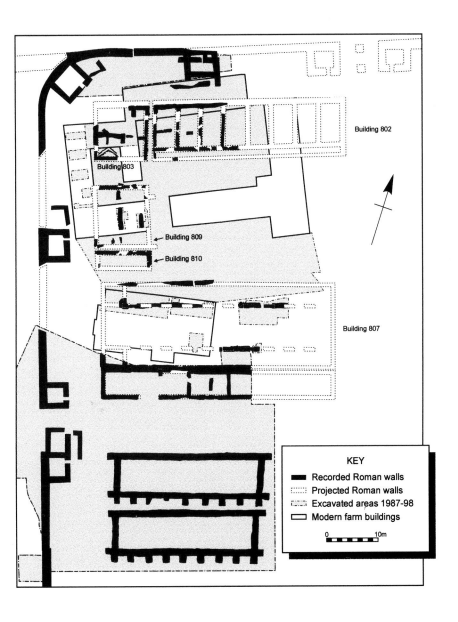

KEY

■ Recorded Roman walls
⠿ Projected Roman walls
⌐⌐ Excavated areas 1987-98
☐ Modern farm buildings

0 ___ 10m

Building 802

Building 803

Building 809

Building 810

Building 807

Figure 49.The north-west quarter of the stone fort at Birdoswald in the later third century.

153

Empire, after which a break in the coin supply seems to exist. The silting of the ditch might have caused the drainage within the fort to back-up, inconceivable if the establishment was in active use. This would provide a context for the collapse and silting of the *praetorium* which is recorded in *RIB* 1912, not least because the *praetorium* occupied the lowest lying part of the fort. It is important to note the contrast between this positive evidence for desertion, and the impression of continued order attested for the Antonine period.

The fourth century (Fig. 50)

The main feature of the early fourth century restoration of the site was the recutting of the silted fort ditch. This deliberately cut off the west gate, and a stone-built bridge was constructed to allow both access to the gate, and the free flow of water around the fort. The buildings of the western *praetentura* had varied histories, though these cannot be dated closely, and are often fragmentary. Certainly the former industrial building on the street frontage was rebuilt at least twice. The instability of this structure was caused by its construction along the line of the former Turf Wall ditch. The basilica appears to have remained largely intact, though at least part of the northern arcade was walled up, hinting at subdivision. To the north of the basilica, post-medieval truncation had removed most fourth century and later stratigraphy; however there were indications that the northern barrack was remodelled to create a row of smaller structures. The evidence, though slight, points towards the familiar 'chalet' plan. The separate officer's quarters of the north barrack showed a sequence of re-floorings and other alterations, culminating in the conversion of the northern half of the structure into a room with a western apsidal end. There is no evidence for the function of this structure, though there has been speculation recently that very late apsidal buildings within the forts at Housesteads (p.127) and Vindolanda (p.135) might have functioned as churches.

The fourth-century history of the granaries was well dated by virtue of the numbers of stratified coins recovered. The buildings were used for their primary purpose until the middle of the century (though the western end of the north granary was given a solid floor). By *c.* 350, the north granary had collapsed and was not rebuilt, while the sub-floor of the southern granary was backfilled and a solid floor installed.

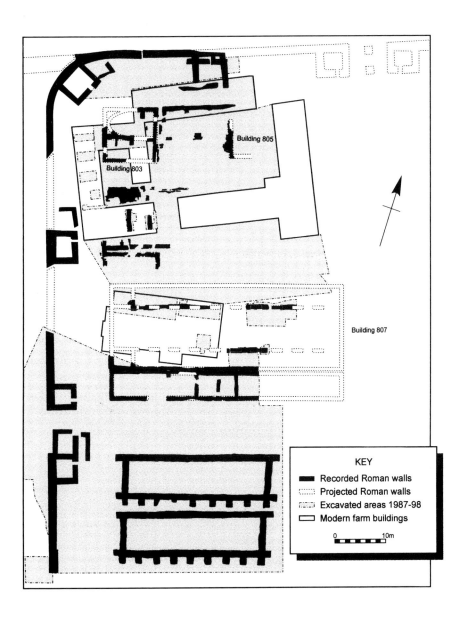

Figure 50. The north-west quarter of the stone fort at Birdoswald showing mid fourth-century structures.

The late fourth century up to the end of the 'Roman' sequence

During the late fourth century and onwards into the fifth, and possibly later, the fort continued in occupation. Within the excavated area, the continuous stratigraphic sequence extended well beyond the accepted end of the Roman period, and was followed by an apparent break, which ended with medieval re-occupation. The use of the south granary continued, leading eventually to patchy reflooring, associated with the use of a large stone-built hearth at the western end of the building. Around this hearth, high quality finds, including a gold earring, glass finger ring, and a Theodosian silver coin were found. This final use of the granary is interpreted in terms of an early post-Roman hall. After the collapse of this granary it appears to have been replaced by a timber building, post-built upon the robbed walls of the north granary, and with a newly laid stone floor. This building was in turn replaced by another timber building, this time built partly over the north granary, and partly over the *via principalis*. This final structure was constructed upon large post-pads and was associated with at least two further buildings which were constructed over the intervallum road. This group of structures is interpreted as a final phase of the hall with associated service buildings.

Extramural activity

An important aspect of the geophysical work recently completed at Birdoswald has been the recognition of an extensive *vicus* located predominantly in the lee of the fort to the east. There was some *vicus* activity to the west also, concentrated along a road which led out of the west gate, curving southwards towards the fort cemetery. The cemetery was located in the 1950s, during ploughing, but was never written up. In 1993 the site notes were discovered in Tullie House Museum, Carlisle, and the surviving finds were located in Corbridge Museum and in private hands. This enabled the publication of a summary account of the cemetery (Wilmott 1993). The burial rite was cremation and funerary vessels survived in good condition. The cemetery site has never been ploughed since its discovery and retains a great deal of potential for future work.

Post Roman occupation

The existence of the fort had a direct influence on the medieval and modern occupation of the site. The earliest documentary references are *c*.1200, which is consistent with findings of pottery of this date. The thirteenth-century structures may be those found in geophysical survey within the *retentura* of the fort. The earliest structure excavated of this period is a tower house, probably built in the fourteenth century. This respects the Roman west gate, which was apparently still in use at this late date. The gate fell during the occupation of the tower house, and a new breach in the wall was made 10m to the north.

During the sixteenth century, a typical bastle house was built, and documents show the site was raided three times. The bastle house was succeded by the earliest phase of the present farmhouse. This was extended in 1745, and acheived its present appearance in 1858. The owner at this time was Henry Norman, who, with Henry Glasford Potter, undertook extensive excavations on the site, which were published in *Archaeologia Aeliana* in 1855. Appropriately, it is thought that the inspiration for this work was the first Pilgrimage in 1849.

T. Wilmott

Note also: Donaldson 1990, a reinterpretation of *RIB* 1912.

Geophysical Survey (Figs 51-52)

A geophysical and topographical survey of Birdoswald fort and *vicus* was conducted in 1997 and 1998. This was initiated as a privately funded academic research project and was completed with grant aid from English Heritage. The fort and many of its buildings are well recognised (Wilmott 1997b), but the extent of the *vicus* was largely unknown, although reference to it had been made by early antiquarians. The survey established the extent of the *vicus*, and to some degree that of the cemetery to the south-west. The results from this survey are significant, but it is only possible in this note to summarise the major archaeological features detected.

The arrangement of the fort, indicated on the interpretative plan (Fig.52) and derived from the initial survey (Fig.51), follows the expected general arrangement. The *principia* (9) and *praetorium* (10) were positioned in the *latera praetorii*, together with a pair of third-century granaries. An earlier granary (12), a building of smaller dimensions, may be sited towards the south and appears to have been subdivided at a later date. The fort is unusual in that a basilica was built within the *praetentura* (8) (Wilmott 1997b, 97-98). Hadrianic stone barracks, with eight *contubernia*, were seen east of the *praetentura* (5, 6, 7), and are probably to be found in the *retentura*. The barracks, particularly those in the southern *retentura*, show considerable alterations. Prominently situated in the east of the *retentura* is a substantial stone building (13) with an attached enclosure. In appearance, this resembles a type of farmstead (barmekin) common in north-east Cumbria (Ramm *et al.* 1970, 49, fig. 13, 52). The absence of documentary evidence suggests that the building represents a period of occupation before the construction of the tower and bastle house found towards its north-west.

Double ditches exist towards the west and south, whilst to the east a more complex pattern is evident. No evidence of the Vallum was observed to the west, but it was clearly identified south and east of the fort (25). The section west of milecastle 49 at Harrow's Scar was clearly defined (A) by the magnetometry survey (Fig.51). The Turf Wall and ditch were not represented on the survey to the west; however the ditch was identified by topographical survey. Towards the east the ditch was detected south of the Stone Wall and west of milecastle 49, at which point the Stone and Turf Walls diverge. The Turf Wall ditch was observed to pass beneath the north guardchambers of the east and west gates of the fort.

The general form of the *vicus* differs markedly to the west and to the east of the fort. To the west, buildings were observed on each side of the road, which widened to form an elongated open space, some 75m long, and *c*. 90m distant from the fort (C). To the south there was strong evidence of burning, possibly linked to a cremation cemetery (D). A group of substantial buildings abuts the road to the north (E), which may be associated with the cemetery and may have ritual significance. There is also evidence that later buildings, constructed on different alignments, overlie these structures. A staggered ditch running north-south and terminating on the southern line of the road (F) appears to delineate the stone buildings to the west. Timber buildings can be seen to the south of those bordering the road, and are also seen adjacent to the fort ditches. The strong linear bi-polar anomalies running east-west and north-south are modern intrusive features.

The eastern settlement revealed a large group of stone structures, constructed in close proximity to the fort, containing heterogeneous groups of buildings, north and south of the road, together with numerous earthworks and ditches.

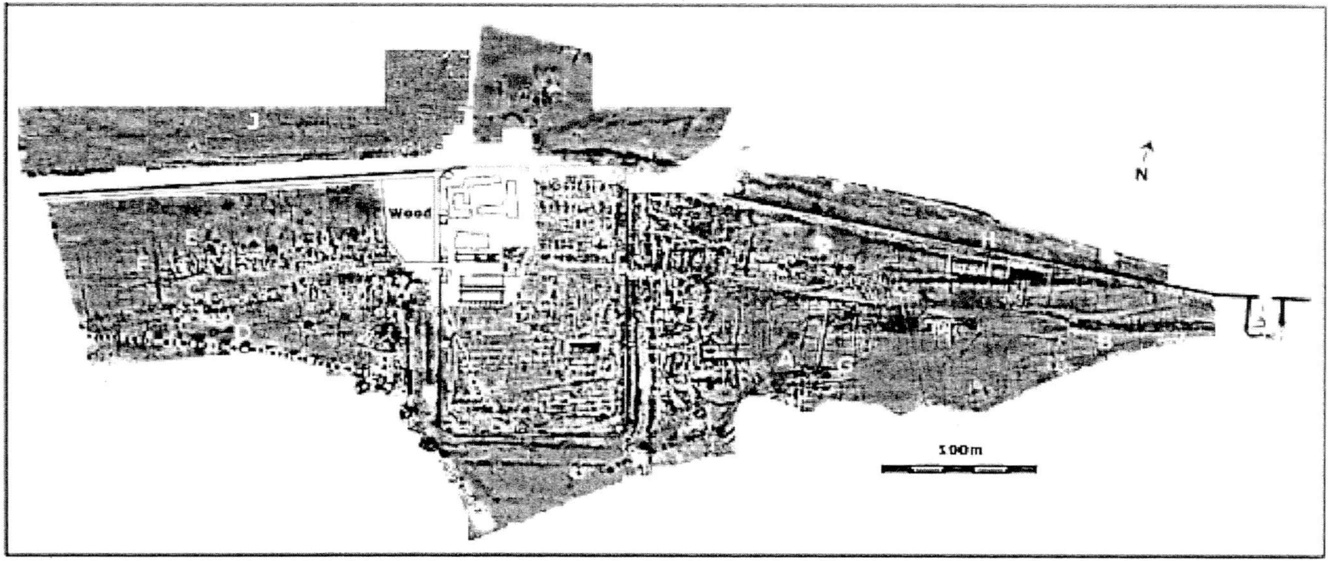

Figure 51. Geophysical survey, Birdoswald.

This complex may represent a military annex surrounded by a ditch (31). A well defined structure (28) is the "good building, twenty feet square....standing thirteen courses high" noted by Richmond in 1931, to which the later linear extension may have been added. This was later cut by a ditch (24), which ran north-south across the site, but appeared not to cut the road. In the centre of the eastern promontory was a prominent enclosure (G) in which traces of a large timber building were identified. Some distance to the east of this, fronting the road, a very strong anomaly identified a building some 15m square. A series of enclosures (H) were seen to the south of the Stone Wall and west of the milecastle; some of the ditches appeared to be contiguous with the line of the Vallum. It is apparent that considerable sections of the southern escarpment containing the eastern settlement have eroded; this area was likely to have included a substantial number of buildings.

The survey found that a significant number of buildings were erected north of the stone wall ditch, especially adjacent to the Maiden Way leading to Bewcastle. These buildings bordering the road extended at least 100m beyond the Wall ditch. A hollow-way, possibly of later date, was observed to run north-east from the north gate. Towards the west of the Maiden Way, the paucity of magnetic anomalies indicates that a parade ground may have been constructed north of the ditch (J). Traces of timber building and other features were seen close to the ditch.

A possible bathhouse was identified, from aerial photography, within the valley south of the fort close to Under Haugh Farm. It is expected to survey this structure in the near future. Full analysis and interpretation of the results from the entire survey has not yet been completed, but a report of the 1997 survey of the fort and a section of the western and eastern *vicus* is forthcoming (Biggins and Taylor 1999).

J.A. Biggins, J. Robinson and D.J.A. Taylor

Note also: Barker and Rushworth 1998 for a survey of the extent and state of preservation of the fort and adjacent lengths of Wall in the guardianship of English Heritage.

Wall Mile 50. The Turf Wall Cutting at Appletree, exposed for every Pilgrimage since the Fourth in 1906, was recorded in detail after the 1989

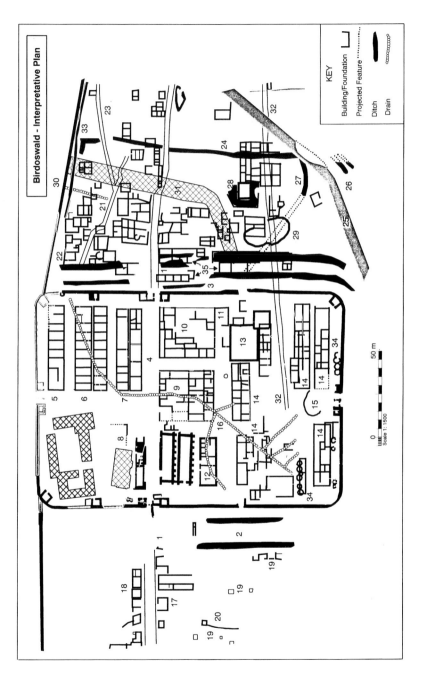

Figure 52. Birdoswald: interperative plan of geophysical survey.

Pilgrimage; pollen and soil analysis was also undertaken (Whitworth 1992).

Wall Miles 51 to 55. For a survey of the extent and state of preservation of the Wall in the guardianship of English Heritage, see Snape 1996.

CASTLESTEADS – *Camboglanna* (Figs 53-54)

In 1934 Richmond and Miss Hodgson established the position of the north-east, south-west and south-east walls of the fort. The north-west part of the fort has fallen away into the Cambeck valley, but if the fort was square, as Richmond and Miss Hodgson argued, its area would have been about 1.5ha (3.75 acres). Nothing is known of its internal plan. The summer house at Castlesteads contains an important collection of altars and other antiquities, including dedications associated with the *cohors II Tungrorum milliaria equitata c(oram?) l(audata?)*, the unit stationed at Castlesteads in the third century. Because of the small size estimated for the fort, the unit is assumed not to have been present in full strength, but if the fort faced south (cf. Stone Fort 1 at Vindolanda), it might in reality have been large enough to accommodate the whole of *cohors II Tungrorum*.

The site has been surveyed by RCHME and remains of the baths were seen in the sides of a burn 200m north of the fort.

Brampton. In 1997 possible remains of timber buildings were found in a field less than 100m north of the Roman tile and pottery kilns (Zant 1998).

Wall Mile 65. Limited investigations by Carlisle Archaeological Unit in 1997, following those by the Central Excavation Unit in 1976 (Smith 1978), located the Stone Wall to the north of Tarraby Lane, whilst work in 1993 also located a counterscarp bank on the northern side of the Wall ditch (*Britannia*, **28** (1997), 415). Two phases of construction were identified, but there was no associated dating evidence. The bank was found to overlie and to preserve plough marks representing pre-Wall agricultural activity (M. R. McCarthy).

STANWIX - *Petriana*
The fort (Fig. 55)

Excavations by Simpson and Hogg in 1932-4 and by Simpson and Richmond in 1939-40 established the positions of the south gate of the Hadrian's Wall fort and of the defences on the north-eastern, south-eastern and south-western sides, as well as the line of the Vallum. Internal buildings, including a granary, were located in the playground of Stanwix Primary School. The results of these investigations are well known and are summarised in the *Handbook to the Roman Wall* (Daniels 1989). From 1940 on very little new information was obtained until the 1980s, when an excavation in the car park of the Cumbria Park Hotel, immediately north of the school playground, located the stone footings of the fort wall and an interval tower on the north-western side, together with two ditches beyond. This important discovery showed that the fort had been enlarged in the Antonine period so that it projected north of Hadrian's Wall. The other key discovery was that of a ditch underlying the interval tower. This ditch, clearly antedating the enlargement of the fort, was presumed to be associated with Hadrian's Wall, the foundations of which had been discovered by Simpson and Hogg in 1932-4 (Dacre 1985; Caruana 1989).

In 1997 further work took place in the playground of the Primary School in advance of the construction of an extension to the school. The earliest identifiable feature consists of a turf deposit, probably a rampart or the Turf Wall. The front and rear faces of the turf were not seen, but the deposit

Period	Date	Feature	Excavator/date	Comments
1	122?	Turf	CAU 1997	Hadrian's Turf Wall?
2	160?	Stone wall	Simpson 1932-4	Hadrian's Stone Wall
3	2nd–4th cent.	fort wall/tower/ditches	Dacre 1985, 1997-8	Enlargement of fort
		?stables/ barracks	Simpson 1932-4	
		granary	Simpson/ Richmond 1940	
		metallings	CAU 1997	
4	4th-5th cent.	Timber buildings	CAU 1997	
5	Med/post-med.	Soils	CAU 1997	
6	Late 19th cent.	School playground	CAU 1997-8	

Table 3: Possible sequence and broad correlation of major features and events in the Stanwix fort (CAU = Carlisle Archaeological Unit).

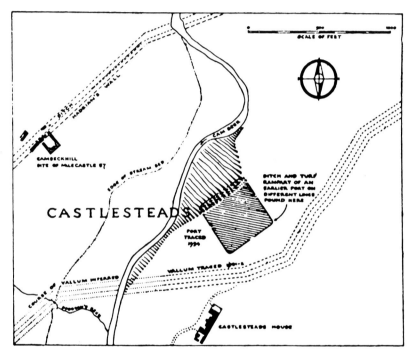

Figure 53. The fort at Castlesteads in relation to Hadrian's Wall.

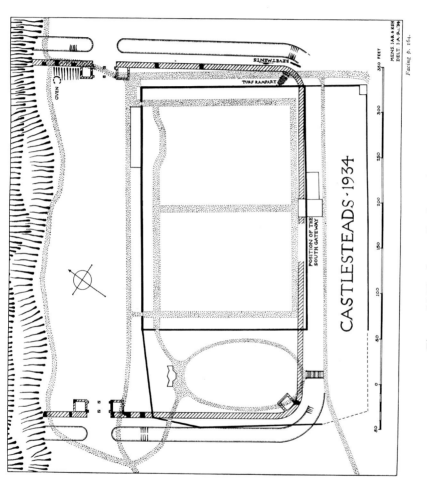

Figure 54. The fort at Castlesteads.

identified was located some metres south of the stone Hadrian's Wall discovered in the 1930s. Overlying the turf was a substantial deposit of clay.

Limitations imposed on the investigations meant that it was impossible to establish a reliable sequence of deposits and to excavate sufficiently widely to determine the layout of the fort in its latest phases. The walls located by Simpson and Hogg were not found, but stone and cobbled surfaces and rubble deposits are presumed to belong with the walls found in the 1930s. A key point, however, was the discovery of timber buildings erected after the deposition of Huntcliff ware in the fourth century.

In 1997 and 1998 two further trenches in a narrow passage immediately adjacent to the north-western side of the Victorian school located the inner ditch and the stone footings of the fort wall. Work in 1993 in Barn Close, Stanwix, revealed two phases of walls and surfaces.

As a result of the work in 1984 and 1997-8 it is now possible to suggest a very broad sequence of events (Table 3).

Extra-mural features
A number of investigations have taken place to the north-east and south-west of the fort. In 1986 deep stratified deposits, including remains of buildings, were found at the former Miles MacInnes Hall at Scotland Road, demonstrating the existence of extra-mural development beyond the west gate. This work was insufficient in scale to enable sequences to be established.

Between the eminence on which the fort is situated and the rising ground to the north-east centred on Wall Knowe is an area of lower ground, where investigations in the grounds of Cumbria College of Art and Design in 1996 revealed an extensive clay platform up to 0.5m thick. The clay is provisionally interpreted as the parade ground for the fort, which a combination of observations suggests may be 7.5 acres (3.15ha) in extent. Between the parade ground and the west gate of the fort is a raised area which can now be tentatively identified as the tribunal. The parade ground clay seals and preserves an old ground surface, extensive areas of plough marks, and field boundary ditches, including some discovered in 1976 by the Central Excavation Unit (Smith 1978). These investigations also revealed traces of

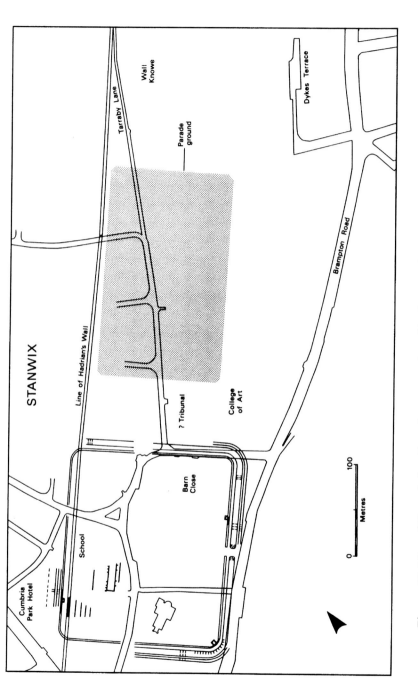

Figure 55. Map of Stanwix locating places mentioned in the text, the Roman fort and parade ground.

buildings close to Dykes Terrace south of the Vallum. In 1998 Carlisle Archaeological Unit located further buildings and possible industrial debris close to the entrance to Cumbria College of Art and Design on Brampton Road. The same investigation showed that within the College campus the Vallum is situated some 75m south of the position indicated on the maps.

M.R.McCarthy

Wall Mile 66. The point at which Hadrian's Wall crossed the River Eden has been known since 1951, when a number of bridge stones were dredged from the river bed. A ground-penetrating radar survey undertaken in 1997 located significant anomalies south of the confluence of the Eden and Caldew at a depth of 2-3m on the projected line of the Wall. No further details about the bridge have been discovered, although an analysis of the stones has identified two probable construction phases (Bidwell and Holbrook 1989, 107-10).

M. R.McCarthy

CARLISLE - *Luguvalium*
Introduction

Carlisle is on the southern bank of the River Eden, at its confluence with the River Caldew. Long the focus of scholarly interest, Carlisle's Roman past as summarised by Salway (1965) and Charlesworth (1978) was based largely on casual discoveries. From 1977 on there has been much excavation, yielding high-quality information from deeply stratified and frequently exceptionally well-preserved deposits. Most of this work has been undertaken by various excavators working for Carlisle Archaeological Unit. Some of this is published, but some is forthcoming or in preparation. The rich waterlogged deposits have been reported on by J. P. Huntley, S. Stallibrass, C. Groves and H. Kenward in a series of AML reports (see Chapter 4).

Carlisle and Stanwix, which is some five minutes' walk away, are sometimes regarded as having been separate and distinct entities in Roman times. Up to a point this may have been true, but although the details of the relationship between the two sites are difficult to discern at present, viewed together they must have represented one of the densest populations in Cumbria, and one of the most significant in the Hadrian's Wall military zone. On the one hand Carlisle exercised a key regional function from very early on, probably becoming the *civitas* capital of the Carvetii, and on the other, Stanwix contained the largest fort on Hadrian's Wall, housing the senior regiment in the province, the *ala Petriana*. Their fortunes must have been inextricably linked together in all aspects of life, especially with regard to military, economic and social matters.

The account set out below is divided for convenience into sections, discussing firstly the forts, beginning with that located between Carlisle Castle and Tullie House Museum and Art Gallery. Other forts or camps in and around Carlisle are also attested, although they are generally less well documented, and their status is not so clear. Secondly, the account of the Roman town of Carlisle attempts to summarise investigations outside the fort and annexe.

The fort and annexe (Fig 56)

On a bluff overlooking the confluence of the rivers Eden and Caldew, a fort was established in the governorship of Q. Petillius Cerialis in 72 or 73. Excavations by the late Dorothy Charlesworth and Carlisle Archaeological Unit have revealed the south gate, rampart with an *ascensus*, two ditches, the main road, probably the *via praetoria*, the *via sagularis* and the southern ends of internal buildings of a turf and timber fort erected in the early 70s. The first fort was deliberately demolished, and the building materials burnt in a series of bonfires, perhaps in 103-5 on the evidence of dendrochronology and associated finds. The next major phase commenced about 105 and entailed a replanning of the site. The defensive perimeter was moved southwards but the line of the main road, one surface of which was laid on a corduroy of timbers, was retained from the Flavian period. During the second century the fort defences were rebuilt further south as a turf and clay rampart, later modified to a clay-fronted rampart on stone blocks at the end of the century. To the east of the road in the second century were latrines and numerous timber buildings which are difficult to interpret. They were followed initially by a courtyard building based on based on clay and cobble foundations, and then by stone-built barracks with a number of well-preserved *contubernia* and metalled roads, all remaining in use into the fourth century. Rebuilding followed in the period 320-360, but there is no positive evidence for the construction of 'chalets' as can be seen elsewhere at this time.

The status of the site in the third and fourth centuries is not clear. That there was a military presence is certain, but there is doubt as to whether it was a conventional fort. A stone wall recorded in sewer trenches in Castle Street and Abbey Street may represent a stone *enceinte,* perhaps comparable with the compound walls at Corbridge, but at the time of writing (January 1999) the evidence for the defences and internal layout is slender.

Work in 1981-2 and in 1990 located an annexe on the southern side of the fort (McCarthy 1991a and b; Caruana 1992). The annexe, which was surrounded by a ditch, contains a tightly dated sequence, including well-preserved rectilinear and circular structures, with scrap metal and other items suggesting the presence of repair and maintenance facilities, and bones of animals, perhaps coralled prior to slaughter. The annexe buildings at this site seem to have been replaced by 'domestic' structures in the late second century.

Excavations in the fort and the annexe have yielded an important series of ink and stylus writing tablets, now known as the *Tabulae Luguvalienses* (Tomlin 1998). Although numerically fewer and less complete than those from Vindolanda, they show that one of the regiments in garrison during the 80s was the *ala Sebosiana.* The correspondence includes a list of barley rations for three days for 16 *turmae (ibid.),* letters referring to missing lances, and names and addresses, including a tablet inscribed *Trimontio aut Luguvalio M Martiali,* indicating perhaps that some units may have been divided between Newstead and Carlisle (Tomlin 1991, 216). One such may have been the Twentieth Legion, whose presence at Carlisle is attested on a promissory note dated 83 (Tomlin 1992, 146-53); detachments of the Second, Ninth and Sixth Legions were also present, as shown by tile stamps and altars. Other units attested on lead sealings and altars include a cohort of Lingones, and the *ala II Asturum.*

The Twentieth Legion is also attested later on through tile stamps, carved stone boars and dedications, and the most important recent discovery, an altar found re-used in Carlisle Castle (Fig. 57; Tomlin and Annis 1989). This altar was dedicated by M. Aurelius Syrio, commanding officer of the legion between AD 213 and 222. Clearly detachments of the Twentieth were brigaded in Carlisle as well as the Corbridge compounds at the same time.

The Roman town (Fig. 56)
Outside the main fort and annexe there grew up a substantial extra-mural settlement, extending south to either side of Botchergate for a distance of at

170

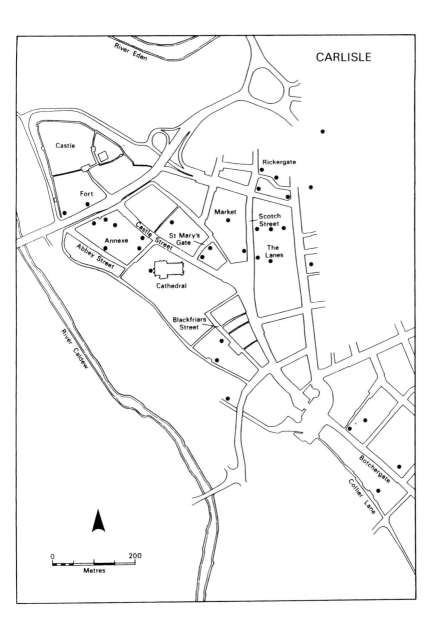

Figure 56. Map of Carlisle locating places mentioned in the text and major investigations since 1977 (dots).

171

least 1km from the fort gate. Amongst the earliest elements recognised so far are the buildings at Blackfriars Street, which began life as open-ended structures broadly comparable to those at Red House, Corbridge in the late 70s. They were succeeded in the late 80s and 90s by simple rectangular multi-roomed, clay-floored timber buildings thought to be domestic in character, perhaps occupied by retired soldiers. The close spacing of the buildings, together with the layout of gable-ends on the metalled road frontage, probably implies dense development along the main road south. This basic arrangement continued throughout much of the Roman period, but there is reason to believe that the function of the buildings changed. In the Trajanic/Hadrianic periods, for example, the plan and structural characteristics of the buildings suggests a storage function, perhaps including a granary (McCarthy 1990).

On the eastern side of Carlisle, the precise nature of the earliest developments is not known because the evidence is too fragmentary. At the southern end of The Lanes, close to the present Old Town Hall, the main east-west road, formerly Crown and Anchor Lane, and possibly the main north-south road heading for the Eden bridgehead, were probably in existence by the 90s. Alongside both roads were relatively large hedged-and-ditched plots containing rectangular timber buildings and associated yards or 'working areas'. The inhabitants of one, at least, were engaged in the manufacture of wooden implements. Although many changes can be recognised throughout the Roman occupation of this area, the essential characteristics of 'strip' buildings associated with yards and fences appears to have remained unchanged into the mid- to late-Roman periods (McCarthy forthcoming).

This was not the case at the northern end of The Lanes. Here, amongst the earliest features, is a large ditched enclosure of which two sides are so far known. The remnants of a fence or palisade lie close to the inner edge of the ditch, but there are no known internal features as yet. It was succeeded by the construction of a very substantial timber building employing fairly sophisticated carpentry and with traces of white plaster on the inside. The building extended for a distance of at least 50m and was 11m wide; the floors in some rooms were of boards on joists, but in others they were earthen. Part of this complex may also have had a hypocaust. In the destruction levels of this short-lived structure were considerable quantities of molten lead. On the eastern side of, and abutting, this building was a metalled road which had a

Figure 57. Altar found at Carlisle Castle.

small timber building on its eastern side. The function and dating of these buildings is problematical. The very large building has been referred to as a *praetorium,* but it has also been suggested that it could be a *mansio.* The small amount of associated pottery includes BB1, implying a date in the first half of the second century, perhaps the 120s or 130s (Zant in preparation).

After the deliberate destruction of the so-called *praetorium/mansio* there was a phase in which extensive buildings employing sill beams were erected. At least two phases of structures can be identified, which seem to have ranges at least 42m in length by 6.5m wide, but although insufficient survived to enable their function to be determined accurately, the general plan is reminiscent of military buildings within a fort or fortress, rather than domestic or agricultural complexes. Either contemporary with these, or with the previous *praetorium/ mansio* phase, was another impressive building comprising two parallel ranges of rooms flanking a small open area or courtyard 8.5m square, and approached on the western side by a series of clay bases for timber columns. The two ranges of rooms, of which at least four, possibly five per range are known, continue east of the courtyard where there is evidence for a wooden colonnade.

173

Once again the dating of these phases is poorly understood because of the relative lack of associated finds, but a *floruit* in the mid-second century is probably near the mark *(ibid.).*

From the mid- to late-Antonine period to the end of the fourth century, or slightly later, on most sites examined so far outside the fort there appears to have been much domestic accommodation with associated industrial or agricultural functions, evidenced by 'strip' buildings, pits, ovens, slag, yards and smaller 'ancillary' structures. This is the case at Blackfriars Street, seemingly in Botchergate, and in The Lanes, where the development of one property excavated can be traced from a simple rectangular timber building to one constructed from stone with multiple rooms including a hypocaust. Hypocausts are also known from nineteenth-century finds, as at 66-8 Scotch Street and elsewhere. Excavated evidence, as at Carlisle Cathedral in 1988 and at St Mary's Gate, together with casual finds (Charlesworth 1978), shows that the whole of Carlisle city centre is underlain by extensive Roman buildings and streets, implying a densely built-up settlement from the second to fourth centuries (McCarthy 1993).

Excavated evidence for public buildings is limited. Substantial foundations located in Abbey Street, tentatively linked with a stone-lined pit in the grounds of Tullie House Museum and Art Gallery, are almost certainly from a public building (Caruana 1996), but whether it is a *mansio,* forum, or some other structure such as a *macellum,* remains unclear. Below Carlisle Market adjacent to a metalled road is a large bathhouse in which a *caldarium, tepidarium* and *frigidarium* were recorded in 1988, but the quality of the dating evidence is poor, and insufficient was exposed to determine whether it stood alone, or whether it was part of a larger complex.

There have been many casual discoveries of stone building remains and architectural fragments, some of which may come from temples or other public buildings. The size of one unprovenanced composite Corinthian capital found in Carlisle points to a building of considerable size. Temples dedicated to Hercules and Mithras seem certain, but sculptures dedicated to the three mother goddesses, *genii loci* and other Celtic deities may have come from niches inside the fort or from private houses. There is no unequivocal evidence for Christianity, but a fourth-century tombstone from London Road commemorating Flavius Antigonus Papias *(RIB* 955) is thought to be Christian on the basis of its *plus/minus* formula.

There is no positive archaeological evidence for Carlisle being encircled by stone walls, despite the reference in The Anonymous Life of St Cuthbert to the saint being shown the *murum civitatis* on his visit in 685. It is possible that St Cuthbert was shown the walls of the late fort or compounds rather than those of the town. In The Lanes, a short stretch of an unfinished earth and timber rampart with signs of unfinished ditches was discovered (McCarthy forthcoming), whilst at Collier Lane, to the west of Botchergate, is a 15m wide earthen bank topped with a double row of posts, excavated in 1998. This may also be a form of defence, perhaps combined with a flood barrier against inundation by the River Caldew. Another large-scale work recently identified is the reclamation of land on the northern side of the city on the former flood plain of the River Eden, part of the former Civic Centre car park, where significant deposits of clay were laid prior to the erection of clay-and cobble-founded buildings.

Evidence for the size and the street plan of Roman Carlisle is slowly emerging. Present evidence suggests that *Luguvalium* may have exceeeded 33ha (80 acres) in area in its heyday, making it one of the largest Roman towns in northern Britain. The key original determinants for the road pattern were almost certainly the fort below Tullie House and Carlisle Castle, and the crossing point of the River Eden. The present A6, the main road from Penrith to Carlisle, leads directly to the fort. The road bifurcates near the present Old Town Hall, leading down Scotch Street and Rickergate to the river. Access to Carlisle from the east seems to have been gained along the former Crown and Anchor Lane leading towards the Greenmarket and the Cathedral, in the grounds of which it linked with the main road from the south. The antiquity of these streets seems certain. Within the city a number of other roads are known, including one near Long Lane, another near St Mary's Gate and a third beneath the Market, whilst nineteenth-century and later observations imply others. There is no evidence that *Luguvalium* had a grid in the early days, indeed a significant element of organic growth is likely. On the other hand recent excavations imply the existence of some more or less square to rectangular *insulae* that are probably not primary features, but which may have been laid out in the mid-Roman period. Evidence for the Roman bridge across the Eden is provided by a small number of bridge stones. Although little is known about the course of the River Eden in Roman times, if recent history is a reliable guide there may have been more than one channel, and hence more than one bridge.

Cemeteries around Carlisle are known mainly from nineteenth-century discoveries of burials and sculptured tombstones (Charlesworth 1978). The best known is at Botchergate, where recent and current excavations have revealed many cremations behind the properties on the street frontage. Other burials are known from near Lowther Street and Dalston Road *(ibid.)*. The quality of the sculpture attested on some gravestones, as well as on other altars and dedications, has led to the suggestion of a Carlisle 'school' of stone sculptors (Phillips 1976).

The essential point arising from large-scale excavations is that every site in Carlisle dating to before the mid- to late-Antonine period has yielded a different sequence of building types, and several examples of forts and/or camps. The implication is that the archaeology of Roman Carlisle in its first century or so is exceedingly complicated. Known as *Luguvalium* from the 80s (Tomlin 1991), and hosting a *centurio regionarius* by around 105 (Bowman and Thomas 1983, 105-11), Carlisle has military sites and other areas such as The Lanes and Blackfriars Street thought to have administrative and supply functions, as well as domestic/agricultural properties that are at least potentially civilian. There are hints of change in the late second and/or early third centuries with a possible grid pattern of streets and an element of civic pride apparent in the initiation of bigger public projects, with the town having an appearance perhaps not unlike Corbridge. It may be that such works coincided with the grant of *civitas Carvetiorum* status in the early third century which Carlisle is assumed to have held (Charlesworth 1978, 123).

The end of Roman Carlisle is less easy to establish. The buildings near the south gate of the fort had fallen from use by the mid-fourth century, and pottery and coins suggest that some buildings and streets may have been abandoned by or during the fourth century, including some close to the Cathedral. Elsewhere, however, there are indications in the stratigraphic sequences and associated finds from sites such as Blackfriars Street, and the Cathedral itself, that occupation continued into the fifth century. At 66-8 Scotch Street, the discovery of a gold *solidus* of Valentinian II sealed in the ducts of a hypocaust beneath a series of floors shows that this building at least had a life extending well into the fifth century (Keevill *et al.* 1989).

Other forts around Carlisle

At the time of writing, a number of other forts are known or suspected around the focus of the Roman settlement of Carlisle. They include a ditch seen in 1993 at Spring Gardens Lane of a size as to imply a major military work dating to the late first or early second century. In Botchergate there is a V-shaped ditch and a possible rampart, together with relatively early buildings, implying the presence of a fort or camp tentatively attributed to the early second century. At Cummersdale and Knockupworth, forts have been found during aerial reconnaissance. The date of these is not yet clear, but that at Cummersdale appears to be large. On the northern side of the River Eden, at St Anns, Etterby, traces of what is thought to be a military ditch with a *clavicula,* but of unknown date, was recognised in 1996. Given the strategic importance of Carlisle, especially in the late first and second centuries, such a profusion of forts or camps is by no means surprising. Indeed, it is likely that more await discovery if the early military landscape here resembles other sites such as Newstead or Wroxeter.

M. R. McCarthy

Note also: studies of finds, Padley 1991 (metalwork, glass and stone objects from Castle Street), Padley 1993 (on two dolphin scabbard runners), Padley and Winterbottom 1991 (wooden, leather and bone objects from Castle Street) and Taylor 1991 (pottery from Castle Street).

BURGH-BY-SANDS II – *Aballava* (Fig. 58)

A number of excavations in and around Burgh-by-Sands over the last two decades has added much to our knowledge of the history and development of the frontier here. The Handbook for the 1989 Pilgrimage (Daniels 1989, 2-4) drew attention in particular to the discovery of two additional forts, Burgh I and Burgh III, both some distance from the Wall, south and south-west respectively of the modern village.

Small-scale excavations within the area of the Burgh II fort in 1992 by Carlisle Archaeological Unit in advance of a new house on the site of three derelict cottages east of Demesne Farm revealed the infilled ditch of Hadrian's Wall with a 4m wide causeway; the ditch showed signs of recutting. This confirmed the projected line of the Wall as established in 1989 at milecastle 72 (see below). The excavations also revealed parts of structures within the fort, identified by clay and cobble foundations which were heavily disturbed. A geophysical survey by the Ancient Monuments Laboratory of English Heritage in the field north and east of the graveyard extension confirmed the north and east defences of the fort as identified by Collingwood. It also showed much activity on the east side of the fort (Linford 1992), including a possible road leading east out of the fort, and extensive anomalies, probably buildings in an eastern *vicus* (*Britannia*, **25** (1994), 263) which are perhaps related to features identified by Jones in the unpublished Vicarage garden investigations in 1982. As well as picking up the eastwards continuation of the Wall ditch, a linear feature running from near the site of Burgh Castle to the north-east corner of the fort can probably be identified as a re-alignment of Hadrian's Wall in the immediate vicinity of the fort to the north so that the fort lay wholly to the

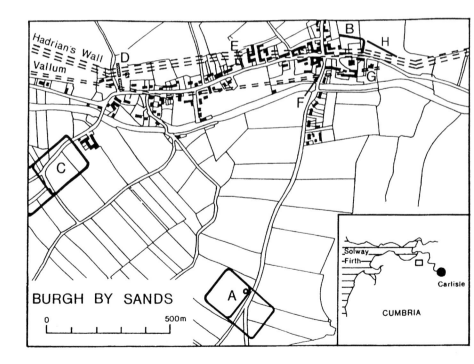

Figure 58. The forts at Burgh-by-Sands.

178

rear of the Wall. This is directly comparable to the re-alignment of the Wall at Birdoswald, although this was carried out at the time of the conversion of the Wall into stone. The combination of evidence - pottery, the line of the Wall in relation to the fort, the dating evidence from the 1980 and 1982 excavations in the former vicarage garden - suggests that Burgh II was a later addition to the Wall in the third century (Austen 1994, 52-3). From the building of the Wall until the third century, one of the detached forts to the south of the Wall, Burgh I or Burgh III, must have continued in use. Moving the fort to the site of Burgh II would afford closer control over the route north across the Solway which is fordable here.

To the south of Burgh II, work behind the cottages at Amberfield confirmed the presence of extensive stratified Roman deposits, including buildings, which probably form a southern *vicus*. Further south, at a site adjacent to the fort at Burgh I, is a masonry building provisionally identified as a bath house (*Britannia*, **28** (1997), 414). North-west of the fort at Burgh II, on land adjacent to Milton House, Carlisle Archaeological Unit has excavated a site believed to be late prehistoric in date. Crossing the site is an unmetalled track flanked by gullies, and associated with Roman pottery. The track appears to be aligned on a causeway crossing the Wall ditch discovered at Demesne Farm.

P.S. Austen and M. McCarthy

MILECASTLE 72.

 Limited excavations in 1989 examined the east wall and part of the north wall in the access track west of Fullwood House (Austen 1994, 44-9). Previous investigations in 1960 had assumed this to be the site of the central road and north gateway. The position of the west wall, located in 1960, was confirmed. The milecastle had initially been constructed in turf and timber, as might be expected in the Turf Wall sector of the Wall, but surprisingly the turf ramparts were laid on a foundation of rounded cobbles, as was a length of Hadrian's Wall 500m to the west, east of turret 72A, excavated in 1986. This is a hitherto unrecorded method of construction of the Turf Wall, but the recording of cobble foundations at Beaumont in 1928 when the churchyard was extended, thought at the time to be foundations for the replacement Stone Wall, would indicate that this method occurs over a distance of at least two miles and may perhaps be a characteristic of the legion engaged in the construction of this part of the Turf Wall.

179

The replacement of the Turf Wall and milecastle in sandstone was undated, but the north wall of the stone milecastle lay on the north edge of the base of the turf rampart while the east and west walls were constructed exactly in the centre of the line of the Turf Wall milecastle walls. The length of the milecastle is not known as the south wall has never been located but the overall width of the stone-phase milecastle was 24.3m (79' 9").

Both the 1986 and 1989 excavations found that Hadrian's Wall did not run as a straight line between West End and the location of the Burgh II fort, as shown by the Ordnance Survey, but veered to the north at West End before turning south- eastwards west of milecastle 72 (Austen 1994, 36-44). The projected line eastwards and its implications for the fort are described above.

P. S. Austen

Wall Mile 72. On the crest of Watch Hill there is a ditch, apparently 12m wide and up to 1m deep, lying about 20m to the north of the Ordnance Survey line of the Wall ditch. Geophysical survey (Geophysical Surveys of Bradford

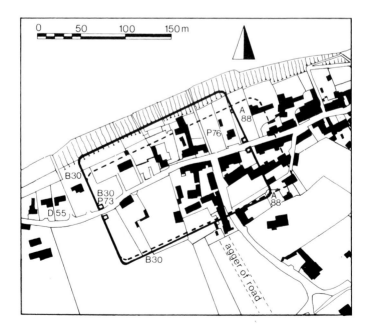

Figure 59. The fort at Bowness-on-Solway.

1991) suggests that this feature continues to the east, parallel to the Ordnance Survey line. There is little, if any, other trace of Wall or ditch in this sector. The newly planned ditch will, if it should prove to be the Hadrian's Wall ditch, have a bearing on the poorly recorded positions of turret 72B and milecastle 73.

M. Bowden, RCHME

DRUMBURGH – *Concavata*
No recent work.

Wall Mile 79. A small camp of 0.6 ha (1.5 acres) north of the Wall might have been an early landing place on the south side of the Solway Firth (Jones 1992; Welfare and Swan 1995, 40, figs 28-9).

BOWNESS-ON-SOLWAY- *Maia* (Fig. 59)
There has been no further work at the western terminal fort of the Wall since the excavations in 1988 which fixed for the first time the position of its eastern defences (see Austen 1991a, augmenting his account in the Handbook for the Eleventh Pilgrimage, Daniels 1989, 19-20).

THE CUMBRIAN COASTAL SYSTEM
Introduction
The existence of smaller installations between the forts on the Cumbrian coast has long been known. Research during the last fifty years has shown that they formed part of a system of milefortlets and towers, reflecting the arrangement of milecastles and turrets on the Wall, but without any form of continuous barrier, at least to the south of Moricambe. In the late 1940s Simpson, Richmond and Miss Hodgson traced the system along the Cardurnock peninsula as far as the exceptionally large milefortlet 5. Then in the succeeding decades Bellhouse was able to follow the system southwards to beyond Maryport. A terminus at St Bees Head, or even as far south as Ravenglass, has seemed possible until recently, but Bellhouse (1989, 54) could find no reason to accept that the system had continued beyond Flimby, the postulated site of milefortlet 27, 4km south of Maryport.

Jones' excavations on the northern part of the system have traced lengths of palisade, parallel ditches and a road, but their evolution and extent are obscured by a fog of controversy which even pervades the interpretation (and sometimes the possible existence) of individual archaeological features (see, most recently,

Bellhouse 1989, Daniels 1990 and Shotter 1996, 72-81). There is some common ground between Bellhouse and Jones: Bellhouse accepts that there were parallel ditches between Herd Hill (turret 80B) and milefortlet 1 and that at some points there were palisades and road metalling as far south as milefortlet 5. Jones, however, sees these elements as part of a continuous system which ran as far as milefortlet 5 and possibly some distance south of Moricambe. At towers 2B and 4B he detected three periods in the evolution of the system, but this has been strongly contested by Bellhouse.

The system was not long-lived. The pottery from milefortlet 21 (p.184) was entirely Hadrianic in date and there is only one sherd from milefortlet 1 (from a samian Dr. 45) which is necessarily post-Hadrianic in date; other sites have occasionally produced later finds but these might well have been casual losses. Only milefortlet 5 was certainly occupied in the later Roman period.

In 1994 the Cumbrian coastal system was surveyed by RCHME. It proved possible to establish accurately the positions of eleven milefortlets and fifteen towers, including milefortlets 4, 17 and 23 where geophysical survey was undertaken.

Tower 2B, Campfield (Fig. 60). Excavations by G. D. B. Jones (1993; plan also published in *Britannia* **25** (1994), 262, fig. 9) explored three successive towers. The earliest was of timber and, at 10 Roman feet square, exceptionally small; the second tower, also of timber, measured 4m by 3.6m. The foundations of the stone tower measured 5.8m by 5.7m. There were also two parallel ditches: the larger, much eroded but surviving to a width of 3.9m, ran 9.5m north of the stone tower; the smaller ditch was earlier than the second timber tower which was built across its line. South of the tower was a road contemporarary with the first tower but re-surfaced and continuing in use when the stone tower was built. Two coins, radiate copies of *c.* 270-90, were found unstratified; preliminary examination of the pottery 'suggests a lengthy period of occupation perhaps extending well into the third century'.

Tower 4B, Cardurnock: Bellhouse (1989, 18-25) has doubted the identification of the site.

Milefortlet 10, Silloth. Bellhouse (1989, fig. 8) suggested that milefortlet 10 had been destroyed by marine erosion, thus rejecting the position marked by

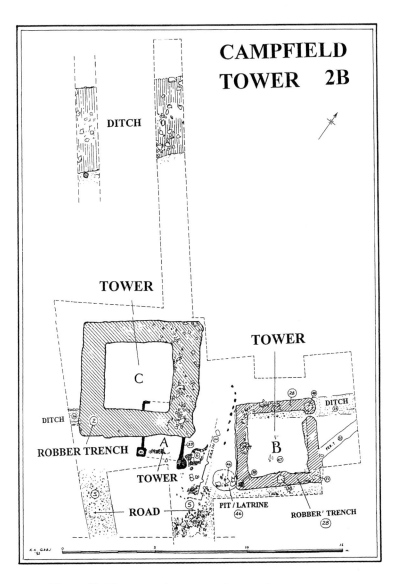

Figure 60. The successive towers at Campfield, tower 2B.

183

the Ordnance Survey. Excavations by Turnbull (1991) confirmed this, showing that the rectilinear platform taken to represent the milefortlet was in fact a truncated dune.

Milefortlet 21, Swarthy Hill (Fig. 61). This milefortlet, some 4.5km north-west of Maryport, was completely excavated in 1990 and 1991 by P. Turnbull for Cumbria County Council; the full report has been published recently (Turnbull 1998). The milefortlet measured 29.5m east-west by 27m north-south measured across the ramparts, which had gates on the east and west sides, and was surrounded on three sides by a ditch up to 7.5m in width. On the landward side the ditch was interrupted by a causeway in front of the east gate; as at milefortlet 22 there was no ditch on the side facing the sea. The interior was bisected by a gravel road. On the south side a range of three rooms was recognised, their walls represented by lines of compacted sand which were cautiously interpreted by Turnbull as having marked the positions of wooden sleeper beams (the editor was struck by the resemblance of these lines to the turf-walled buildings at South Shields: Bidwell and Speak 1994, 52-5, figs 3.6-8, 111, fig.4.5). North of the road there was also a range of rooms, probably four in number, represented by a line of post-holes, occupation deposits and ovens.

The milefortlet displayed only one period of construction and none of the pottery was necessarily later than the mid-second century. Turnbull (*ibid.*, 104) concluded that the site was abandoned at the end of the Hadrianic period and never re-occupied.

MARYPORT (Fig. 62)

In recent decades advances in knowledge about Roman Maryport have been achieved largely without archaeological interventions on the fort or *vicus*. The last excavation at the site remains the campaign of 1966. Since that date the two major developments have been the securing of the Netherhall collections, culminating in the opening of the Senhouse Roman Museum in 1990, and the publication of *Roman Maryport and its Setting: Essays in Memory of Michael G. Jarrett* (Wilson 1997).

In the modern town a watching brief by Percival Turnbull (1996) was important for its negative results. It produced the highly significant observation that the large expanses of red sandstone recorded on either side of the River Ellen

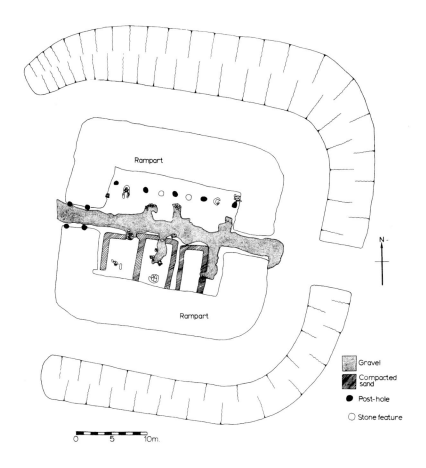

Figure 61. Milefortlet 21.

by J. B. Bailey (1926) were almost certainly natural bedrock, thereby removing the evidence for a built harbour at Maryport.

Field survey work by staff of the RCHME on the site of the fort has produced a detailed plan and interpretation of the earthworks of the fort, together with an assessment of the aerial photographic coverage of the *vicus* to the north (Lax and Blood in Wilson 1997). Greater accessibility of the collections from the site has allowed for various re-interpretations of known material. Shirley Waldock, quoted by David Breeze (1997), has shown that the idea that the Jupiter altars found in pits in 1870 were by a parade-ground is pure guesswork. A much more likely context was in a temple of a type now known from Osterburken and Sirmium. Breeze's paper also reviews the information on the units in residence and their commanders. Other important surveys examined the stone sculptures (Coulston 1997), the coins (Shotter 1997), and the women of Roman Maryport (Allason-Jones 1997).

One further point worth noting is the role of Maryport in the Cumberland coast defences. In the past Richard Bellhouse has argued that the system was laid out from the corners of Maryport fort. In the light of recent discoveries of towers and milefortlets in the vicinity of Maryport, it is now much more plausible that the fort replaced tower 23B (as is typical of Wall forts) and a coherent system of towers ran through Maryport to tower 25B (Rise How) (Daniels 1990; Wilson 1997, fig. 1.4).

The history of the site can be summarised briefly. The visible fort of 2.58ha (6.5 acres) was built for a milliary cohort (*cohors I Hispanorum equitata milliaria*) in the early 120s. In the early 130s the unit was split and half of it left the province, never to return. Although effectively occupied by a quingenary unit for the rest of the Hadrianic period, the fort was not reduced in size. Under Antoninus Pius a new unit, *cohors I Delmatarum*, was in garrison for some or all of the time. In turn it was replaced by *cohors I Baetasiorum cR ob virtutem et fidem* which was in garrison until the mid 180s. The later history of the fort is obscure but in the fourth century the presence of late Roman military belt fittings suggests that the soldiers were of a higher grade than the frontier units in most of the Wall forts.

I.Caruana

RAVENGLASS - *Tunnocelum*

In 1995 a diploma dated to 158 was found on the beach below the fort at Ravenglass (Holder 1997). The name of the recipient does not survive, but he was a cavalryman in *cohors I Aelia classica*. Ravenglass has also produced a lead sealing of the same unit (*RIB* 2411.94) and there is now a strong case for identifying the fort with *Tunnocelum*, which is where the *Notitia Dignitatum* (XL, 51) placed *cohors I Aelia classica*. Ravenglass was formerly thought to have been *Glannoventa*, a name Holder (*ibid.*, 9) would now apply to Ambleside. There are difficulties with this, as also with the identification of

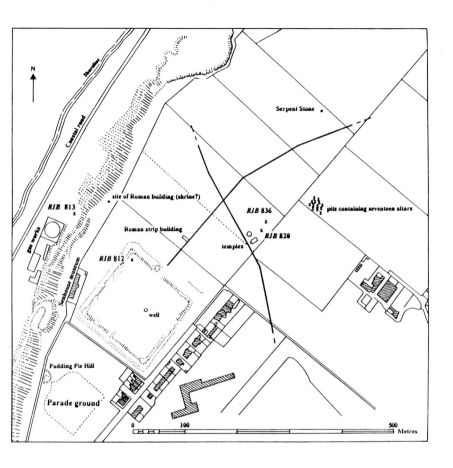

Figure 62. The fort at Maryport in its setting. Roman roads (solid black lines) plotted from aerial photography.

other forts on the Cumbrian coast and elsewhere in north-west England (cf. Mann 1989b; Shotter 1993, 105-9).

THE OUTPOST FORTS

RISINGHAM – *Habitancum*

There have been no excavations in the fort since 1935, but in 1990 two trenches were cut through the 'groyne' immediately beyond the north wall (Anderson

1992, 45-7, figs 25-9). Originally thought to have been a defence against river erosion, and latterly claimed as a barge-wharf, the 'groyne' was shown by the 1992 excavations, and by geomorphological analysis undertaken at the same time, to have been a platform of natural alluvium cut away on two sides by palaeo-channels of the River Rede.

M. P. Speidel (1998) has read the name of the same officer, Arruntius Paulinus, on fragmentary inscriptions from Corbridge and Risingham (*RIB* 1152, 1229); he argues that the letters '*praet[...]*' on the Corbridge inscription are probably to be restored as '*praeten[sione]*', 'a line of manned posts linking a rearward base [ie Corbridge] to an outlying fort [ie Risingham]'.

HIGH ROCHESTER - *Bremenium* (Figs 63-5)

The site of the Roman fort of High Rochester (*Bremenium*) occupies a distinct platform, today occupied by a cluster of later houses. Few Roman fort sites are as well preserved and at the west gate, uncovered in the last century, not only does the gate arch survive to the moulded impost block with a voussoir above it, but remains of internal walls abutting against the gate stand to over a metre in height. Excavations in 1852 and 1855 revealed the outline of the curtain wall and the plan of many of the internal stone buildings, providing one of the earliest near-complete plans of any fort in the Britain. Further small-scale excavations were undertaken in 1935 and the main accounts of the site are by Richmond (1940) and by Daniels (1978, 295-301). Since 1992 a research programme, initiated by Northumberland National Park Authority and English Heritage, has been carried out by the Department of Archaeology, Newcastle University. The project has combined detailed topographical and geophysical survey of the fort and its environs with a programme of limited excavation and consolidation of the exposed Roman masonry.

The fort lies close to the line of Dere Street which passes to the east of the fort and crosses the deep valley of the Coalcleugh Burn to the north before turning and crossing the Sills Burn beyond. Throughout its history the Roman presence at High Rochester was linked with Dere Street, the principal invasion route into Scotland and the vital communication to the garrisons further north. At other times and especially in the third and fourth centuries it was an outpost to Hadrian's Wall, and for a long time the most northerly garrison in Britain. The surviving fort covers 5 acres and the earliest attested garrison was *cohors*

I Lingonum equitata, mentioned on a building inscription of Q. Lollius Urbicus, governor from 139-43 (*RIB* 1276). In the early third century a number of inscriptions refer to the garrison as *cohors I fida Vardullorum milliaria equitata* (*RIB* 1265, 1272, etc). This was one of only five such milliary equitate cohorts known from Britain (a similar unit was stationed at Risingham to the south) and this no doubt reflects the military significance and importance of the fort to the Romans. Another late inscription refering to the *exploratores Bremenienses,* the 'Bremenium Scouts', is a further indication of the role of the outpost garrisons (*RIB* 1270). Other building inscriptions refer to vexillations from the Sixth and Twentieth Legions (*RIB* 1283-4); these could either have been part of the garrison or solely engaged in building work.

The remains of two phases of turf and timber fort ramparts considered to be of Flavian date have been found underlying the north-west angle of the stone fort. However, recent geophysical survey has revealed an earlier, double ditched, D-shaped enclosure in the field west of the fort. The east side was overlain by the later fort platform, but the enclosure occupied the full extent of the spur as far as the steep valley of the Sills Burn to the west. In shape and size it is virtually identical with other iron age fortified settlements in central Northumberland, such as Manside Cross and Witchy Nook. The D-shaped enclosure constitutes rare evidence for an Iron age predecessor to a Roman fort location. Three and a half miles south of High Rochester another Flavian fort with a small annexe is known at Blakehope (Richmond 1940, 70-72). Whether both sites were occupied simultaneously is not clear, but by the later first century High Rochester, on the site of an earlier native centre, became the dominant Roman station. The first Flavian defences of the fort comprised a turf rampart on a base of stone flags with a narrow ditch on the outside. Re-excavation of Richmond's trench (1940, 88) combined with geophysical survey showed that the later Flavian foundations he recorded were part of an annexe to the west of the fort, in part lying over the earlier D-shaped enclosure. The annexe is trapezoidal in shape and projects a maximum of 59m west of the west gate with a maximum length from north-south of 81.5m. On the north side of the line of the rampart a test pit revealed the fill of a ditch and further excavations on the south side showed that the turf base still survived to a height of 0.25m. The rampart had been demolished and the remains of decayed turfwork was found slumped into the south ditch. Rectangular geophysical anomalies within the annexe may indicate some later use of this area, but there was no trace of a built settlement or other significant buildings. Indeed

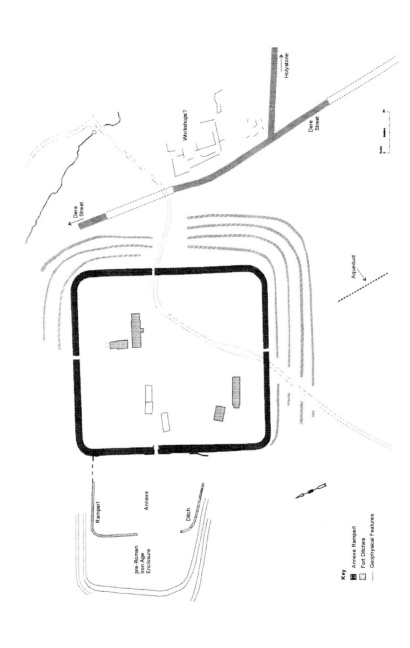

Figure 63. High Rochester: plan showing the location of features outside the fort based on topographical and geophysical surveys. Scale 30m in length.

once the annexe was demolished the parallel, multiple ditches of the later forts ran across the east half of it and the inner ditch of these defences was located by excavation 2.7m from the fort wall at the north-west angle.

All three outpost forts in the western sector of Hadrian's Wall have evidence of Hadrianic inscriptions, but none is known from the Dere Street sites and it is generally accepted that Risingham and High Rochester were not reoccupied until the mid-second century when there was a need to secure the routes to the new Antonine frontier. Earlier excavations had revealed the plans of the principal stone buildings within the fort: these were the north-facing headquarters, flanked on both sides by two sets of double granaries. It can be assumed that the commanding officer's house was located to the east, closest to the gate leading to Dere Street, but this area was not investigated in the nineteenth century. South of the central range two blocks of buildings, comprising a number of small, parallel rooms, are thought to represent late-Roman chalet-barracks which replaced earlier long barracks aligned across the width of the fort from east-west. It is likely that there were two pairs of back-to-back barracks immediately south of the central range, with another pair of single barracks to the south of these. Also apparent from the nineteenth century plan is the number of buildings constructed against the rear of the rampart. These are shown on the south-west curtain and against the south wall, behind the interval tower. Limited excavations in these areas have confirmed the accuracy of the earlier plans. During the consolidation of the stonework of the south interval tower a group of pottery dateable to the third century was found incorporated in the blocking of the entrance to the tower indicating that the rampart buildings on either side predated that event.

The north-west angle (Lambing Garth) was not investigated in the last century, although Richmond carried out limited trenching south of the north curtain (1940, 83). Geophyscal survey of this area showed the outline of three barracks aligned east-west with little or no trace of the later chalet-type structures. The same sequence can be seen from Richmond's trench, where he identified an earlier barrack and the fragmentary walls of later structures. Elsewhere in the fort Roman stonework is still visible close to the surface of the village green. But in the Lambing Garth it seems that when the field was cultivated, probably in the eighteenth century, the stones near the surface were cleared off, effectively removing the later chalet phase and enabling the geophysicists to

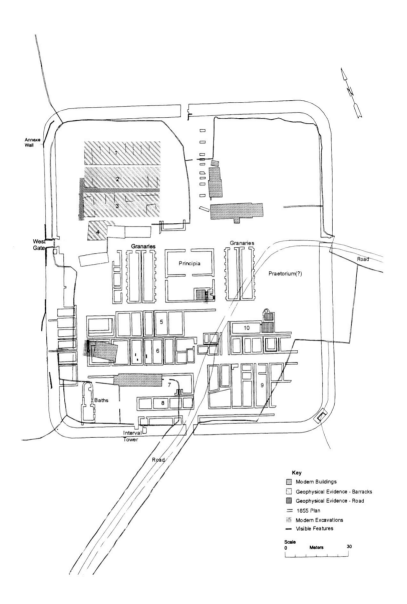

Figure 64. Plan of the internal buildings within the fort. Based on the nineteenth-century excavations and modern geophysical survey, the results have been merged using the surviving stonework and excavated details as a guide. Note that this is a preliminary plan and some details are not yet included. Building 1, 2 and 3 represent the site of earlier barracks preceding the 'chalet phase'.

record the outline of the earlier second- or third-century barracks. As was suggested for the buildings in the south range of the fort the pattern of internal buildings is of closely spaced barracks, with some further buildings against the inner face of the curtain. Around the edge of the field piles of stones could be recognised from the geophysical survey and these probably masked the stone-built platform against the north rampart identified by Richmond as *ballistaria* or gun-platforms. The construction of *ballistaria* from High Rochester is noted on two Severan inscriptions (*RIB* 1280-1), although recent discussions have interpreted these as either 'sheltered emplacements for light arrow shooters' (Campbell 1984, 84) or 'a magazine or workshop for the *tormenta* assigned to the High Rochester garrison' (Donaldson 1990, 211). Without further excavation either interpretation is to be preferred to Richmond's 'gun-platforms' for stone throwing *onagri*.

Recent excavations within the fort have been limited to the re-excavation of the south-east rooms of the headquarters showing part of the heated rear room and the exterior angle of the building. Palaeomagnetic dating of the flue indicates that the last date of firing was AD 190. It is clear that in some areas of the fort the later levels are very well preserved, but in the centre the remains have been extensively robbed out. In the south-west quadrant part of a chalet-type barrack was exposed confirming the basic reliability of the plan from the 1850s excavations. Included on that is an internal bath house in the south-west corner; the remains of an aqueduct channel were reported near the south gate and further evidence for the line of this channel from the south-east was confirmed by the resistivity survey south of the well-preserved south ditch system.

On the west curtain following cleaning and recording of the stonework it is possible to distinguish four stone phases:

I.   Foundations indicating a double-portal gate, probably belonging to the first stone (Antonine) phase.
II.   A single portal west gate with the adjacent curtain constructed with thin levelling slabs (Severan).
III.   Repairs with large bonding slabs, seen at the north-west angle.
IV.   Rebuilding with large irregular blocks seen at the north-west angle and in late repairs close to the location of the interval tower.

This final phase may be compared with the fourth-century restorations to the

Figure 65. Part of the headquarters building with the bastle in the background. In the foreground can be seen the flue and two standing pillars of the hypocaust of a heated room in the rear range of the building (1997).

curtain wall seen at Housesteads and Vindolanda. Studies of the coins known from High Rochester by Casey and Savage (1979) suggested that the site was largely abandoned early in the fourth century, but the structural evidence from the west curtain wall, the chalet-type barracks and also an unusual type of construction seen in the interior of the fort known as 'park railing stones' all invite comparison with structures on Hadrian's Wall dating later in the fourth century.

The evidence from the field west of the fort has already been discussed and further extensive geophysical surveys were undertaken using resistivity, magnetometer and ground penetrating radar survey to investigate Roman activity and settlement outside the fort. Much of the resulting evidence was negative in nature: possible anomalies to the south of the fort were tested by excavation and proved to be either natural features or of recent date. Similar results were found along the line of Dere Street towards the tombs, where no additional cemeteries were discovered. The most productive area was the

194

field immediately east of the fort. The line of the Roman road was clearly defined as well as the course of the branch road to Holystone (see *Archaeology in Northumberland 1995-96*, 41-42). Between Dere Street and the fort the only significant features were the lines of the multiple ditch system and some areas indicating intensive bonfires, probably associated with scrub clearance. East of the road a number of sub-rectangular magnetic anomalies were apparent which were thought to be the foundations of structures aligned with the road. Excavation in the field to test these results produced clear evidence for Dere Street as a paved stone road flanked by parallel ditches; one was sampled and provided evidence for cereal pollen dating before the mid-third century. West of the road, towards the fort, an extensive area of cobbles was found although without any associated structural features such as walls or post-holes, apart from a single drain. Beyond the road to the east, dense layers of burnt soil and rubbish were discovered, but once again without any recognisable structural elements. Rather than a roadside settlement as the geophysics had indicated, this seems to have been an area used for craft activity with areas of hard standing, possibly associated with the passage of armies north into Caledonia. From the sheltered garrisons of Hadrian's Wall we are familiar with extra-mural settlements clustering around the forts; what emerges at High Rochester is a closely packed military settlement within its walled and ditched enclosure. The known annexe only dates to the Flavian period, although like the early fort when it was abandoned is not known.

Richmond's excavations north of the fort in 1935 recorded the profile of six ditches (1940, fig.8); as a result of our survey it is likely that at least two of the outer ditches were part of a system of rigg-furrow of nineteenth-century date. On the east side we were able to recognise the continuation of the four inner ditches. The ground radar profile of these indicated that they had been recut. This hypothesis was tested by excavating a machine-dug trench across the line. Like the profile that Richmond had published, the ditches were not especially deep and the high mounds which survive to the south of the fort had been removed by ploughing, but there were clear traces in the sections that two had indeed been recut in Roman times. We have no indication when this occurred but it reinforces the overall impression that the maintenance of the security of the outpost fort was a high priority throughout the Roman occupation.

J.Crow

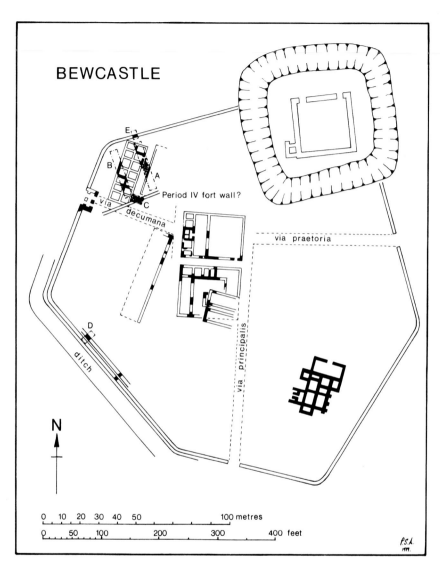

BEWCASTLE

E

B

A

Period IV fort wall?

via decumana

C

via praetoria

D

ditch

via principalis

N

| 0 | 10 | 20 | 30 | 40 | 50 | | 100 metres |
| 0 | | 50 | 100 | | 200 | 300 | 400 feet |

P.S.A.
1999.

Figure 66. The fort at Bewcastle.

Devil's Causeway. See Moorwood and Hodgson (1992) for a discussion of the point at which this Roman road crossed the River Coquet.

BEWCASTLE – *Fanum Cocidii* (Fig. 66)
An earthwork survey has been published by RCHME (Sainsbury and Welfare

1990). The report on the 1977-78 excavations by P. Austen (1991) sets out a new chronology for the fort. In the Hadrianic period the defences were of turf and the internal buildings of timber, although there were stone gates and a stone *principia* (see p.17) for the likelihood that the fort was built in the governorship of A. Platorius Nepos). The remainder of the fort was rebuilt in stone in the mid-Antonine period or possibly later. There was further rebuilding in the third century and the fort was abandoned in the early fourth century, perhaps *c*. 312. A full account of the internal baths, discovered in 1949 and excavated in 1954 and 1956, has also appeared (Gillam, Jobey and Welsby 1993). The baths are another example of the Hadrianic blueprint best seen at Chesters.

There have been no excavations at Bewcastle since 1978. Nothing of the fort structures is visible, although the fort platform is prominent. The site is dominated by the remains of the fourteenth-century castle and in the churchyard stands the Bewcastle Cross.

THE BEWCASTLE CROSS
The church at Bewcastle lies within the Roman fort, to the south of the medieval castle. It is small and typical of the remote northern dales, although there are features within it which are of thirteenth-century date. The Anglo-Saxon cross standing in its churchyard, however, is one of the finest of its genre, matched in completeness and sophistication only by the Ruthwell cross on the northern shore of the Solway, a little to the east of Dumfries.

The cross would appear to be in its original position, set on a roughly pyramidal base over 1m high which tapers to an irregular octagon; the cross itself stands over 4m high. The juxtaposition of such a cross and a church within the Roman fort strongly suggests an important centre, either royal or religious (or both, as in the case of Whitby, where the ruling house established the monastery). The presence of inscriptions on the monument (see below) implies literacy, and the sundial a community who could and would use it.

The cross is now headless, and the head is lost, although it is recorded in an unpublished eighteenth-century drawing, held by the Society of Antiquaries, as lying against a gravestone nearby. There is also reference to it in the correspondence between Lord William Howard and Sir Robert Cotton in the early seventeenth century. It would appear to have expanded terminals, as does Ruthwell, and the whole of its west face was covered with chequers.

The origin of inspiration for a monument of this calibre must be the insular manuscripts of Northumbria. In terms of stone sculpture, however, both stylistically and iconographically, there are clear links with Ruthwell, which in many respects is the closest parallel, although there are also significant differences between the two monuments. In addition, there are obvious stylistic links with material from Durham and Northumberland. For instance, whilst the elegant and varied plant forms at Bewcastle are unique in Cumbria, these elements are paralleled elsewhere, such as at Ruthwell, Jarrow, Rothbury and Jedburgh. Bewcastle is however the only monument to have a complete inhabited vine scroll, thereby giving scope for a larger-scale treatment.

The work is clearly that of a single mason or master designer, who demonstrates a remarkable ability to relate the ornament to the form of the monument. In particular, the sophistication with which the scale of detail is varied is striking, so that each element makes an impact. There is clearly a dependence on Mediterranean prototypes for the figural sculpture, both at Ruthwell and Bewcastle, but the carvers varied their models sufficiently to develop the style, and the confident classical control and originality set both apart from all other crosses in western Britain. It is generally felt that the training for a craftsman of this calibre is likely to have been east of the Pennines, perhaps at Jarrow itself, where the only parallels for the deep relief can be found (Bailey and Cramp 1988). Perhaps surprisingly, given this sophistication, there is little doubt that the Bewcastle Cross is early in the sequence of pre-Conquest stone sculpture in Britain. Both Bewcastle and Ruthwell clearly belong to the same generation as the early sculpture east of the Pennines, and there are justifiable arguments in seeing Bewcastle as the innovatory piece of the two. In terms of parallels in eastern Northumbria, both in stone and other media, and in historical terms, its date range sits most comfortably in the first half of the eighth century, some fifty years after stone working was reintroduced to Monkwearmouth by Benedict Biscop in 674 (according to the Venerable Bede).

Many analyses of the Bewcastle Cross have been written during the last two hundred years; for a synthesis of sources and a detailed description of the iconography, see Bailey and Cramp (1988), on which the following description heavily depends.

West face

Below a small area of wear, a square-headed panel edged by fine roll-moulding encloses a standing figure. He supports a lamb with nimbus, gazing back at the viewer, on his left arm, and his right hand appears to point across his body. The figure is clearly male and wears a long garment with a scarf-like feature draped between his arms. Whilst there have been many interpretations of this panel, since it was first identified as the Virgin and Child in 1685, there is now almost universal agreement that this is John the Baptist with the Lamb of God.

Below is a small panel with the inscription '*Jesus Christ*' in runes, which identifies the figure in the next major panel. This is round-headed, again edged with roll-mouldings and again enclosing a standing figure facing the viewer. This figure is also clearly male, his head surrounded by a dished halo, with long hair and a central parting, and the garments are long, but expose the feet, which are placed on the heads of two beasts. The left hand holds a scroll angled across the body and the right arm is raised. The animals emerge from the two bottom corners of the panel, and their muzzles touch in the centre, as does a front foot of each; the other is raised towards the hem of Christ's tunic. The similarities between this representation and that in an identical position on the Ruthwell cross must imply that they come from a common model, yet these two are unique in the entire corpus of Anglo-Saxon sculpture.

A long runic inscription follows which sadly is now largely illegible, although it clearly begins: *This token of victory [victory cross, victory memorial] Hwaetred……. and……….. set up in memory of……* From this, it would appear to be commemorative and probably funerary. Again, the style is particularly close to Ruthwell in the type of runes used.

The bottom panel has engendered more debate over its interpretation than any other part of the monument. Again, the panel is round-headed and edged by roll-moulding enclosing a standing figure, which on this occasion is half turned towards the viewer. The right hand holds a long rod or stick and the left arm is extended in front of a large bird, below which is a T-shaped object.

Figure 67. Bewcastle Cross, west face.

The figure is also clearly male, though dressed in a significantly different manner to those above, with long curling hair, a calf-length tunic and cloak, and what may perhaps be gloves. The two interpretations given the most credence are that it is a precocious example of a secular figure, presumably the person commemorated in the inscription above, in which case it predates any similar representations by as much as two hundred years, or that it represents St John the Evangelist, with his symbol, the eagle. This latter interpretation has the advantage of unifying the iconography: Christ recognised as the Lamb of God by the Baptist, Christ himself, and the Evangelist who recorded the incident.

South Face
The south face consists of five ornamental panels, each one different, enclosed by fine roll-mouldings. The ornament is a mixture of interlace and complex plant trails, with possible traces of fragmentary inscriptions at the top and between the fourth and fifth panels. The most interesting feature of the face is the incorporation of a sundial, attached like a large leaf to the stem of the upper panel of plant scroll. This is a unique survival on a stone cross of the pre-Conquest period.

East Face
The east face comprises an individual vine scroll springing from a single root, inhabited by pairs of beasts. These display a remarkable awareness of perspective, those at the top being considerably smaller than those at the base. Each munches on a bunch of berries, a unique feature. Near the top is a pair of squirrel-like creatures in profile, below which are two thrush-like birds, the upper facing right and the lower full-frontal. Two bipeds can be seen below these, their tails seemingly growing from the vine scroll. At the base of the scroll is a quadruped, perhaps a canine, leaping up to grasp fruit in its front paws.

North Face
The north face is the least weathered, having been sheltered from the elements by the church. It again is formed of a series of panels, interspersed by short inscriptions. The majority of the panels comprise either interlace or plant scroll, but the third is unique in sculpture of this period, in that it is formed of 25 rows of sunken and raised chequers, placed alternately. At the top of the face, there are traces of the word '*Jesus*', and between the fourth and fifth

panels is the inscription '*Kynibur*g*'.

R.Newman

Barron's Pike. A possible signal tower, situated 3.3k m east of Bewcastle, was sampled in 1987 (Woolliscroft 1990).

NETHERBY - *Castra Exploratorum*

The Roman outpost fort at Netherby was recorded by antiquaries in the sixteenth and eighteenth centuries, but there has been little subsequent research, and most of what can be said is based upon altars and other casual discoveries (Birley 1961, 229-30). The position of the fort defences is not known, and even the position of the bath house, first recorded in 1732, cannot be precisely located. The building of the present Hall in the eighteenth century and the subsequent extensions in the early nineteenth century have obscured the Roman topography so apparent to Stukeley, Gale and their contemporaries. In view of the importance of the site, and its uncertain future, Carlisle Archaeological Unit undertook limited work immediately west of Netherby Hall in 1996 and confirmed the presence of complex archaeological deposits under post-medieval landscaping. A substantial wall was tentatively identified as part of a granary.

M. R. McCarthy

BIRRENS – *Blatobulgium*

Geophysical survey has revealed further details of the north and west annexes (*Britannia*, **28** (1997), 410-11, fig. 8). Two Roman inscriptions have been found at the Anglian monastery of Hoddom, 5km from Birrens: one is a dedication to the *numina Augustorum*; the other mentions vexillations of *legio VIII Augusta* and *legio XXII Primigenia*, apparently responsible for the early Antonine rebuilding of Birrens and otherwise unattested in Britain at this period (*Britannia*, **23** (1992), 317-8).

BIBLIOGRAPHY

The bibliography includes references to all substantial publications on Hadrian's Wall which have appeared between 1989 and the end of April 1999, but excludes annual summaries (but cf p. 73) and interim reports superseded by definitive publications. The more important 'grey literature' is also cited. These comprise laboratory reports, some academic theses and documentary surveys (i.e. catalogues and assessments of publications and archives relating to specific sites) commissioned by English Heritage; their entries are enclosed in square brackets to distinguish them from conventional publications. They are only available from the commissioning bodies or relevant universities (which are noted in the bibliographical entries) and access may be subject to certain restrictions. They nevertheless include material of primary importance. Publications before 1989 are included where cited in the text. For full bibliographies of the sites, readers are referred to the various editions of the *Handbook to the Roman Wall*.

Abbreviations

AA^{1-5}: *Archaeologia Aeliana, series 1-5.*
CW^{1-2}: *Transactions of the Cumberland and Westmorland Antiquarian and Archaeological Society, old and new series.*

Adams, J. N., 1995 'The language of the Vindolanda Tablets: an interim report', *J. Roman Stud.*, **85**, 86-134.

Allason-Jones, L., 1989 *Women in Roman Britain*, London.

Allason-Jones, L., 1991 'Roman and native interaction in Northumberland', in (eds) Maxfield and Dobson 1991, 1-5.

Allason-Jones, L., 1994 'A stone head from Walker', AA^5, **22**, 263-5.

Allason-Jones, L., 1996 'Roman military and domestic artefacts from Great Chesters', AA^5, **24**, 187-214.

Allason-Jones, L., 1997 'The women of Roman Maryport', in (ed.) Wilson 1997, 105-111.

Allason-Jones, L., and Dungworth, D. B., 1997 'Metalworking on Hadrian's Wall', in (eds) Groenman-van Waateringe *et al.*1997.

Anderson, J. D., 1992 *Roman Military Supply in North-East England: An Analysis of and an Alternative to the Piercebridge Formula*, BAR Brit. Ser. **224,** Oxford.

Austen, P. S., 1991a 'How big was the second largest fort on Hadrian's Wall at Bowness-on-Solway?', in (eds) Maxfield and Dobson 1991, 6-8.

Austen, P. S., 1991b *Bewcastle and Old Penrith: A Roman Outpost Fort and a Frontier Vicus, Excavations 1977-8*, CWAAS Res. Ser. **6**, Kendal.

Austen, P. S., 1994 'Recent excavations on Hadrian's Wall, Burgh-by-Sands', *CW²*, **94**, 35-54.

Baatz, D., 1997 'The eighth Horsley Memorial Lecture: Keeping watch over the *limes*', *AA⁵*, **25**, 1-20.

Bailey, J. B., 1926 'Further notes on Roman roads at Maryport and on the Netherhall Collection', *CW²,* **26**, 414-22.

Bailey, R. N., and Cramp, R. J. C., 1988 *The British Academy Corpus of Anglo-Saxon Stone Sculpture: Cumberland, Westmorland and Lancashire North-of-Sands*, **2**, London.

Bakker, L., 1993 'Raetien unter Postumus – Das Siegesdenkmal einer Juthungenschlacht im Jahre 260 n. Chr. aus Augsburg', *Germania*, **71**, 369-86.

Balaam, N.,1978 'Pollen analyses of the buried soils', in Smith 1978, 54-56.

Balaam, N.,1983 'Pollen analysis', in Bennett and Turner 1983, 76-77.

Barber, K. E., 1981 *Peat Stratigraphy and Change. A Palaeoecological Test of the Theory of Cyclic Peat Bog Regeneration*, Rotterdam.

Barber, K. E., Chambers, F. M., Dumayne, L., *et al.*,1993 'Climatic change and human impact in north Cumbria: peat stratigraphic and pollen evidence from Bolton Fell Moss and Walton Moss', in (eds) J. Boardman and J. Walden, *The Quaternary of Cumbria: Field Guide,* Oxford, Quaternary Research Association.

[Barker, L., and Rushworth, A., 1998 *Hadrian's Wall at Birdoswald*, English Heritage.]

Bartley, D. D., Chambers, C. and Hart-Jones, B., 1976 'The vegetational history of parts of south and east Durham', *New Phytologist* , **77,** 437-468.

Bellhouse, R. L., 1989 *Roman Sites on the Cumberland Coast*, CWAAS Res. Ser. **3**, Kendal.

[Bennett, J., 1990 *The Setting, Development and Function of the Hadrianic Frontier in Britain*, unpublished PhD thesis, University of Newcastle upon Tyne.]

Bennett, J., 1998 'The Roman frontier from Wallsend to Rudchester Burn reviewed', *AA⁵*, **26**, 17-37.

Berry, J., and Taylor, D. J. A., 1997 'The Roman fort at Halton Chesters: a geophysical survey', *AA⁵*, **25**, 51-60.

Bewley, R. H., 1994 *Prehistoric and Romano-British Settlement in the Solway Plain*, Oxbow Monograph **36**, Oxford,

Bidwell, P. T., 1985 *The Roman Fort of Vindolanda*, HBMCE Archaeol. Rep. **1**, London.

Bidwell, P. T., 1991 'Later Roman barracks in Britain', in (eds) Maxfield and Dobson 1991, 9-15.

Bidwell, P. T., 1996a 'The exterior decoration of Roman buildings in Britain', in (eds) Johnson, P, and Haynes, I, *Architecture in Roman Britain*, CBA Res. Rep. **94**, London, 19-29.

Bidwell, P. T., 1996b 'Some aspects of the development of later Roman fort plans', *Arbeia J.*, **5**, 1-18.

Bidwell, P. T., 1997a 'A water-colour of a culvert through Hadrian's Wall at West Denton, Newcastle upon Tyne', *AA⁵*, **25**, 151-2.

Bidwell, P. T., 1997b *Roman Forts in Britain*, London.

Bidwell, P. T., and Holbrook, N., 1989 *Hadrian's Wall Bridges*, EH Archaeol. Rep. **9**, London.

[Bidwell, P. T., Holbrook, N. and Snape, M. E., 1991 *The Roman Fort at Benwell and its Environs*, English Heritage].

[Bidwell, P. T., and Snape, M. E., 1993 *The Roman Fort of Chesters and its Environs*, English Heritage.]

Bidwell, P. T., and Speak, S. C., 1994 *Excavations at South Shields Roman Fort, Vol. I*, Soc. Antiq. Newcastle upon Tyne Mon. **4**, Newcastle upon Tyne.

Bidwell, P. T., and Watson, M., 1989 'A trial excavation on Hadrian's Wall at Buddle Street, Wallsend', *AA⁵*, **17**, 21 8.

Bidwell, P. T., and Watson, M., 1996 'Excavations on Hadrian's Wall at Denton, Newcastle upon Tyne, 1986-89', *AA⁵*, **24**, 1-56.

Biggins J. A. and Taylor D. J. A., forthcoming 'Survey of the Roman fort and settlement at Birdoswald, Cumbria', *Britannia*, **30.**

Birley, A., 1997 *The Small Finds: Security: The Keys and Locks*, Vindolanda Res. Rep. (n. s.) **4**, Fasc. **2**, Bardon Mill.

Birley, A. R. (ed.), 1969 *The Ninth Pilgrimage of Hadrian's Wall*, Kendal.

Birley, A. R., 1991 'Vindolanda; new writing tablets', in (eds) Maxfield and Dobson 1991, 16-20.

Birley, A. R., 1995 'Vindolanda: Das Alltagsleben in einer römischen Grenzenbefestigung in Britannien zu Beginn des 2. Jahrhunderts n. Chr.', in (ed.) Busse, G, *Burg und Schloss als Lebenorte im Mittelalter und Renaissance*, Dusseldorf, 9-18.

Birley, A. R., 1997a 'Supplying the Batavians at Vindolanda' in (eds) Groenman-van Waateringe *et al.* 1997, 273-80.

Birley, A. R., 1997b *Hadrian, the Restless Emperor*, London.

Birley, A. R., 1998 'A new tombstone from Vindolanda', *Britannia*, **29**, 299-306.

Birley, E., 1961 *Research on Hadrian's Wall*, Kendal.

Birley, E., Birley, R., and Birley, A., 1993 *The Early Wooden Forts: Reports on the Auxiliaries, The Writing Tablets, Inscriptions, Brands and Graffiti*, Vindolanda Res. Rep. (n. s.) **2**, Bardon Mill.

Birley, R., 1994 *The Early Wooden Forts*, Vindolanda Res. Rep. (n. s.), **1**, Bardon Mill.

Birley, R., 1996 *The Small Finds: The Weapons*, Vindolanda Res. Rep. (n. s.) **4**, Fasc. **1**, Bardon Mill.

Birley, R., 1999a *Writing Materials*, Vindolanda Res. Rep. (n. s.) **4**, Fasc. **4**, Greenhead.

Birley, R., and Birley, A., 1994 'Four new writing-tablets from Vindolanda', *Zeitschrift für Papyrologie und Epigraphik*, **100**, 431-46.

Birley, R., Birley, A., and Blake, J., 1999 *The 1998 Excavations at Vindolanda: the* Praetorium *Site, Interim Report*, Greenhead.

Birley, R., Blake, J., and Birley, A., 1998 *The 1997 Excavations at Vindolanda: The* Praetorium *Site, Interim Report*, Greenhead.

Bishop, M. C. 1993 'Excavations in the Roman fort at Chester-le-Street (*Concangis*), Church Chare 1990-91',*AA⁵*, **21**, 29-85.

Bishop, M. C. 1994 *Corstopitum, An Edwardian Excavation: Photographs from the 1906-14 Excavations of the Roman Site at Corbridge, Northumberland*, London.

Bishop, M. C., 1995a 'A new Roman military site at Roecliffe, North Yorkshire', *Yorks. Archaeol. Soc. Roman Antiq. Sect. Bull.*, **12**, 3-5.

Bishop, M. C., 1995b 'A 'new' tile-stamp from Corbridge and legionary dispositions on the Tyne-Solway isthmus', *AA⁵*, **23**, 311-2.

Bishop, M. C., 1998 'An old Corbridge bath-house revisited', *AA⁵*, **26**, 39-47.

Bishop, M. C., and Dore, J. N., 1988 *Corbridge: Excavations of the Roman Fort and Town, 1947-80*, HBMCE Archaeol. Rep. **8**, London.

Blood, K., and Bowden, M. C. B., 1990 'The Roman fort at Haltonchesters: an analytic field survey', *AA⁵*, **18**, 55-62.

Bowden, M. C. B., and Blood, K., 1991 'The Roman fort at Rudchester: an analytical field survey', *AA⁵*, **19**, 25-31.

Bowman, A. K., 1994 *Life and Letters on the Roman Frontier, Vindolanda and Its People*, London.

Bowman, A. K., and Thomas, J. D., 1983 *Vindolanda: The Latin Writing-Tablets* (Tabulae Vindolandenses **I**), Britannia Mon. Ser. **4**.

Bowman, A. K., and Thomas, J. D., 1994 *The Vindolanda Writing Tablets (*Tabulae Vindolandenses **II***)*, London.

Bowman, A. K., and Thomas, J. D., 1996 'New writing tablets from Vindolanda', *Britannia*, **27**, 299-328.

Breeze, D. J., 1985 'Roman forces and native populations', *Proc. Soc. Antiq. Scotland*, **115**, 223-8.

Breeze, D. J., 1989 'The Northern Frontiers', in (ed.) Todd 1989, 47-60.

Breeze, D. J., 1991 'The frontier in Britain, 1984-1989', in (eds) Maxfield and Dobson 1991, 35-43.

Breeze, D. J., 1992 'Cavalry on frontiers: Hadrian to Honorius', *Univ. London Inst. Archaeol. Bull.*, **29**, 19-35.

Breeze, D. J., 1993 *Hadrian's Wall, A Souvenir Guide to the Roman Wall* (revised edn), London.

Breeze, D. J. 1997 'The regiments stationed at Maryport and their commanders', in (ed.) Wilson 1997, 67-89.

Breeze, D. J., and Dobson, B., 1976 *Hadrian's Wall*, London.

Breeze, D. J., and Dobson, B., 1987 *Hadrian's Wall* (third edn), London.

Bruce, G., 1905 *The Life and Letters of John Collingwood Bruce, LL.D., D.C.L., F.S.A., of Newcastle-upon-Tyne*, London.

Bruce, J. C., 1867 *The Roman Wall* (third edn), London.

Campbell, D. B., 1984 '*Ballistaria* in first to mid-third century Britain: a reappraisal', *Britannia*, **15**, 75-84.

Caruana, I. D., 1989 'Carlisle-*Luguvalium*', in (ed.) Daniels 1989, 24-31.

Caruana, I. D., 1992 'Carlisle; excavation of a section of the annexe ditch of the first Flavian fort, 1990', *Britannia*, **23**, 45-109.

Caruana, I. D., 1996 'A forum or *mansio* at Carlisle', *Britannia*, **27**, 345-53.

Caruana, I. D., 1997 'Maryport and the Flavian conquest of North Britain', in (ed.) Wilson 1997, 40-51.

Caruana, I. D., forthcoming *The Early Roman Forts of Carlisle: Excavations at Annetwell Street 1973-84.*

Caruana, I. D., Shotter, D. C. A., and Pirie, E. J. E., 1994 'Roman and medieval coins found during sewer renewal in Carlisle, 1983-87', *CW²*, **94**, 65-76.

Casey, P. J., 1985 'The coins', in Bidwell 1985, 103-16.

Casey, P. J., 1987 'The coinage of Alexandria and the chronology of Hadrian', in (eds) Huvelin, H., Christol, M., and Gautier, G., *Mélanges de Numismatique offerts á Pierre Bastien à l'occasion de son 75ᵉ anniversaire*, Wetteren, 65-72.

Casey, P. J., 1992 'The end of garrisons on Hadrian's Wall: an historico-environmental model', *Univ. London Inst. Archaeol. Bull.*, **29**, 69-80.

Casey, P. J., 1994 'The end of fort garrisons on Hadrian's Wall: a hypothetical model', in (eds) Vallet, F., and Kazanski, M., *L'Armée Romaine et les Barbares du IIIᵉ au VIIᵉ Siécle*, Paris, 259-68

Casey, P. J., and Hoffmann, B., 1995 'Excavations on the Corbridge bypass', *AA⁵*, **23**, 17-45.

Casey, P. J., and Hoffmann, B., 1998 'Rescue excavations in the *vicus* of the fort at Greta Bridge, Co. Durham', *Britannia*, **29**, 111-83.

Casey, P. J., Noel, M., and Wright, J., 1992 'The Roman fort at Lanchester: a geophysical survey and discussion of garrisons', *Archaeol. J.*, **149**, 69-81.

Casey, P. J., and Savage, M., 1980 'The coins from the excavations at High Rochester in 1852 and 1855', *AA⁵*, **8**, 75-87.

Charlesworth, D., 1978 'Roman Carlisle', *Archaeol. J.*, **135**, 115-37

Coello, T., 1996 *Unit Sizes in the Late Roman Army*, BAR Int. Ser. **645**, Oxford.

[Connell, B., and Davis, S. J. M., submitted *Animal bones from Roman Carlisle, Cumbria: the Lanes (2) excavations, 1978-1982,* Ancient Mons Lab. Report.]

Corbet, G. B., and Harris, S., 1991 *The Handbook of British Mammals*, Oxford.

Corfe, T., 1997a 'Hexham before Wilfrid?', in (ed.) Corfe, T., *Before Wilfrid: Britons, Romans and Anglo-Saxons in Tynedale*, Hexham Historian **7**, 87-93.

Corfe, T., 1997b 'The Battle of Heavenfield', in (ed.) Corfe 1997a, 65-86.

Coulston, J. C. N., 1997 'The stone sculptures', in (ed.) Wilson 1997, 112-31.

Croom, A. T., 1995 'A hoard of military equipment from South Shields', *Arbeia J.,* **4**, 45-53.

Croom, A. T., and Snape, M. E., 1996 'Lost small finds from South Shields Roman Fort and *vicus*', *Arbeia J.,* **5**, 19-47.

Crow, J. G., 1988 'An excavation of the North Curtain Wall at Housesteads 1984', *AA⁵*, **16**, 61-124.

Crow, J. G., 1989 *Housesteads Roman Fort*, London.

Crow, J. G., 1991a 'Construction and reconstruction in the central sector of Hadrian's Wall', in (eds) Maxfield and Dobson 1991, 44-7.

Crow, J. G., 1991b 'A review of current research on the turrets and curtain of Hadrian's Wall', *Britannia*, **22**, 51-63.

[Crow, J. G., and Rushworth, A., 1994, *Housesteads Roman Fort and Its Environs*, English Heritage.]

Crow, J. G., 1995 *Housesteads*, London.

Crow, J. G., and Jackson, M., 1997 'The excavation of Hadrian's Wall at Sewingshields and the discovery of a long cist burial', *AA⁵*, **25**, 61-9.

Dacre, J. A., 1985 'An excavation on the Roman fort at Stanwix, Carlisle', *CW²*, **85**, 53-69.

Daniels, C. M., 1978 *Handbook to the Roman Wall,* 13th edn, Newcastle upon Tyne.

Daniels, C. M., 1979 'Fact and theory on Hadrian's Wall', *Britannia*, **10**, 357-64.

Daniels, C. M., 1980 'Excavation at Wallsend and the fourth-century barracks on Hadrian's Wall', in (eds) Hanson, W. S., and Keppie, L. J. F., *Roman Frontier Studies 1979*, BAR Int. Ser. **71**, Oxford, 173-93.

Daniels, C. M., (ed.) 1989a *The Eleventh Pilgrimage of Hadrian's Wall*, Newcastle upon Tyne.

Daniels, C. M., 1989b 'The Flavian and Trajanic Northern Frontier', in (ed.) Todd 1989, 31-5.

Daniels, C. M., 1990 'How many miles on the Cumberland Coast?', *Britannia*, **21**, 401-6.

Daniels, C. M., 1991 'The Antonine abandonment of Scotland', in (eds) Maxfield and Dobson 1991, 48-51.

Dark, K. R., 1992 'A sub-Roman re-defence of Hadrian's Wall?', *Britannia*, **23**, 111-20.

Dark, K. R., and Dark, S. P., 1996 'New archaeological and palynological evidence for a sub-Roman reoccupation of Hadrian's Wall', *AA⁵*, **24**, 57-72.

Davies, G. and Turner, J., 1979 'Pollen diagrams from Northumberland', *New Phytologist*, **82**, 783-804.

Davies, R.W., 1971 'The Roman military diet', *Britannia*, **2**, 122-43.

De la Bédoyère, G., 1998 *Hadrian's Wall: History and Guide*, Stroud.

Dixon, K. R., 1989 'A Roman bronze openwork buckle from Corbridge', *AA⁵*, **17**, 211-3.

Dobson, B., 1979 *The Tenth Pilgrimage of Hadrian's Wall*, Kendal.

Dobson, B., 1986 'The function of Hadrian's Wall', *AA⁵*, **14**, 1-30.

Donaldson, A.M. and Turner, J., 1977 'A pollen diagram from Hallowell Moss, near Durham City, UK', *J. Biogeography*, **4**, 25-33.

Donaldson, G. H., 1988a 'Signalling communications and the Roman Imperial Army', *Britannia*, **19**, 349-56.

Donaldson, G. H., 1988b 'Thoughts on a military appreciation of the design of Hadrian's Wall', *AA⁵*, **16**, 125-37.

Donaldson, G. H., 1989 '*Tormenta, Auxilia* and *Ballistaria* in the environs of Hadrian's Wall', *AA⁵*, **17**, 217-9.

Donaldson, G. H., 1990 'A reinterpretration of *RIB* 1912 from Birdoswald', *Britannia*, **21**, 207-14.

Donaldson, G. H., 1991 'The location of *armamentaria* and *ballistaria* in Roman auxiliary forts', *AA⁵*, **19**, 133-4.

Dumayne, L., 1994 'The effect of the Roman occupation on the environment of Hadrian's Wall: a pollen diagram from Fozy Moss, Northumbria', *Britannia*, **25**, 217-24.

Dumayne, L. and Barber, K. E., 1994 'The impact of the Romans on the environment of northern England: pollen data from three sites close to Hadrian's Wall', *The Holocene*, **4**, 165-173.

Dumayne, L., Stoneman, R., Barber, K. E., *et al.* 1995 'Problems associated with correlating calibrated radiocarbon-dated pollen diagrams with historical events', *The Holocene*, **5**, 118-123.

Dumayne-Peaty, L., 1998 'Forest clearance in northern Britain during Romano-British times: re-addressing the palynological evidence', *Britannia*, **29**, 315-22.

Dumayne-Peaty, L. and Barber, K., 1997 'Archaeological and environmental evidence for Roman impact on vegetation near Carlisle, Cumbria: a comment on McCarthy', *The Holocene*, **7**, 243-245.

Edwards, J., 1984 *The Roman Cookery of Apicius*, London.

Esmonde-Cleary, A. S., 1989 *The Ending of Roman Britain*, London.

Evans, J., and Scull, C., 1990 'Fieldwork on the Roman fort site of Blennerhasset', *CW²*, **90**, 127-37.

Fernández Ochoa, C., and Morillo Cerdán, A., 1997 '*Cilurnum* and *Ala II Asturum*. A new epigraphic document relating to the Spanish origin of a military toponym in Britannia', in (eds) Groenman-van Waateringe, W., *et al.* 1997, 339-41.

Funari, P. P. A., 1991 'Dressel 20 amphora inscriptions found at Vindolanda: the reading of the unpublished evidence', in (eds) Maxfield and Dobson 1991, 65-72.

[Gidney, L.J., 1998 'Wallsend 2: the animal bone. Publication report', *Durham Environmental Archaeol. Rep.* **32/98**.]

Goulty, N. R., Gibson, J. P. C., Moore, J. G., and Welfare, H. G., 1990 'Delineation of the Vallum at Vindobala, Hadrian's Wall, by a shear-wave refraction survey', *Archaeometry*, **32**, 71-82.

Green, D., 1992 *Discovering Hadrian's Wall*, Edinburgh.

Griffiths, W., 1992 'Survey of the remains of Chesters Roman bridge in the River North Tyne', *Arbeia J.*, **I**, 40-5.

Griffiths, W., 1993 'Excavation to the north-east of Wallsend Roman fort - 1993', *Arbeia J.*, **2**, 25-36.

Griffiths, W., 1995 'A reinstated section of the Branch Wall at Wallsend', *Arbeia J.*, **4**, 55-9.

Groenman-van Waateringe, W., van Beek, B. L., Willems, W. J. H., and Wynia, S. L., (eds) 1997 *Roman Frontier Studies 1995: Proceedings of the XVIth International Congress of Roman Frontier Studies*, Oxbow Monograph **91**, Oxford.

Hanson, W. S., 1996 'Forest clearance and the Roman army', *Britannia*, **27**, 354-8.

Harbottle, B., Fraser, R., and Burton, F. C., 1988 'The Westgate Road milecastle, Newcastle upon Tyne', *Britannia*, **19**, 153-62.

Hartley, B. R., 1972 'The Roman occupations of Scotland: the evidence of samian ware', *Britannia*, **3**, 1-55.

Hassall, M. W. C., 1984 'The date of the rebuilding of Hadrian's Turf Wall in stone', *Britannia*, **15**, 242-4.

Henig, M., 1984 *Religion in Roman Britain*, London.

Heywood, B., 1965 'The Vallum - its problems restated', in (eds) Jarrett, M. G., and Dobson, B., *Britain and Rome: Essays Presented to Eric Birley on his Sixtieth Birthday*, Kendal.

Hill, P. R., 1991 'Hadrian's Wall: some aspects of its execution', *AA⁵*, **19**, 33-9.

Hill, P. R. 1997a 'The Maryport altars: some first thoughts', in (ed.) Wilson 1997, 92-104.

Hill, P. R., 1997b 'The Stone Wall turrets of Hadrian's Wall', *AA⁵*, **25**, 27-49.

Hill, P. R., and Dobson, B., 1992 'The design of Hadrian's Wall and its implications', *AA⁵*, **20**, 27-52.

Hodgson, N., 1991 'The *Notitia Dignitatum* and the later Roman garrison of Britain' in (eds) Maxfield and Dobson 1991, 84-92.

[Hodgson, N., 1993 *The Military Limes: Aspects of the Comparative Development, Function and Significance of the Linear Frontier Systems of the Roman Empire up to AD 200*, PhD thesis, University of Newcastle upon Tyne.]

Hodgson, N., 1995a 'Were there two Antonine occupations of Scotland?',*Britannia*, **26**, 29-49.

Hodgson, N., 1995b 'A view of Roman frontiers for the 1990s', *Arbeia J.*, **4**, 73-84.

Hodgson, N., 1996 'A late Roman courtyard house at South Shields and its parallels', in (eds) Johnson, P., and Haynes, I., *Architecture in Roman Britain*, CBA Res. Rep. **94**, 135-51.

Holbrook, N., 1991 'A watching brief at the Roman fort of Benwell-*Condercum*', *AA⁵*, **19**, 41-5.

Holbrook, N., and Speak, S. C., 1994 'Washingwells Roman fort - a transcription of the aerial photographs and an assessment of the evidence', *Arbeia J.*, **3**, 33-45.

Holder, P. A. 1997 'A Roman military diploma from Ravenglass, Cumbria', *Bull. John Rylands Univ. Lib. Manchester*, **79,** 3-41.

Hopkins, T., 1993 *Walking The Wall*, Newcastle upon Tyne.

[Huntley, J. P., 1987 *Woodland management studies from Carlisle: Castle Street 1981*, Ancient Mons Lab. Rep. **119/87**, 31.]

Huntley, J. P., 1988 'Palaeoenvironmental investigations', in Harbottle *et al.* 1988, 160-163.

[Huntley, J. P.,1989a *Plant remains from Annetwell Street, Carlisle, Cumbria: the bulk samples*, Ancient Mons Lab. Rep., **1/89**, 103.]

[Huntley, J. P., 1989b *Woodland management studies from Carlisle: Annetwell Street, 1983-4*, Ancient Mons Lab. Rep., **51/89**, 81.]

[Huntley, J. P., 1991 *Botanical remains in samples from the Tullie House extension (ANN D and ANN E) and Tullie House Basement (ABB B) sites (Carlisle)*, Durham

Environmental Archaeol. Rep., **1/91**.]

[Huntley, J. P., 1992a *Carbonised plant remains from Chesters Roman Bridge Abutment*, Ancient Mons Lab. Rep., **29/23**, 6.]

[Huntley, J. P., 1992b *Plant remains from excavations at The Lanes, Carlisle, Cumbria: part I - CAL, OGL, OBL and LEL*, Ancient Mons Lab. Rep., **51/92** (2 parts), 201.]
[Huntley, J. P., 1995. *Buddle Street, Wallsend: BS94. The pollen evidence*, Durham Environmental Archaeol. Rep., **9/95**, 3.]

[Huntley, J. P., 1996 *Thornbrough Farm, Catterick. CAS452 and 482. The charred and waterlogged plant remains*, Durham Environmental Archaeol. Rep. and AML Rep., **21/96** and **105/97**.]

Huntley, J. P., 1997 'Macrobotanical evidence from the horrea', in Wilmott 1997, 141-44.

[Huntley, J. P. 1998a *Black Carts, Northumberland: CAS-623. Assessment of bulk environmental samples and pollen monoliths from sections across Hadrian's Wall*, Durham Environmental Archaeol. Rep., **18/98**.]

Huntley, J. P. 1998b 'The environmental samples' , in Birley *et al.* 1988, 68-80.

Huntley, J. P., and Stallibrass, S. M. 1995 *Plant and Vertebrate Remains from Archaeological Sites in Northern England: Data Reviews and Future Directions*, Architect. Archaeol. Soc. Durham Northumberland Res. Rep. **4**.

Innes, J. B. and Shennan, I., 1991 'Palynology of archaeological and mire sediments from Dod, Borders Region, Scotland', *Archaeol. J.*,**148**, 1-45.

Jacobson, G. L., and Bradshaw, R. H. W., 1981 'The selection of sites for palaeoecological studies', *Quaternary Research*, **16**, 80-96.

Jarrett, M. G., 1994 'Non-legionary troops in Roman Britain: part one, the units', *Britannia*, **25**, 35-77.

Jobey, I., 1979 'Housesteads Ware – a Frisian tradition on Hadrian's Wall', *AA[5]*, **7**, 127-43.

Johnson, G. A. L., 1997 *Geology of Hadrian's Wall*, Geol. Assoc. Guide **59**, London.

Jones, G. D. B., 1991 'The emergence of the Tyne-Solway frontier', in (eds) Maxfield and Dobson 1991, 98-107.

Jones, G. D. B., 1992 'Old Police House camp, Bowness-on-Solway', *Britannia*, **23**, 230-1.

Jones, G. D. B., 1993 'Excavations on a coastal tower, Hadrian's Wall: Campfield Tower 2B, Bowness-on-Solway', *Manchester Archaeol. Bull.*, **8**, 31-9.

Jones, G. D. B., 1994-5 'Farnhill, excavations on the Solway Frontier', *Manchester Archaeol. Bull.*, **9**, 23-7.

Keevill, G. D., Shotter, D. C. A., and McCarthy, M. R., 1989 'A *solidus* of Valentinian II from Scotch Street, Carlisle', *Britannia*, **20**, 254-5.

Kendal, R., 1996 'Transport logistics associated with the building of Hadrian's Wall', *Britannia*, **27**, 129-52.

[Kenward, H., Dainton, M., Kemenes., I. and Carrott, J., 1992 *Evidence from insect remains and parasite eggs from the Old Grapes Lane B site, The Lanes, Carlisle,* Ancient Mons Lab. Rep., **76/92**.]

Kenward, H., and Hall, A., 1997 'Enhancing bioarchaeological interpretation using indicator groups: stable manure as a paradigm', *J. Archaeol. Science*, **24,** 663-73.

King, A.C., 1978 'A comparative survey of bone assemblages from Roman sites in Britain', *Bull. Univ. London Inst. Archaeol.*, **15,** 207-232.

Lax, A., and Blood, K., 1997 'The earthworks of the Maryport fort: an analytical field survey by the Royal commission on the Historical Monuments of England', in (ed.) Wilson 1997, 52-66.

Lewis, M. J. T., 1995 'A *festuca* from Chesters?', *AA⁵*, **23**, 47-50.

[Linford, N., 1992 *Geophysical Survey: Burgh-by-Sands, Cumbria,* E. H. Ancient Mons Lab. Rep. 88/92.]

Mackay, D., 1990 'The Great Chesters aqueduct: a new survey', *Britannia*, **21**, 285-9.

Mann, J. C., 1989a 'The Housesteads latrine', *AA⁵*, **17**, 1-4.

Mann, J. C., 1989b 'Birdoswald to Ravenglass', *Britannia*, **20**, 75-9.

Mann, J. C., 1990a 'Hadrian's Wall west of the Irthing: the role of *VI Victrix*', *Britannia*, **21**, 289-92.

Mann, J. C., 1990b 'The function of Hadrian's Wall', *AA⁵*,**18**, 51-4.

Mann, J. C., 1992a '*Loca*', *AA⁵*, **20**, 53-5.

Mann, J. C., 1992b '*Armamentaria*', *AA⁵*, **20**, 57-62.

Mann, J. C., 1992c 'A note on *RIB* 2054', *Britannia*, **23**, 236-8.

Manning, A., Birley, R., and Tipping, R., 1997 'Roman impact on the environment at Hadrian's Wall: precisely dated pollen analysis from Vindolanda, northern England', *The Holocene*, **7.2**, 175-86.

Masé, A. 1995 *Hier endet Rom ... : Die Hadriansmauer im römischen Britannien*, Thun.

Mawer, C. F., 1995 *Evidence for Christianity in Roman Britain*, BAR Brit. Ser. **243**, Oxford.

Maxfield, V. A., 1990 'Hadrian's Wall in its imperial setting', *AA⁵*, **18**, 1-27.

Maxfield, V. A., and Dobson, M. J., (eds) 1991 *Roman Frontier Studies 1989: Proceedings of the XVth International Congress of Roman Frontier Studies*, Exeter.

McCarthy, M. R., 1990 *A Roman, Anglian and Medieval Site at Blackfriars Street, Carlisle: Excavations 1977-9*, CWAAS Res. Ser. **4**, Kendal.

McCarthy, M. R., 1991a *The Roman Waterlogged Remains and Later Features at Castle Street, Carlisle: Excavations 1981-2*, CWAAS Res. Ser. **5**, Kendal.

McCarthy, M. R., 1991b *The Structural Sequence and Environmental Remains from Castle Street, Carlisle: Excavations 1981-2* (Fasc. **1** of McCarthy 1991a).

McCarthy, M. R., 1993 *Carlisle: History and Guide,* Stroud.

McCarthy, M. R., 1997 'Archaeological and environmental evidence for Roman impact on vegetation near Carlisle, Cumbria: a reply to Dumayne-Peaty and Barber', *The Holocene*, **7**, 245-6.

McCarthy, M. R., forthcoming *Excavations at The Lanes, Carlisle, Volume 1*.

Moorwood, R. D., and Hodgson, N., 1992 'Roman bridges on the Devil's Causeway?', *Britannia*, **23**, 241-5.

Nollé, J. 1997 'Neue Militärdiplome', *Zeitschrift für Papyrologie und Epigraphik*, **117**, 227-76.

Nouwen, R., 1995 'The Vindolanda Tablet 88/841 and the cohors I Tungrorum milliaria', in (ed.) Lodewijcx, M., *Archaeological and Historical Aspects of West-European Studies (Album Amicorum André van Doorselaer)*, Acta Archaeologica Lovaniensia **8**, Leuven, 123-34.

Padley, T. G., 1991 *The Metalwork, Glass and Stone Objects from Castle Street, Carlisle: Excavations 1981-2* (Fasc. **2** of McCarthy 1991).

Padley, T. G., 1993 'Two dolphin scabbard runners from Carlisle', *J. Roman Milit. Equip. Stud.*, **4**, 101-2.

Padley, T. G., and Winterbottom, S., 1991 *The Wooden, Leather and Bone Objects from Castle Street, Carlisle: Excavations 1981-2* (Fasc. **3** of McCarthy 1991).

Passmore, D., O'Brien, C. F., and Dore, J., 1991 'Roman period riverine deposits at Castle Stairs, Sandhill', *AA⁵*, **19**, 17-24.

Phillips, E. J., 1976 'A workshop of Roman sculptors at Carlisle', *Britannia*, **7**, 101-8.
[Phillips, S. J .F. S., 1995 *The animal bones from South Shields Roman fort,* Dept Archaeol. Univ. Durham, unpub. BA dissertation.]

Potter, T., 1977 'The Biglands milefortlet and the Cumbrian coastal defences', *Britannia*, **8**, 149-83.

Poulter, J., 1998 'The date of the Stanegate, and a hypothesis about the manner and timing of the construction of Roman roads in Britain', *AA⁵*, **26**, 49-56.

[Pratt, K. E., 1996 *Development of methods for investigating settlement and land-use using pollen data: a case study from north-east England circa 8000 cal BC - cal AD 500*. Depts Archaeol. Biological Sciences, Univ. Durham. unpub. PhD thesis.]

Ramm, H. G., McDowall, R. W., and Mercer, E., 1970, *Shielings and Bastles*, RCHME, London.

Ratcliffe, D. A., and Walker, D., 1958 'The Silver Flow, Galloway, Scotland', *J. Ecology*, **46**, 407-55.

RIB Collingwood, R. G., and Wright, R. P., 1965 *The Roman Inscriptions of Britain: I, Inscriptions on Stone*, Oxford (reprinted with addenda and corrigenda by R. S. O. Tomlin, Stroud, 1995).

RIB II Frere, S. S., and Tomlin, R. S. O. (eds), 1990-1995, Collingwood, R. G., and Wright, R. P., *The Roman Inscriptions of Britain: II,* Instrumentum Domesticum *(Personal Belongings and the Like)*, Fascs 1-8 and Index Volume, Stroud.

Richards, M., 1993 *Hadrian's Wall Vol. 1: The Wall Walk*, Milnthorpe.

Richmond, I. A., 1940 'The Romans in Redesdale', *Northumberland County History*, **15**, 63-154.

Richmond, I. A., 1950 'Hadrian's Wall 1939-1949', *J. Roman Stud.*, **40**, 43-56.

Roberts, B. K., Turner, J., and Ward, P. F., 1973 'Recent forest history and land use in Weardale, Northern England' in (eds) H. J. B. Birks and R. G. West, *Quaternary Plant Ecology*, 207-220.

Rowell, T. K., and Turner, J., 1985 'Litho-, humic and pollen stratigraphy at Quick Moss, Northumberland', *J. Ecology*, **73**, 11-25.

[Rushworth, A., and Barker, L., 1997 *Hadrian's Wall at Winshield Crags, Cawfield Crags and Walltown Crags*, English Heritage.]

[Rushworth, A., and Lucas, C., 1997 *Hadrian's Wall at Heddon-on-the-Wall, Planetrees, Brunton and Blackcarts*, English Heritage.]

Sainsbury, I., and Welfare, H., 1990 'The Roman fort at Bewcastle: an analytical field survey', *CW²*, **90**, 139-46.

Salway, P., 1965 *The Frontier People of Roman Britain*, Cambridge.

Shotter, D. C. A., 1993 *Romans and Britons in North-West England*, Lancaster.

Shotter, D. C. A., 1994 'Rome and the Brigantes: early hostilities', *CW²*, **93**, 21-34.

Shotter, D. C. A., 1996 *The Roman Frontier in Britain: Hadrian's Wall, the Antonine Wall and Roman Policy in the North*, Preston.

Simpson, F. G., and Richmond, I. A., 1932 'Report of the Cumberland Excavation Committee for 1931, Excavations on Hadrian's Wall: I, Birdoswald', *CW²*, **32**, 140-5.

Simpson, F. G., and Richmond, I. A., 1937 'The fort on Hadrian's Wall at Halton', *AA⁴*, **14**, 151-71.

Smith, G. H., 1978 'Excavations near Hadrian's Wall at Tarraby Lane 1976', *Britannia*, **9**, 19-57.

Smith, I. G., 1997 'Some Roman place-names in Lancashire and Cumbria', *Britannia*, **28**, 372-83.

Snape, M. E., 1991 'Roman and native: *vici* on the north British frontier', in (eds) Maxfield and Dobson 1991, 468-71.

Snape, M. E., 1992 'Sub-Roman brooches from Roman sites on the northern frontier', *AA⁵*, **20**, 158-60.

Snape, M. E., 1993 *Roman Brooches from North Britain: A Classification and a Catalogue of Brooches from Sites on the Stanegate*, BAR Brit. Ser. **235**, Oxford.

Snape, M. E., 1994a 'An excavation in the Roman cemetery at South Shields', *AA⁵*, **22**, 43-66.

[Snape, M. E., 1994b, *Carrawburgh Roman Fort and Its Environs*, English Heritage.]

[Snape, M. E., 1994c *Hadrian's Wall at Sewingshields*, English Heritage.]

Snape, M. E., 1995 'Watching brief at Morton Walk, South Shields', *AA⁵*, **23**, 312-4.

[Snape, M. E., 1996 *Hadrian's Wall from Piper Sike Turret (51A) to Dovecote Bridge (Near 55B)*, English Heritage.]

Snape, M. E., and Bidwell, P. T., 1994 'The *vicus* of the Roman fort at Wallsend, Tyne and Wear', *Arbeia J.*, **3**, 13-32.

[Snape, M. E., Bidwell, P. T., and Croom, A. T., 1995 *Hadrian's Wall in Wall-Mile 48*, English Heritage.]

Snape, M. E., and Speak, S. C., 1995 'An excavation on Dere Street at Riding Mill', *Arbeia J.*, **4**, 21-34.

Sommer, C. S., 1995 ' "*Where did they put the horses?*", Überlegungen zu Aufbau und Stärke römischer Auxiliartruppen und deren Unterbringung in den Kastellen', in *Provincialrömische Forschungen: Festschrift für Günter Ulbert zum 65. Geburtstag*, Eselkamp, 149-68.

Speidel, M. A., 1996 *Die römischen Schreibtafeln von Vindonissa*, Brugg.

Speidel, M. P., 1998 'The Risingham *praetensio*', *Britannia*, **29**, 356-9.

[Stallibrass, S., 1991 *A Comparison of the Measurements of Romano-British Animal Bones from Periods 3 and 5, Recovered from Excavations at Annetwell Street, Carlisle*, Ancient Mons Lab. Rep., **133/91**.]

[Stallibrass, S., 1993 *Animal Bones from Excavations at Old Grapes Lane, Trenches A and B, The Lanes, Carlisle, 1982*, Ancient Mons Lab. Rep. **93/93**.]

[Stallibrass, S., 1997 *Thornbrough Farm, Catterick, North Yorkshire: CAS sites 452 & 482. The animal bones from excavations of Roman deposits in 1990 & 1993 by Peter Wilson for CAS*, Durham Environmental Archaeol. Rep., **29/97**.]

[Stallibrass, S., 1998 *Vindolanda, Northumberland: VIN97. An assessment of the animal bones from the area of the third/fourth century* praetorium *of the second stone fort*, Durham Environmental Archaeol. Rep., **33/98**.]

[Stokes, P. R. G., 1992 *Observations on the Roman military diet and culinary practices from the Commandant's House, South Shields*, Dept Archaeol., Univ. Durham, unpub. B.A. Dissertation.]

[Stokes, P. R. G., 1993 *The animal bones from the 1990-91 excavations at Chesters Bridge, Northumberland (NY 913701)*, Durham Environmental Archaeol. Rep., **9/93**.]

Stoneman, R. E., 1993 *Holocene palaeoclimates from peat stratigraphy: extending and refining the model*, Univ. Southampton.

Stuiver, M. and Kra, R. S., 1986 'OxCal radiocarbon dating calibration program', *Radiocarbon*, **28**, 805-1030.

Swan, V. G., 1992 'Legio VI and its men: African legionaries in Britain', *J. Roman Pottery Stud.*, **5**, 1-33.

Taylor, D. J. A., 1997 'The Roman fort at Benwell: a re-examination of its size',

Durham Archaeol. J., **13**, 61-4.

Taylor, J., 1991 *The Roman Pottery from Castle Street, Carlisle: Excavations 1981-2* (Fasc. **4** of McCarthy 1991).

Thomas, E., and Witschel, C., 1992 'Constructing reconstruction: claim and reality of Roman rebuilding inscriptions from the Latin West', *Pap. Brit. School Rome*, **60**, 135-77.

Tipping, R., 1995 'Holocene evolution of a lowland Scottish landscape: Kirkpatrick Fleming. Part 1, peat- and pollen-stratigraphic evidence for raised moss developoment and climatic change', *The Holocene*, **5**, 69-81.

Todd, M., (ed.) 1989 *Research on Roman Britain*, Britannia Mon. Ser. **11**, London.

Tomlin, R. S. 0., 1991 'The writing tablets', in Padley and Winterbottom 1991.

Tomlin, R. S. O., 1992 'The Twentieth Legion at Wroxeter and Carlisle in the first century: the epigraphic evidence', *Britannia*, **23**, 141-58.

Tomlin, R. S. O., 1996 'The Vindolanda tablets', *Britannia*, **27**, 459-63.

Tomlin, R. S. O., 1998 'Roman manuscripts from Carlisle: the ink-written tablets', *Britannia*, **29**, 31-84.

Tomlin, R. S. 0., and Annis, R. G., 1989 'A Roman altar from Carlisle Castle', *CW²*, **89**, 77-91

Turnbull, P., 1991 'The position of milefortlet 10 (Silloth)', *CW²*, **91**, 267-8.

Turnbull, P., 1996 'The supposed Roman harbour at Maryport', *CW²*, **96**, 233-5.

Turnbull, P., 1998 'Excavations at Milefortlet 21', *CW²*, **98**, 61-106.

Turner, J., 1979 'The environment of northeast England during Roman times as shown by pollen analysis', *J. Archaeol. Science*, **6**, 285-90.

van der Veen, M., 1991 'Native communities in the frontier zone - uniformity or diversity?', in (eds) Maxfield and Dobson 1991, 446-50.

van der Veen, M., 1992 *Crop Husbandry Regimes: An Archaeobotanical Study of Farming in Northern England 1000 BC - AD 500*, Sheffield Archaeol. Mon. **3**, Sheffield.

van der Veen, M., 1994 'Reports on the biological remains', in Bidwell and Speak 1994, 243-68.

van Driel-Murray, C., 1990 'The Roman army tent', *Exercitus*, **2**,137-44.

van Driel-Murray, C., Wild, J. P., Seaward, M., and Hillam, J., 1993 *The Early Wooden Forts: Preliminary Reports on the Leather, Textiles, Environmental Evidence and Dendrochronology*, Vindolanda Res. Rep. **3**, Bardon Mill.

Webster, J., 1986 'Roman bronzes from Maryport in the Netherhall Collection', *CW²*, **86**, 49-70.

Welfare, H., and Swan, V., 1995 *Roman Camps in England: The Field Archaeology*, RCHME, London.

Welsby, D., 1985 'The pottery from the two turrets at Garthside on Hadrian's Wall', *CW²*, **85**, 71-6.

Welsby, D., 1991 'A recently discovered moulded stone from Hexham', *AA⁵*, **19**, 131-2.

Wenham, L. P., and Heywood, B., 1997 *The 1968 to 1970 Excavations in the* Vicus *at Malton, North Yorkshire*, Yorks. Archaeol. Rep. **3**, Leeds.

Whittaker, C. R., 1994 *Frontiers of the Roman Empire: A Social and Economic Study*, Baltimore.

Whitworth, A. M., 1992 'The cutting of the Turf Wall at Appletree', *CW²*, **92**, 49-55.

Whitworth, A. M., 1994 'Recording the Roman Wall', *AA⁵*, **22**, 67-77.

Whitworth, A. M., 1997a 'Recording of Hadrian's Wall at Willowford Farm', *CW²*, **97**, 57-61.

Whitworth, A. M., 1997b 'Five stones from Great Chesters fort', *AA⁵*, **25**, 153-7.

Wilmott, T., 1993 'The Roman cremation cemetery in New Field, Birdoswald', *CW²*, **93**, 79-85.

Wilmott, T., 1995 *Birdoswald: A Short History and Souvenir Guide*, Carlisle.

Wilmott, T., 1997a 'The Birdoswald basilica: a new type of building in an auxilliary fort', in (eds) W. Groenman van Waateringe *et al.* 1997, 581-6.

Wilmott, T., 1997b *Birdoswald, Excavations of a Roman Fort on Hadrian's Wall and Its Successor Settlements: 1987-92*, EH Archaeol. Rep. **14**, London.

Wilson, R. J. A. (ed.) *Roman Maryport and Its Setting: Essays in Memory of Michael G. Jarrett*, CWAAS Extra Ser. **28**, for the Senhouse Museum Trust.

Wiltshire, P. E. J., 1997 'The pre-Roman environment', in Wilmott 1997, 25-40.

Woolliscroft, D. J., 1989a 'The outpost system of Hadrian's Wall', *CW²*, **89**, 23-8.

Woolliscroft, D. J., 1989b 'Signalling and the design of Hadrian's Wall', *AA⁵*, **17**, 5-19.

Woolliscroft, D. J., 1990 'Barron's Pike, possible Roman signal tower', *CW²*, **90**, 280.

Woolliscroft, D. J., 1994 'Signalling and the design of the Cumberland coast system', *CW²*, **94**, 55-64.
Woolliscroft, D. J., 1996 'Signalling and the design of the Antonine Wall', *Britannia*, **27**, 153-77.

Woolliscroft, D. J., Swain, S. A. M., and Lockett, N. J., 1992 'Barcombe B, a second Roman 'signal' tower on Barcombe Hill', *AA⁵*, **20**, 57-62.

Younger, D. A., 1994 'The small mammals from the forecourt granary and the south west fort ditch', in Bidwell and Speak 1994, 266-68.

Zant, J. M., 1998a 'An archaeological evaluation at William Howard School, Brampton, Cumbria', *CW²*, **98**, 298-9.

Zant, J. M., in preparation *Excavations at The Lanes, Carlisle, Volume 2.*